The
Lean Product
Development
Guidebook

Everything Your
Design Team Needs to Improve
Efficiency and Slash Time-to-Market

Ronald Mascitelli

TECHNOLOGY PERSPECTIVES

Northridge, CA

Editorial and Sales Offices: Technology Perspectives
18755 Accra Street, Northridge, CA 91326
(818) 366-7488

Publisher's Cataloging-in-Publication
(Provided by Quality Books, Inc.)

Mascitelli, Ronald.
  The lean product development guidebook : everything
your design team needs to improve efficiency and slash
 time-to-market / Ronald Mascitelli.
    p. cm.
  Includes bibliographical references and index.
  LCCN 2006905344
  ISBN-978-0-9662697-3-4
  ISBN 0-9662697-3-X

  1. Product management. 2. Industrial management.
3. Time to market (New products)   I. Title.

HF5415.15.M353 2006   658.5
                    QBI06-600318

10 9 8 7 6 5
First Edition

This book is printed on acid-free recycled paper meeting
the requirements of the American National Standard for
Permanence in Paper for Printed Library Materials.

Manufactured in the United States of America

Dedication

To all those
who have dedicated their
lives to protecting the
natural world.

Table of Contents

Acknowledgements

As with an acceptance speech, there are always far too many people to thank. I would like, however, to single out several individuals for their contributions to this guidebook, and to the field of lean product development in general. First, of course, are the good people at the Lean Enterprise Institute (www.lei.org), embodied in James Womack and his coworkers, for their continuing energy and ongoing support of lean enterprise endeavors. Dr. Allen Ward has contributed groundbreaking work in translating the subtleties of the Toyota product development process into useful tools and ideas. His work has been carried on by Michael Kennedy, Durward Sobek, Jeffrey Liker, and others. Don Reinertsen has continued to build on his already considerable contribution to slashing time-to-market, most recently with a specific focus on lean product development. Finally, several other authors have brought their unique perspectives to the field, including Clifford Fiore, John Bicheno, and Mary Poppendieck to name a few.

From the standpoint of influence on the material contained in this guidebook, however, the true credit goes to my client firms and professional peers for enabling me to test, refine, and retest many of the tools and methods found herein. In particular, I would like to thank Tim Matuseski, Norm Raffish, Maria Elena Stopher, Doug Carlberg, Kaye Treese, Dave Hogg, Phil Ebeling and his team, Tim Mitchell, Mike Barre, and Jon Simons. Finally, I owe an enormous debt of gratitude to my wife, Renee, who is my editor and publisher. She has worked with me on four books (so far) and has managed not to kill me in my sleep (so far).

Ron Mascitelli
September, 2006

"Nothing is more simple
than greatness; indeed, to be
simple is to be great"

Ralph Waldo Emerson

About This Guidebook

Over the past decade, tremendous progress has been made toward the elimination of waste on the factory floor. It is not surprising, therefore, that as lean manufacturing has matured, attention has been drawn to the upstream process of new product development. After all, even the most efficient factory cannot design the products that it produces. If new product introductions are being launched "fat and slow" then all the lean manufacturing in the world cannot ensure a company's long-term success. Indeed, implementation of lean manufacturing is not enough: competitiveness depends on establishing a product development process that can feed the factory with great, cost-optimized products at a lightening pace.

Herein lies the challenge: product development is different from manufacturing - fundamentally, inexorably different. Yet the compelling need to eliminate waste remains the same. Why is it different? Let me count the ways. Product development is cross-functional, making communication, consensus, and coordination, both complex and difficult. Customer requirements don't come in the form of drawings and work instructions. Instead they often arrive through ambiguous channels, in a language that requires interpretation and translation. While manufacturing is inherently a recurring process, the design of each new product is, at least in some respects, unique. Risks are higher, the probability of success is lower, and showstoppers such as excessive cost and intractable new technologies lurk around every corner.

The very good news is that, although product development is truly a different animal from operations, much of the knowledge and indeed many of the tools of lean manufacturing can also be applied to this critical upstream process...with a little modification. As you will see in the pages that follow, a practical, proven, and immediately deployable toolbox has evolved over the past decade that can help any firm achieve significant reductions in time-to-market. Moreover, by following a systematic approach to implementation, achieving these gains can be relatively straightforward.

This book is the second in a series of practical manuals for eliminating waste throughout the design and development process. The first installment, entitled *The Lean Design Guidebook*, focuses on strategies for eliminating unnecessary cost. This latest guidebook's aim is to eliminate *wasted time*, in both the broad, strategic sense of time-to-market, as well as in the more tactical sense of the day-to-day activities of design team members. The intended audience is practitioners: scholars should be warned that they might find their hands a bit dirty after reading this book. The foundation for the material that follows is rooted in an exhaustive study of the literature, but it is the implementation experiences and improvement successes of dozens of firms that give the lean tools and methods described in this guidebook their credibility. Executives and managers should view this manual as a comprehensive roadmap to process improvement and strategic deployment. Team leaders will learn practical time-saving tools and detailed instructions on how to use them. Working-level designers and developers will discover many ways to make their daily efforts more efficient, of higher value, and frankly, a lot more fun. Finally, those of you who are consulting and training professionals will find this guidebook to be an invaluable resource in crafting your own customized improvement programs.

The material is presented in chronological order from the earliest stages of project selection and prioritization to the transition of a new product design to the factory floor.

The term "lean method" is used to identify individual tools or techniques that attack a specific type of waste (e.g., endless meetings, poor communication, disruptive change, e-mail overload, etc.). Those of you who have read *The Lean Design Guidebook* will notice that there is a small but necessary overlap of material. However, both the figures and the text within these overlapping sections have been recreated with a fresh, updated, and time-sensitive perspective, so they are worth a second look.

The writing style is fast and informal, with extensive graphics (over 150 figures and drawings), and a bit of humor thrown in to keep both the reader and the author stimulated. Important concepts are illuminated through a combination of step-by-step instructions and real-world examples. Although the actual experiences of many firms are described, their names have been omitted to protect their privacy and competitive advantage. Near the end of the guidebook, I've identified some useful resources for the serious practitioner of lean product development. A section entitled "Recommended Reading in Lean Product Development" provides a sampling of books that I believe significantly contribute to the field. The bibliography lists over eighty additional references that were used as source material. Finally, a glossary is provided to ensure that we all share a common language.

In closing, I will offer a brief motivational speech. All of us in the lean community know that Toyota Motor Company is great (okay, "great" may not be a strong enough word), but many other fine firms have independently solved problems of waste, risk, and time-to-market in unique and valuable ways. Certainly Toyota's insights are deeply embedded in this material, but the innovations and successes of many other firms are also represented – truly a "best-in-class" approach. Yet reading about other firms' successes can take you only so far. Why not step out on your own and achieve some of your own lean breakthroughs? All it takes is some independent thinking and problem-solving ability to adapt the lean toolbox presented herein to your firm's specific needs. This guidebook will help you and your firm make significant progress toward faster time-to-market and greater product development efficiency...wherever you may be on the path to perfection.

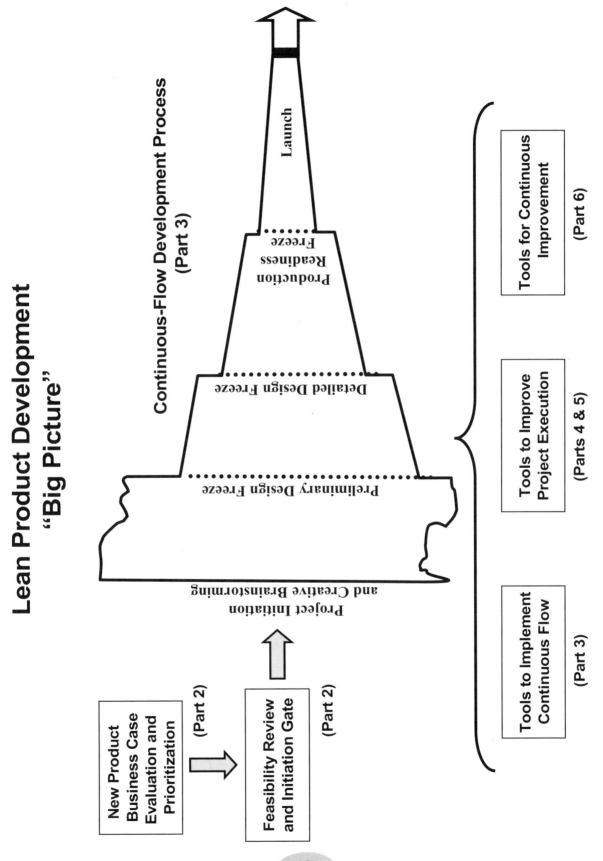

Lean Product Development
"Big Picture"

*"Common sense is something
that you already know,
once someone points
it out to you"*

Ron Mascitelli

Part 1

The Benefits of Lean Product Development

*"I'm working to improve my
methods, and every
hour that I save
is an hour added to my life"*

Ayn Rand

How Time Impacts New Product Success

To quote the theme song from a popular television series; "It's a jungle out there." I can't think of an industry sector that has not been shaken to its core by the events of the past twenty years. The combined impacts of globalization and information technology have changed competition from a walk-a-thon to a drag race. Certainly if your firm produces high-technology or biomedical products, this reality must be embedded in your DNA by now. But even the most mature industries are not immune. Whether you produce hose fittings, farm implements, or the latest high-tech gadget, there is a big factory somewhere in China that is cranking out increasingly competitive products at costs that make your head swim. The following sections describe how product development fits within this new competitive landscape, and provides some initial ground rules for meeting the challenge. Andrew Grove of Intel once famously stated, "Only the paranoid survive." Taken a step further, one could easily say that "only the *fast* survive".

The Three Dimensions of Lean Product Development

The challenge of achieving excellence in lean product development is illustrated in Figure 1.1. For a firm to be competitive, there are three distinct dimensions of design and development that must be addressed; neglecting any one dimension can be a recipe for market failure. First, the development process must yield products that respond to a market need and can garner an acceptably high *price*. Naturally, unique and innovative products command higher prices, so the first dimension of product development can be enhanced through innovation. Tools that foster innovation include structured brainstorming, methods for capturing the "voice of the customer," and systematic design techniques such as Set-Based Design (covered in Section 4.3).

Second, the cost of a product must allow for a substantial profit to be made by the firm that produces it. This implies that *cost optimization* is also a critical dimension of product development. There is a pantheon of tools that support integrated cost reduction, including Toyota's "3P" process, Design for Six Sigma (DFSS), Design for Manufacture and Assembly (DFMA), and Value Engineering (VE). (Reader note: Integrated cost reduction is the subject of the first installment of this guidebook series, entitled *The Lean Design Guidebook*.)

The third and final dimension of new product development is *time*. Historically, time-to-market has been the weak sister of the trio. It is only in the past two decades that speed and efficiency have been considered the equals of price and cost. In fact, in many industries today, this relationship has been turned on its head: the difference between the total profits generated by a "first-to-market" product and a "fast-second" product can be so great that time-to-market ultimately determines success or failure.

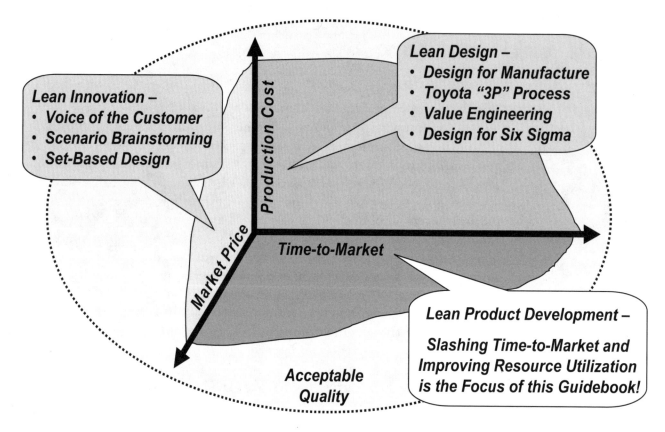

Figure 1.1: For a firm to achieve excellence in product development, there are three dimensions of capability that must be addressed: maximizing price, minimizing cost, and accelerating time-to-market. The latter dimension is the focus of this guidebook.

It is this third dimension that is the focus of this guidebook, and a challenging dimension it is. Henry Ford once said, "Wasted time is the hardest form of waste to eliminate, because it doesn't lay on the floor where you can trip on it." In truth, the hardest part about achieving lean product development is simply identifying what is waste and what is value. In the factory, we can see buildups of work-in-process (WIP) inventory or the unnecessary movement and handling of materials simply by walking the floor. Can you "see" waste by walking through the cubicles of a design department? Unfortunately, a messy desk is not necessarily an indication of waste; some of the most productive designers that I've worked with have had offices that bordered on being a health hazard. What about general activity level? Surely lots of communication and collaboration are indicative of a tight-running ship. Again, not really. Depending on the type of work being done, silence might indicate deep thought and intense concentration, whereas lots of "communication" might be nothing more than idle chitchat. Even the old standby of team collocation (something which, in principle, you could see) has been successfully cast aside in many cases in favor of geographically dispersed virtual teams. In short, there is no obvious (i.e., superficial) means by which you can evaluate the efficiency of a product development group.

Before we begin enhancing your eyesight for waste throughout the design process, however, some additional motivation for improving time-to-market is in order. There are several compelling reasons to focus on speed and efficiency. As you will see, this mandate applies to virtually every industry, and can make or break your next new product introduction.

The "Market Clock"

Perhaps the most familiar motivation for slashing time-to-market is the "market clock". Ever since the first early bird snatched a juicy earthworm, it has been a well-established axiom that getting to market first is a very good thing. The reasons why it is good are related to how markets behave relative to the timing of a new product introduction, as illustrated in Figure 1.2. The market clock begins ticking when a new product becomes desirable by customers, and ends when that product either becomes obsolete or is intentionally replaced. Note that the former is not necessarily "as soon as someone gets it to market". Whereas most new products address an existing need in a new and improved form, revolutionary products can actually be introduced *too early*. If a new product enters the market prematurely, it may die from lack of interest despite having a bright (albeit distant) future. Consider, for example, the initial introduction of HDTV, or perhaps the Apple Newton personal digital assistant. For most products most of the time, however, faster is better.

Assuming that being too early is not your problem, the products that your firm produces probably follow the behaviors shown in the figure. Sales revenue generally goes through an initial rampup as a new product penetrates the market, followed by a period of slow or no sales growth as the market for the product matures. Once penetration is complete, the market will slowly saturate, resulting in a decline in revenue. This decline is typically accelerated by the entry of many competitors who must divide up an already mature market. Finally, some firm will introduce a new and improved product that renders the current generation obsolete, and the whole cycle begins anew. Although the timeframe for this behavior can vary dramatically for various product categories (e.g., refrigerators versus microprocessors), the general trend is much the same.

What is fascinating about all of this is that profits don't typically track with revenue. In most cases, the first product of a given generation to hit the market captures a disproportionate share of total profits. This can be understood by considering three possible points of entry, as shown in the lower half of Figure 1.2. If a firm reaches the market first (point "A" in the figure), it can often command a relatively high price due to its monopoly position in the marketplace. With essentially one-hundred percent early market share, the margins can be huge. However, once even a single competitive product reaches the market, margins typically begin to shrink. If a firm were to enter the market at point "B," for example, they would have sacrificed all of those monopoly profits, and would be forced to price their product competitively from the very start. Introduction at point "B" is representative of the fast-second strategy that many firms have embraced. You wait for someone else to define a new market, enter it as fast as possible, and try to eat their lunch. Certainly the risk is lower with this approach, but so are the benefits. Even in this case, speed is of the essence if a firm wishes to avoid the vast wasteland known as "commoditization". If a company delays market entry until point "C" in the figure, a number of competitors will have already entered the market, so clear differentiation no longer exists. Price becomes the only source of competitive advantage, much to the benefit of the consumer and to the great disbenefit of the competing firms. Product introduction at this late stage can result in a net loss for the firm: the paltry remaining profits may not cover the cost of development and capital investment.

Certainly the behaviors exhibited in the figure are an oversimplification, however the general story remains much the same. If you're late to market, you can never go back and capture those lost profits. The market clock keeps ticking whether you are in the market making money, or still dithering over whether your product needs just one more added feature.

More Projects Per Design Team Member

Here's an interesting twist on the same theme. A large percentage of firms cannot unilaterally decide when they introduce a new product. This may result from seasonal effects (snowblowers generally do poorly during the dog days of summer), or could be driven by the demands of key customers. Many firms, for example, are forced to time their new product entries based on one or more "windows" that are set by major big-box retailers such as Home Depot or Wal-Mart. At Home Depot, for example, changes to their product mix are only considered a few times per year. If a manufacturing firm misses one of these periods, they may wait up to a year before getting another shot at shelf space. Trade shows can also dramatically distort the market landscape. Sporting goods manufacturers, for example, must have new products ready for spring and fall trade shows or they risk losing an entire season of sales. In this surprisingly common situation, speed to market is morphed into "speed to the next market window".

The two most common market conditions are contrasted in Figure 1.3. The upper portion of the figure represents an open-market situation, in which getting the product out as soon as possible is the best revenue- and profit-maximizing strategy. The lower half of the figure illustrates how a firm might respond to a market window imposed, for example, by a big-box retailer. Rather than focusing on speed alone, the total number of projects that will be completed by the next time-window must also be considered. In a sense, firms in this situation must aim for the highest *productivity* from their design team; maximizing total revenue and profit per market-defined period.

So how might firms in this environment focus their improvement efforts? Naturally, if speed is all that matters (top of Figure 1.3), any benefits gained through the application of lean tools and methods should be applied exclusively to the slashing of time-to-market. Firms constrained to fixed market time-windows, however, would be better off using a split approach, striving for a balance between achieving enough speed to hit the window while

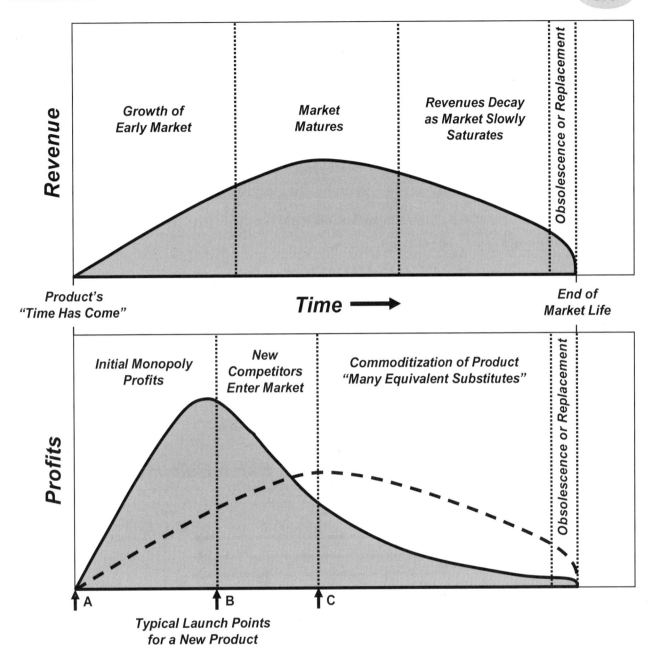

Figure 1.2: An illustration of market behavior over time, often referred to as the "market clock". The top graph represents a typical trend for the revenue of a new product, beginning when the product first becomes desirable by the marketplace and ending when the product is rendered obsolete. The lower graph shows how profits often behave over the same time period, demonstrating the significant benefits of early market entry. A firm that introduces a product at point "A" captures a disproportionate percentage of the total profits, as compared to entry at point "B," or (heaven forbid) point "C".

increasing their capacity to complete more development projects per period. Although most of the waste-slashing methods described in this guidebook will help firms in both situations, there are a few exceptions which will be duly noted as we proceed. If you find that your product timing is being driven by a dictatorial market, take special note of my comments on this topic throughout the remainder of this guidebook.

Case 1 – Time-Sensitive Products Released ASAP

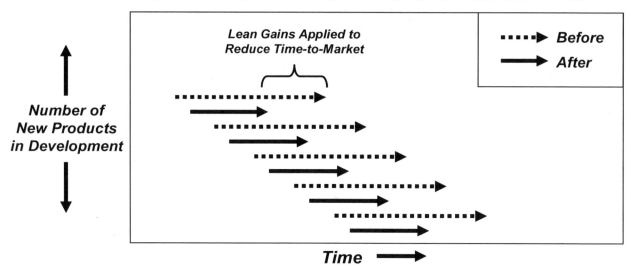

Case 2 – Market Forces Batch Release of Products

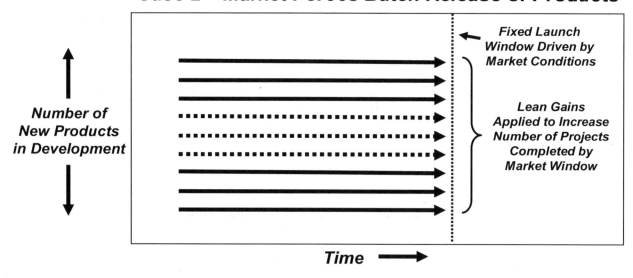

Figure 1.3: A comparison between the two most common situations with respect to the timing of market entry. The top graph illustrates the familiar "get to market as quickly as possible" condition. The lower graph shows how a fixed market window can distort the timing of new product entries.

Lower Development Cost

Here's one you might not have thought of: Eliminating waste from new product development will almost certainly reduce the cost of non-recurring engineering. Now this might not seem important, particularly if development costs in your firm are buried in operational overhead. Even if they are not directly visible, however, these costs can mean the difference between turning a *real* profit on a product and taking a net loss. As you will soon learn (see Section 3.3), the cost of design and development must be considered when choosing which products to produce, and is subtracted from total profits when developing the business case for a new product. There is really no need to belabor this point; faster products are also cheaper products. Enough said.

A Mandate for Speed and Efficiency

I doubt that you would have purchased this guidebook if you were not already convinced of the need for faster and more productive new product development. Therefore, I will assume that you are sold on the goal. From this point forward, we will get down to brass tacks. In the next section we will begin to develop your "sixth sense" for waste and value within the product development process. Rather than whispering, "I see dead people" (from the movie, *The Sixth Sense*), however, you will find yourself walking the halls of your firm whispering, "I see waste."

Notes

Learning to See New Product Development Waste

Improving new product development can be an intimidating prospect. Defining an effective cross-functional process can be daunting, requiring buy-in and support from myriad functions, support groups, suppliers, and, of course, executive management. Once a new and improved process is in place, sorry to say, you have only taken the first step. The real gains in speed and efficiency come from improving the way that process is executed on a daily basis. This reality is often neglected; improvement teams and lean champions tend to focus on high-level, strategic initiatives, while ignoring grassroot improvements. As mundane as it may seem, an hour wasted in a poorly run meeting is just as important as an hour wasted due to an inefficient product development process. Strategic thinking is great, as far as it goes. But as I will reiterate throughout this guidebook, *the only way a company can improve product development is by changing the way people work every day.* The best weapons for fighting waste are basic, commonsense, and practical. It is reasonable to identify targets from 40,000 feet, but to attack problems effectively, you need to be flying down near the treetops.

The "Five Principles"...Adapted

This just wouldn't be a lean book without a reference to the "five principles of lean thinking". These core principles involving value, pull, and flow, are what originally attracted me to the lean improvement philosophy. There is not much room for ambiguity here; waste is bad and value is good, and you are unquestionably better off doing less of the former and more of the latter. That being said, the five principles that were originally presented in the groundbreaking book, *Lean Thinking*, by James Womack and Dan Jones, don't quite fit the world of new product development. Therefore, I've taken the liberty of adapting them to the subject at hand, and adding a bit of personal insight as well:

Principle #1 – Precisely specify the *value* of a new product.
Principle #2 – Identify the *value stream* for creating the new product.
Principle #3 – Allow value to *flow* without interruptions.
Principle #4 – Let the customer *pull* value from the development team.
Principle #5 – Continuously pursue (economical) *perfection.*

The first principle begs the question, "Who is the arbiter of value?" The answer is, of course, the customer. Therefore specifying the value of a new product cannot be accomplished without actually listening to customers. The marketplace can speak to us in many ways, from the labyrinthine intricacies of market research and data mining to the anecdotes heard every day by sales people, field engineers, and technical support representatives. Indeed just listening to customers is not enough to specify value (although it is certainly a good start). The voice of the customer must be interpreted through several levels of the organization before a detailed product specification can be created (see Section 4.1).

Once product value has been specified, the design and development process can begin. In the jargon of lean, this process is often referred to as the "value stream". Hence, Principle #2 demands that an efficient, low-waste methodology be defined and communicated to all those who touch new product development. There are many opinions on what a "best practice" looks like in this regard; I will put my oar in the water on this subject in Section 3.2. In truth, however, it really doesn't matter all that much which best practice you choose (do I hear a gasp from the reader?). Certainly there are some awful processes out there, but within reason almost any sensible methodology can be leaned-out to achieve acceptable time-to-market. As long as your firm utilizes cross-functional teams and doesn't let administrative overhead sap too much productivity, almost any process can achieve lightening speed.

The real breeding-ground for waste is often not in the process itself, but in its execution, as is highlighted in Principle #3. Obstacles to the flow of value are everywhere, as shown in Figure 1.4 (we used to say in the aerospace community that it's a target-rich environment). Inefficient handoffs among development team members are a common obstacle, as are draconian reviews and approvals. Poor initial requirements definition is a barrier that is frequently exacerbated by disruptive changes as the design of the product progresses. The batching of activities can cause significant delays; waiting for a monthly executive review to receive approval to proceed, for example, represents a "time batch" that can add weeks to the development process. Lack of needed information, available resources, and effective communication all represent rocks in the river of value. In fact, a majority of the lean tools and methods presented in this guidebook are focused on eliminating obstacles to the flow of value.

Principle #4 calls for the development team to respond to the "pull of the customer". In this case, "pull" means responding to the articulated and unarticulated needs of the customer (both external paying customers and internal process customers), rather than guessing at what is needed and throwing it over the wall. Product designs should be a collaboration between design teams and customers, even when the "customer" is really a broad and inhomogeneous segment of the marketplace. In this sense, business-to-business enterprises may be better off than firms that sell to the open market. Being a supplier to other firms is hard, but at least you can develop collaborative relationships with your key customers over time. It is far more difficult to read the minds of the general public, particularly for products that depend on taste rather than necessity.

Finally we arrive at the fifth principle of lean thinking, and this is where I must insert an editorial comment. As it is traditionally stated, firms should "continuously pursue perfection". Here's the problem that I have with that statement; it can lead to as much waste as it eliminates. We are all familiar with the concept of diminishing returns. Business is not a hobby that we can obsess over and pursue without practical limitations.

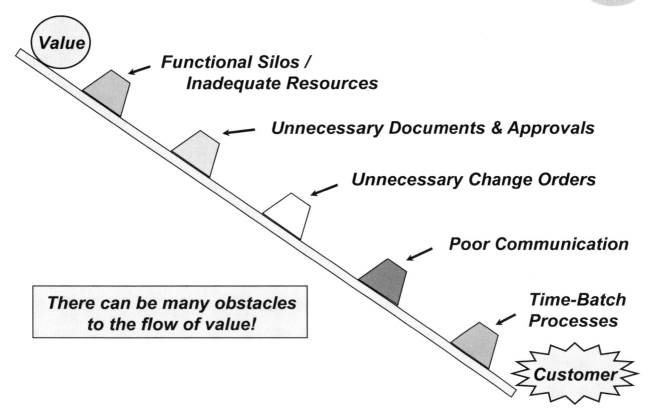

Value

**Functional Silos /
Inadequate Resources**

Unnecessary Documents & Approvals

Unnecessary Change Orders

Poor Communication

**Time-Batch
Processes**

**There can be many obstacles
to the flow of value!**

Customer

Figure 1.4: Obstacles to the flow of value can include barriers caused by functional silos, lack of needed resources, unnecessary documentation, excessive approvals, disruptive changes to specifications, delays caused by "time batches," and, as always, poor communication.

Business is an *economic pursuit* that demands constant attention to how time and money are invested. If an improvement initiative takes a week to implement and saves months of time, that would be a worthwhile investment of both time and money. If, however, an improvement requires months of effort to save a few hours here and there, it is waste in sheep's clothing. The trick to avoiding this trap is to constantly review opportunities for improvement and *set priorities*. As long as a significant payback can be demonstrated, go for it. Don't squander your precious resources working on trivial problems.

Finding the Target: A Top-Ten List

Taiichi Ohno is famous for enumerating the types of waste found within the manufacturing environment. Is it possible to create a finite list of the types of waste in new product development? While I can't say that it is impossible, I can assure you that creating such a list would not be of much use. I suppose, for example, that one could group together poorly run meetings, unnecessary e-mails, wasteful handoffs, etc., into a single category entitled "waste due to poor communication". It's just not clear how that would help us solve the problem. Specific problems require very specific solutions. The method we might use to address poorly run meetings (see Section 5.5), for example, is completely different from the approach needed to improve handoffs among team members (see Section 3.2). In fact, I have thus far identified twenty-eight tools and methods that can help slash waste throughout product development, with each method attacking a unique target. Hence, I'll leave the semantic grouping of the types of waste to the academics, and proceed with helping you become faster and more productive. What I can provide is an experience-based list of what I consider to be the "top-ten" sources of waste in new product development, as shown in Figure 1.5. Although the order might be different for your firm, it is almost certain that you are experiencing most, if not all, of these forms of waste on a daily basis. Let's go through the list in reverse order (David Letterman style).

"Top-Ten" Sources of Product Development Waste

Chaotic work environment – constant interruptions	Section 5.3
Lack of available resources – resource bottlenecks	Section 5.6
Lack of clear prioritization of projects / tasks	Section 4.2
Poor communication across functional barriers	Section 5.2
Poorly defined product requirements	Section 4.1
Disruptive changes to product requirements	Section 3.3
Lack of early consideration of manufacturability	Section 3.4
Overdesigning, analysis paralysis, gold-plating	Section 4.1
Too many @!%&* meetings	Section 5.5
E-mail overload – the "e-mail avalanche"	Section 5.5

Figure 1.5: The author's "top-ten" list of sources for product development waste. Although the order may be different within your firm, it is likely that most, if not all, of these sources are eating away at your productivity and speed.

Starting with e-mail waste may seem anticlimactic until one adds up the time spent on dispositioning the avalanche of e-mails that most workers receive on a daily basis. 3M Corporation recently performed an in-house survey of its development team members and found that over an hour per day is spent on such activities, with only a small fraction of that time considered to be necessary and valuable. Any of you who have watched coworkers banging away at their Blackberries instead of participating in important meetings will understand how distracting and time-consuming this can be. There is no question that e-mail is an essential business tool. However, the lack of commonsense guidelines for its use has resulted in a significant (and frustrating) time-waster. And speaking of time-wasters, the most common complaint that I hear in working with companies is that team members spend far too much time in meetings. All that I said about e-mail waste applies here as well; meetings are essential, but in the absence of disciplined tools, waste abounds.

On a different note, even the act of designing a new product can lead to an insidious form of waste. It goes by many names: design overshoot, analysis paralysis, gold-plating. Designers are driven to pursue perfection, both by personal commitment and often by management direction. For a given product, however, there is a clear point at which the marketplace will neither recognize nor reward an excessive design. In most cases, a "good-enough" product will fare just as well as an overdesigned product, provided that the customers' true needs are completely addressed. Time spent on "gilding the lily" represents an insidious form of waste, since it is difficult to know when good enough is actually good enough.

When is the right time to consider the manufacturability of a new product? The answer is early and often. Although cross-functional teams were intended to bring together the perspectives of all key disciplines, I've found that teams often delay addressing manufacturability well beyond the point of highest leverage. There are some seemingly legitimate reasons for this delay: "We just don't know enough about what the product will look like to bring in the manufacturing folks." Toyota has virtually negated this issue by forming process development teams at the very inception of new product development, and running them in lockstep with the design teams themselves. This represents true product-and-process co-development, wherein a conceptual product design is mirrored by a conceptual design of the processes needed to manufacture it.

Requirements are at the root of the next two sources of waste. Whether it be a lack of definition at the initiation of new product development, or disruptive changes during the design process, a moving target virtually precludes optimal time-to-market. Some changes are driven by compelling reasons; a competitor comes out with a product that undermines your design-in-process, for example. Yet there is much that we can do to harvest more accurate information at the earliest stages of product definition, and a disciplined approach to managing in-process change can alleviate many of the disruptions.

I've never come across a firm that has completely eliminated the barriers to communication that occur across functions. In most organizations, functions develop their own way of thinking, their own jargon, and often a different set of goals from other functions. Certainly cross-functional teams are a positive step in bringing down barriers, but the differences run deep. It is important that a more proactive stance be taken, including the use of lean methods that gently force a meeting of the minds on critical issues within product development.

In real estate, it is said that all that matters is "location, location, location". Well, in new product development, particularly in a multi-project environment, (almost) all that matters is "priorities, priorities, priorities". Most of us are familiar with the concept of *opportunity cost*. If you choose to spend time on one project, you must, of necessity, neglect other projects. The more projects on the table, the more likely it is that, in the absence of clear priorities, you will pick something to work on that is not the best use of your time. Those projects that are the most critical to your firm's future should be elevated above the rest, and that distinction should be communicated to all who are involved in development. Egalitarian concepts such as "first in, first out" have no place in a business environment; it should always be "most important in, first out".

We have now arrived at number two on my top-ten list: the lack of available resources. Imagine that you are planning to drive a rather large truck through a series of mountain tunnels. Assuming that you are wise enough to plan ahead, which tunnel would determine the maximum height of your truck? Well, of course it would be the tunnel with the lowest ceiling. The same is true for new product development. The number and speed of projects is limited by the essential resource that is in shortest supply. In the factory, this type of resource bottleneck can usually be identified; the recurring nature of production implies that bottlenecks tend to stay put long enough to be pinpointed. Since each product development effort is unique, however, bottlenecks can move around quite a bit. Transient "peaks" can occur that will cause one function or another to appear to be a constraint, only to be replaced a short time later by a peak that occurs somewhere else. Although the challenge might be greater than for production, it is still essential that development capacity be managed, and that the number and size of projects be matched to resource limitations.

And last but certainly not least, my number-one pick for the most problematic source of waste in new product development: a chaotic and disruptive work environment. It continues to amaze me that firms invest tremendous effort in bringing together highly qualified professionals, and then force them into an environment in which productive work is virtually impossible. How can highly intelligent and creative designers and developers be expected to accomplish great things when they can't find a moment's peace? When you were attending college, where did you go to study for a tough exam? I'm guessing that you might have chosen the library over your fraternity or sorority house. Yet most firms allow a work environment that more closely resembles a frat party than a study hall. Frequent communication among coworkers is a very positive thing, but constant low-value inter-ruptions, frivolous meetings, loud voices, beeping pagers and ringing cell phones, etc., can sap the productivity of creative professionals. Again, some sensible guidelines can make a world of difference, allowing your firm to become a great design house, rather than an animal house.

In summary, there are myriad sources of waste that impact the product develop-ment process. Each of the lean tools presented in this guidebook focuses on a specific type of waste, or situation that can cause waste, and all of the top-ten sources of waste are directly addressed by tools discussed herein. Just like strains of the influenza virus, however, as new sources of waste are identified, we will need to evolve new lean tools and methods to treat them.

A Working Definition of Value

1.3

To begin our assault on waste, we will need a working definition of value. If this seems backward to you, consider this: It is far easier to identify *what is not value*, than it is to define *what is waste*. Hence, we will use a subtractive approach. If we can agree on a reasonably specific definition of which activities are value-added within new product development, then we can simply say, "If it's not value, it's an opportunity for improvement."

What Is a Customer Willing to Pay For?

While I'm sure that other words could be used, I propose the definition of value given in Figure 1.6. To ensure that the reader is clear on my meaning, I will break it down phrase by phrase. First, the term "activity or task" includes anything that consumes the time of development team members – no exceptions. It is all too easy for waste to hide behind semantic definitions (e.g., "That is really not a task, so it doesn't count."). If you spend time on it, then it should be counted in your waste / value equation. In this context, the term "transform" means to make more complete. I suppose you could transform a product to make it *less* complete, but I'll assume that my readers know which way development is supposed to go. This transformation is not limited to the product design itself; the launch of a new product requires a complex suite of deliverables, including drawings, documentation, promotional strategy, tooling, logistics, and so on. I use the term "deliverable" to denote any essential item that must be in place for the successful commercialization of a new product. (Note that this broad terminology can be abused; deliverables must be *essential*, not superfluous). In fact, it can be said that *all value in product development is embodied in the deliverables needed to launch a new product.*

The last phrase in my definition states that customers must be both "aware of the transformation and willing to pay for it". It seems reasonable that value would be closely linked to customers' willingness to pay. Altruism aside, business is an economic endeavor, therefore getting paid is our best measure of the value placed on a new product. But what about this "aware of it" stuff? As you will soon learn (see Section 4.1), not all transformations increase customer value. It is quite possible to overshoot customers' needs, or to provide "hidden" features or benefits that are not well-communicated to the marketplace. In these instances, your firm has invested time and money, but the customer doesn't reward you with extra revenue. Note that I consider any transformation that results in cost reduction (without sacrificing customer benefits) to be within the scope of my definition. My justification is that, ultimately, the customer is better off paying a lower price for the same product, even if you don't pass along the cost savings until competition forces a price reduction.

> **"Any activity or task is <u>value</u>-<u>added</u> if it transforms a new product design (or the essential deliverables needed to produce it) in such a way that the customer is both aware of it and willing to pay for it."**

"Value"   **= Value-added (essential) tasks**

"Type 1" (Enabler)   = Non-value-added but currently necessary

"Type 2" (Waste)   = Non-value-added and not necessary

Figure 1.6: A proposed definition for value throughout the new product development process, and the three categories of activity that are derived from it.

Finally, one caveat: Insightful readers may have noticed that there are many activities related to product development that don't meet my rather strict definition. What about general market research, training, competency development, investigation of new technologies, and so on? These activities fall into the category of "strategic investments," and as such, create value for the *firm* (at least in the short term), rather than the customers for a specific product. These are certainly essential activities, but to get a handle on waste and value within the development process, I have chosen to exclude strategic efforts, since they don't (or perhaps I should say, *shouldn't*) affect time-to-market.

Three Categories of Development Activity

Based on the definition of value presented in Figure 1.6, we can identify three categories of activity that might take place during new product development. The first category we will simply call "value". This group includes any time-consuming task that meets our value definition. The second category is "enablers" (often referred to in the lean literature as "Type 1" activities). Tasks within this group are not directly value-creating, but they enable value to be generated in some essential way. Team coordination, for example, is an enabler, as is configuration control. In principle, neither of these activities actually transforms the product, but it would be difficult, if not impossible, to create a valuable product without them. Finally, whatever is left over after all of the value-creating and enabling activities are subtracted away, is by definition "waste" (referred to as "Type 2" in the lean literature). Everything that consumes the time of development team members must fall into one of these three categories – again, no exceptions.

With a working definition of value and the three categories of activity in place, our goal for improving product development becomes quite clear, as shown in Figure 1.7. We should eliminate the pure waste wherever possible, and reduce the time spent on enablers whenever possible. The time freed from these non-value-added activities can be redirected toward developing more products in less time. While pure waste represents the low-hanging fruit of lean product development, many of the lean methods presented in this guidebook offer more efficient ways of performing essential, enabling activities. For example, we can't eliminate team coordination meetings entirely (despite the wishes of some downtrodden team members that I've met). We can, however, find a way to accomplish the same goals in less time and with better results.

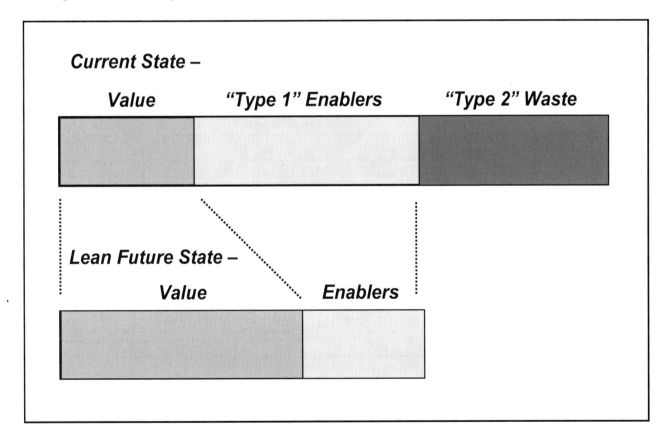

Figure 1.7: Our goal in implementing the methods of lean product development is to eliminate the pure "Type 2" waste wherever possible, and reduce the time spent on "Type 1" enablers whenever possible. The resulting time savings can be applied to improving both product development capacity and time-to-market.

Sizing the Opportunity – Some Results from the Field

Here's a question for you to consider: Based on the value definition and categories described above, how many hours per workday do you spend creating value? No fair counting early mornings, working lunches, late evenings, and weekends. Just the eight (ha!) hours you are *supposed* to be working. If you said to yourself, "One to two hours, if I'm lucky," you're not alone. Consider the results shown in Figure 1.8. Over a three-year period, I harvested data from ten firms spanning a broad range of industry sectors. The data was gathered informally; in some cases through workshop exercises, in others through a daily log sheet filled out by design team members. Although this was certainly not a scientific (i.e., statistically large) study, these anecdotal results send a clear message. Across this disparate study group, the time spent on value creation averages less than two hours per day. In all of these firms, team members complained about long workdays and lost weekends; indeed it was left to the workers themselves to achieve the goals of the company, to a great extent, on their own time.

Firm No.	Description	Approx. No. of Employees	Hours of Value	Hours of Enablers	Hours of Waste
1	Major Aerospace Firm	100,000	1.2	4.0	2.8
2	Major Aerospace Firm	80,000	1.1	4.3	2.6
3	Factory Controls and Sensors	10,000	1.5	5.0	1.5
4	Auto Parts Manufacturer	7,000	1.5	3.9	2.6
5	Aerospace Supplier	4,000	1.8	3.4	2.8
6	High-Technology Hardware	1,500	1.0	4.5	2.5
7	Sporting-Goods Manufacturer	400	2.4	2.0	3.6
8	Division of Insurance Firm	250	1.4	2.8	3.8
9	Solar Energy Systems	150	2.3	2.5	3.2
10	Farm Equipment Manufacturer	130	3.0	1.5	3.5
	Industry Averages ⟶		1.7	3.4	2.9

Figure 1.8: Results of surveys performed by the author over a three-year period with ten firms spanning several industry sectors. Although not a statistically large sampling, the trend is quite clear; only a few hours of value is typically produced by design team members in an average workday.

The time not spent on value-added activities was almost equally divided between enablers and pure waste. Without putting too sharp a point on this small statistical sampling, it appears that there is a trend toward spending more time on enablers in larger firms, with more time squandered on pure waste in smaller firms. This might be explained by the fact that larger firms tend to have more "standard operating procedures" in place to address known wasteful situations. Ironically, it appears that these firms may have simply moved time from the pure-waste category into the enabling-waste category, with little benefit from a value perspective.

Why not perform your own survey? Select a typical product development team and ask them to track their activities for a week or so. Have each member fill out an informal time sheet that records their efforts during each standard workday (in fifteen-minute increments, if you can get that kind of buy-in). At the end of your study period, meet with the team and ask them to help you sort their time based on the three categories described above. (Note that you might need to spend a few minutes discussing the definitions of value, enablers, and waste, to avoid confusion.) If your goal is to kick off an improvement initiative within your firm, you might find that such an exercise will give you a strong lever to gain management attention and commitment. After all, if you can move just one hour per day from the waste / enabler columns into the value column, your firm could realize a very significant improvement in time-to-market efficiency.

Commonplace Problems – Commonsense Tools

At this point, you should be salivating like Pavlov's dogs for solutions to the waste you now (hopefully) see all around you. Fear not. We will begin exploring our lean toolbox in Part 2. Keep in mind as we move forward that this guidebook is organized both chronologically, from the earliest stages of project selection through project execution and launch, as well as conceptually, from a high-altitude, strategic perspective to a workaday tactical viewpoint. Hence, if you are looking for quick hits and easy gains (and lack the patience to read this book in the order that the author intended), you might consider skipping ahead to Parts 4 and 5. There is no real risk in doing so, other than missing out on some very important strategic tools and concepts.

Whether you read this material in order or skip around, one thing should become quite clear. Lean product development tools and methods are just good common sense, as illustrated in Figure 1.9. Personally, I like the second quote in the figure (perhaps because it is my own): "Common sense is something that you already know...once someone points it out to you." In other words, the tools and methods described in this guidebook should closely match your work experience and intuition. If they seem obvious, don't be fooled. As one of my mentors once said about lean manufacturing, "The beauty is in the simplicity."

> *"Common Sense is genius dressed in its working clothes."*
> **- Ralph Waldo Emerson**
>
> *"Common Sense is something that you already know...*
> *once someone points it out to you."*
> **- Ron Mascitelli**

Figure 1.9: Lean product development tools and methods are rooted in common sense. Don't let the practical nature of these concepts cause you to underestimate their power, however. After all, lean manufacturing methods can appear almost childishly simple, yet they have caused a revolution in efficient production.

Selecting and Prioritizing Development Projects

*"We work not only to
produce, but to give
value to time"*

Eugene Delacroix

What Defines a Great Product?

In Part 2, we will discuss the most important step in product development: selecting and prioritizing new product opportunities. It is easy to dismiss this critical activity as being far too "strategic" for mere mortals. However, choosing the wrong projects can be the greatest source of waste in many firms. Hence, even if this topic seems to be above your pay grade, understanding how new product ideas should be identified, quantified, filtered, and rank-ordered is essential knowledge. After all, you just might be running things someday. Well...at least you can sound really smart in executive meetings.

Attributes of a Great Product

There is a common misconception as to what constitutes a "great" product opportunity. Most people are familiar with legendary breakthroughs such as the Walkman, Palm Pilot, IMac, IPod, and so on. These high-visibility icons appear to be what every firm wants; a moneymaker so powerful that it can elevate a firm above the miasma of everyday competition to new and lofty heights. What is not visible to the general public, however, is the significant risk, pain, cost, and sheer luck involved in creating such products. For every IPod there are literally dozens of failures, many of which have cost their respective firms their financial health and well-being. Even mighty Apple nearly collapsed under the billion-dollar loss caused by the "breakthrough" Apple Newton.

While we shouldn't ignore the possibility of a breakthrough, obsessing over such opportunities is like moving to Hollywood with the hope of being discovered. It could happen, but it is more likely that you'll end up waiting tables and nursing broken dreams. Far better to take a more practical and sustainable approach. In Figure 2.1, I've identified six important criteria for selecting new development projects. For a new opportunity to be truly great, it must satisfy *all* of these criteria to a reasonable extent. Even one missing element can lead to a suboptimal outcome; failing at more than one should be grounds for sending an idea to the bone yard.

First up on our list of key criteria is the need for clear differentiation. Although many companies have based their business models on a "me-too" strategy, this is a tough way to survive. Without an obvious advantage over other products in its class, a new product must enter the market at a lower price point to gain any notice. This puts immediate pressure on margins; a pressure that will only increase as competitors respond to the new challenge. How different does a product need to be? Enough that a clear niche can be identified with sufficient interested customers to provide adequate returns. More

Figure 2.1: There are six key attributes of a "great" new product opportunity. If any one of these criteria is missing, the risks to a product's success increase dramatically. More than two missed criteria should be grounds for setting the idea aside.

will be said about how customers perceive and reward products with unique advantages in Section 4.1.

Risk must also be considered when weighing new product opportunities. There are three general categories of risk that can turn a promise into a curse: financial, market, and technical. Financial risks can include the magnitude of required investment, the availability of needed funds, the returns that might have been generated by lower-risk investments, and so on. Assuming that the financial risk is acceptable (i.e., you would not be betting the company on the product's success or failure), your next question should be: "Is the market forecast relatively firm and objective?" There is a common joke among manufacturers: "The only thing we know for sure about forecasts is that they are wrong." If the predicted sales volumes are based on solid market data and seem reasonable when compared to existing products, the market risk is probably manageable. Alternatively, if the product is being pushed ahead based on gut feel or wishful thinking, step away from the opportunity until adequate data is available. Here's a hint: If the words, "seems like a good idea" come up in a project selection meeting, you don't have enough market data. Finally, the technical risks must be balanced with the potential rewards. A great product does not necessarily require breakthrough (aka, "bleeding-edge") technology, nor does its use guarantee success. Keep high-risk technology out of new products, unless your business model depends on such things to survive.

The next three criteria demand alignment with the existing capabilities and strategy of your firm. A nice analogy might be to consider how one walks on thin ice. Most sensible people would carefully place one foot on a nearby area and test it for firmness. If you can shift your weight to this new position without causing the ice to crack, the move is relatively safe. The farther out you reach, however, the more likely it is that your jump to the new position will end in disaster. Does your firm have manufacturing capability, capacity, and capital equipment that can be substantially leveraged when the new product enters the factory? Does your design or engineering organization have adequate internal competency to handle the technical aspects of the project (or at least enough understanding to manage outside consultants)? I've often said that the ideal manufacturing firm produces products that appear highly differentiated to the marketplace, but the designers and operations folks can't tell the difference between them. An exaggeration to be sure, but trying to be something that you are not is generally a bad idea in life and in business.

The final criterion mandates the need for financial discipline when weighing a new product opportunity. All of the other criteria are subjective, whereas the need for quantitative evaluation through solid financial techniques stands out as being coldly objective. As will be discussed below, there are several metrics that can be used to assess the value of a new product opportunity. Whichever metric you choose, keep in mind that performing due diligence prior to project selection can save significant time and effort on the part of your precious design resources.

Applying Financial Discipline to Project Selection

I've come across a number of firms that essentially ignore financial metrics when selecting new products for future development. I believe this is due to either intellectual laziness or a form of denial. Some executives believe that performing business-case calculations (such as estimating net present value) is just too difficult to be worth the effort. This is analogous to saying that optimizing your 401k investments is just too much trouble. If being blithely unaware of lost wealth is your cup of tea, then by all means skip over that nasty financial stuff.

The other common reason for not applying solid metrics to new product selection is denial. What if the numbers don't look good? Then we might have to shoot down an idea that we really like. I suppose it is human nature to put faith in intuition and hunches, but turning a blind eye to objective information is irrational. Avoid the trap of "don't confuse me with facts, I've made up my mind". Great products will stand up under scrutiny, and the ramifications of selecting weaker projects are just too great to put forth anything less than your best effort.

A number of possible metrics for evaluating the business case for a new product opportunity are shown in Figure 2.2. I'll be honest; there is no better cure for insomnia than discussing finance. Hence, I will offer the reader a moment to refill your coffee, suck on a sugar cube, or splash cold water on your face. There, now you should be able to focus your attention for just a few pages of vital, albeit dusty, information. First, let me offer some relief. I will not be describing all of the metrics mentioned in the figure. My personal favorite is net present value (NPV), and as such I will use it as an archetype. Besides, if your firm is sophisticated enough to understand the subtle advantages of expected commercial value (ECV), for example, you can probably skip this section.

The basic NPV calculation is shown in Figure 2.3. In a sense, we are trying to capture all aspects of the business case (i.e., revenue, price, cost, and profit) in a single straightforward number. In fact, the output of the NPV equation is in dollars (or the currency of your choice). Moreover, understanding the meaning of this output is child's play; positive dollars *good*, negative dollars *bad*. Now a financial person would define NPV as "the total discounted future cash flows from a product, minus the non-recurring investment". Actually, in English, all of that jargon simply means that we add up the profits and subtract what it costs to earn them. The "net" result is a measure, in today's dollars, of what we can expect to earn from the product over its entire market life.

Let's dig just a bit deeper into this calculation. What is meant by "discounted future cash flows"? In this context, cash flows translate into profits. Hence, we must subtract the estimated cost from the estimated price of the product for each year that we expect it to be in production. This estimated profit margin is then multiplied by a forecast of the annual sales volume, yielding a total profit for each year of the proposed product's anticipated life. Before we go any further, you might have already detected a fundamental weakness of NPV (or any other such financial metric). If we must guess at the market price, estimate the marginal production cost, and forecast the sales volume, how much confidence can we have in the number that we generate? The answer is somewhere between throwing darts at a dartboard and holding a wet finger up to the wind. I never take the numeric output of NPV very seriously, but as you will soon see, it is a useful tool for sanity-checking an opportunity and rank-ordering it relative to other possible new products.

After we've estimated the cash flow for each year, we must correct these numbers by applying a discount rate. Here is where some artistry is required. The discount rate used for NPV is not simply a "future value of money" correction. Certainly inflation will reduce the value of profits in future years when compared to the present, but this is only the tip of the iceberg. The discount rate actually represents *lost opportunity*. For example, if you keep your money in a mattress, inflation will degrade your savings over time. Not a very good retirement strategy to be sure, but it gets worse. In reality, you could have put that mattress money into a certificate of deposit that would earn more than the inflation rate. So you aren't just throwing away inflation, you are actually losing the interest that could have been earned in the CD. Now if you have a brother-in-law who is a stock analyst, your money-bed strategy is poorer still, since he could likely have helped you earn even more than the CD on an annual basis. Hence, your lost opportunity is actually the difference between investing with your brother-in-law and earning zero in your mattress (this, of course, ignores the emotional cost of trusting your brother-in-law).

For a firm, the lost opportunity should be based on what other product investments typically earn. If the average net return on recent product investments is ten percent, for example, this is a reasonable number to use as your discount rate. Many firms refer to this number as an "internal rate-of-return threshold" or IRR threshold. When used as the discount rate for NPV calculations, the IRR threshold ensures that the profitability of new development projects is comparable to (or better than) other recent successful projects. A negative NPV in this case means a lower projected return than the IRR threshold, while a positive NPV implies higher than average profitability.

Profitability Metric	Formula	Advantages	Disadvantages

Net Present Value (NPV)	$= \text{Sum}_{t=0,n} \dfrac{(\text{After-Tax Cash Flow})_t}{(1 + \text{Discount Rate})^t} - \text{NRI}$
	
	NRI = Non-recurring Investment
		• Fairly comprehensive.
		• Widely used.
		• Enables easy decisions:
		  NPV > 0 Profitable
		  NPV < 0 Cancel Project
			• Depends on soft data such as market forecasts.
			• Some complexity involved.
			• Needs enhancements to accommodate risk.

Internal Rate of Return (IRR)	= Discount Rate at which NPV=0	• Easily understood and has intuitive meaning. • Considers time value of money, but ignores other risks.	• Tedious to calculate, but no harder than NPV. • Fails to recognize the varying size of investments in competing projects.
Profitability Index (PI)	$= \dfrac{\text{Net Present Value}}{\text{Initial Investment}}$	• A nice concise number for project ranking. • Optimizes utilization of capital; important if cash is scarce.	• Not intuitive – can only be used for ranking. • Puts weight on available cash, rather than on available resources.
Expected Commercial Value (ECV)	$= ((NPV \times P_{cs} - C) \times P_{ts} - D)$ P_{ts} = Probability of Technical Success P_{cs} = Probability of Commercial Success D = Development Costs Remaining on Project C = Commercialization (Launch) Costs	• Has at least the potential to be highly accurate. • Captures risks better than any other approach. • Provides job security for your finance department.	• Gives the impression of accuracy and validity, but is still subject to the same risky data. • Far too complex for most organizations.

Figure 2.2: An overview of several financial metrics that can be used to estimate the future potential of a proposed new product opportunity. The most commonly used are net present value (NPV), internal rate of return (IRR), or a combination thereof.

$$
NPV = \left\{ \frac{\text{All the Net Profits You Expect to Make from a New Product}}{\text{Corrected for Inflation and Financial Risk}} \right\} - \left\{ \begin{array}{c} \text{Upfront Costs} \\ \text{such as Tooling,} \\ \text{Product Design, etc.} \end{array} \right\}
$$

NPV > 0

(GOOD Product)

NPV < 0

(BAD Product)

Figure 2.3: The calculation of net present value (NPV) is based on several estimates: future price, future cost, and forecasted sales volume for all years that the product will be in production. Although these estimates result in significant inaccuracy, NPV is quite useful as a sanity check on the validity of a business case, and as a ranking tool for new product opportunities.

Okay, so we now have a number for the total estimated future profits in today's dollars. To earn these dollars, however, we must first spend some money. Design team members must be paid throughout development, capital equipment and tooling must be purchased, promotions must be funded, and so on. The non-recurring investment (NRI) term in the NPV equation is a catchall for these initial investments. Once subtracted from the estimated profits, we get a number that represents the net value of the proposed project. As I mentioned above, all of these financial machinations yield an output of dubious accuracy. However, when compared to other similar calculations, the NPV can be used effectively as a prioritization tool. In other words, even if the absolute values of the calculations are of limited use, their *relative* values are typically good enough to rank your opportunities.

Correcting for Project Risk

I wish that I could tell you we are done, but unfortunately there is still more to be considered before we select our next great product development project. Our goal throughout this section has been to effectively rank-order opportunities so that we can apply our finite resources in the most profitable way. To do this, however, we need to be sure that we are comparing apples with apples. If we must choose between two possible projects, for example, knowing the NPV of each is not quite enough. Suppose that Product A has an NPV of $1M, and Product B has an NPV of $2M, which development project would you pick? Very good. Now suppose that I told you that Product A is a straightforward extension of an existing product, with no new technology, and an anxious and well-established market. Product B, on the other hand, is a totally new initiative, using high-risk technologies, and with a sales forecast based on nothing more than a guess by the head of marketing. Feeling a little insecure about your choice? Perhaps a million dollars in the hand is worth two in the bush.

The only way that we can reasonably compare Products A and B is to somehow compensate for the very different *risks* involved. Market risk results from uncertainty in the sales forecast of a new product. Sources of this risk include a lack of history in the proposed product's category, a very long time-horizon (the farther out we must go with a forecast, the more inaccurate it becomes), and weak market research. The easiest way to compensate for this variance is to insist that the forecasts for both products be equalized for risk. A relatively firm forecast can stand without adjustment, whereas a highly uncertain forecast must be derated sufficiently to reflect its proportionally higher risk. In this case, the NPV calculation for Product B should use the most conservative end of the forecast range. Assuming that your marketing group is capable of something other than irrational optimism, it should be possible to balance market risk in this way, so that the two possible development projects can be effectively compared.

All well and good, but what about *technical risk*? Unfortunately, this is a tougher nut to crack. Technical risk can cause significant schedule slips, higher than expected engineering costs, increased capital investment, and if the technology fails to perform, a worthless product. Probably the easiest way to adjust for differing technical risk is to increment the non-recurring investment term in the NPV calculation to account for the added costs mentioned above. This really doesn't capture the whole story, but frankly I'm not certain there is any rigorous way to quantify this intangible risk factor more accurately. Instead, I will propose in Section 2.3 a method for mitigating technical risk before the development process actually begins. By performing an early, low-level feasibility study, a firm can filter out projects with unacceptably high technical risk, while allowing projects with manageable risk to move forward.

As I used to say to my father as a child, "Are we there yet?" Unfortunately, then as now, the answer is "Almost." In the next section, I will bring this project prioritization process to a close by incorporating two more factors that just cannot be ignored: the strategic importance of new product opportunities, and their impact on scarce design resources.

Notes

Too Many Projects, Too Few Resources

In Section 2.1 we discussed a practical approach for evaluating the business case for a new product opportunity. Although the risk-corrected net present value (NPV) for a product has a high degree of uncertainty, it can be a useful indicator of which opportunities should be placed high on your priority list. As will be demonstrated in this section, however, there are still two factors that should be considered before we are ready to pick our dream product(s) and unleash the development team(s). Both the "strategic importance" of a new product and its demands on design-team resources must be considered when creating an optimized priority list. Fortunately, these considerations can be incorporated into our prioritization approach in a simple and straightforward way.

The Reality of Finite Capacity

A few years ago, the hot book among manufacturing types was *The Goal*, by Eli Goldratt. This industrial parable highlighted the critical importance of identifying resource constraints throughout a factory. Whether referred to as a "bottleneck," or the "weak link in the chain," a resource constraint represents the point in a process that has the smallest relative capacity. By relieving these constraints and matching demand to capacity, the overall output of a factory can be significantly increased. It seems odd to me that although the idea of managing *finite capacity* has become a no-brainer for the operations folks, this concept has been largely ignored in the context of the product development process. Time for a reality check; your firm *does* have a finite development capacity, whether you like it or not. Moreover, that capacity directly determines the number and value of new products coming down the pipeline to fill your factory (not to mention your balance sheet).

It is disturbingly common to hear general managers or engineering directors say something like, "I don't need to set priorities; my people know what to work on." Or here's one that's even scarier: "I won't set priorities for the development group because that will just give them an excuse not to do it all." Failure to set priorities for finite development resources is frankly unacceptable in a competitive environment. Let me be clear about this; *it is the responsibility of every manager to set priorities for their direct reports*. The big question should not be, "Should I set priorities?" but rather, "How do I go about doing it?"

The answer to this question might surprise you. Despite the effort invested in calculating a risk-adjusted NPV, prioritizing your new product opportunities on that basis alone *would almost certainly be suboptimal*. To prove my point, consider the example presented in Figure 2.4. Let's assume that a firm has identified six exciting opportunities for new product development (Products A through F in the figure). Each product has a positive NPV, even after risks have been considered. Now I admit that if management were to use the magnitude of NPV alone to prioritize these projects, they would certainly be better off than setting no priorities at all. However, we can actually do much better. Suppose that our fictional firm has an available design capacity of 10,000 hours per year (I will explain how to arrive at this number for your own firm later in this section). Based on an NPV-only prioritization, the available capacity could accommodate just the first two products (Products A and B) on our list. (Note: For simplicity, I've assumed that these products all take about a year to develop and that they all start development at about the same time. These assumptions can easily be generalized to more realistic situations without loss of validity.)

At this point, you might be thinking; "In our firm, we would just work on all six products and take two or three years to get them done." Sad but true in many cases, however it should be obvious after reading Part 1 of this guidebook that a much slower "do-it-all" approach will cost your firm significant profits. Assuming we agree that faster is better, why not just develop Products A and B over the next year, take our $17M to the bank, and feel satisfied? Well, because we could actually make considerably more money with the same finite resources. Consider what would happen if we rank-ordered our opportunities by the NPV for each project *divided by the estimated number of design hours required to complete it.* As can be seen in Figure 2.4, the resulting priority list would look quite different, and the profits generated with our finite capacity of 10,000 hours would jump by $7M! By taking the ratio of NPV to estimated design hours, we are prioritizing not by future profits alone, but by the *productivity* of the design organization. Product opportunities with higher NPV per design hour make better use of those precious designers and developers. This result is summarized in Figure 2.5.

How might a firm come up with the design-hour estimates mentioned above?   The topic of resource capacity management and optimization throughout the product development process is discussed in detail in Section 5.6. For now, however, a high-level estimate will be adequate. A rough assessment of design capacity can be determined by identifying the key functions required to execute your development process and adding up the available hours per year for each function. Note that "available hours" should take into account the typical corrections for vacation, sick leave, weekends, etc., as well as any recurring demands on these resources (e.g., sustaining factory support, improvement initiatives, training, and so on). To estimate the number of design hours required to complete the proposed projects on your wish list, compare each opportunity to similar projects from your firm's recent history. You will probably have to guess at how many hours were spent, and make some corrections for differences in complexity, technical risk, etc., but even a rough order-of-magnitude estimate will work.

Based on these ballpark numbers, you can calculate the NPV-per-design-hour ratio for each project and generate your priority list. How many of those projects can actually be completed in a timely manner? Compare your list to the overall capacity estimate you generated, and you can clearly see which projects can fit within your available capacity, and which fall below the line.   The real challenge for you and your firm will be to resist the temptation to force additional projects onto the development organization beyond their

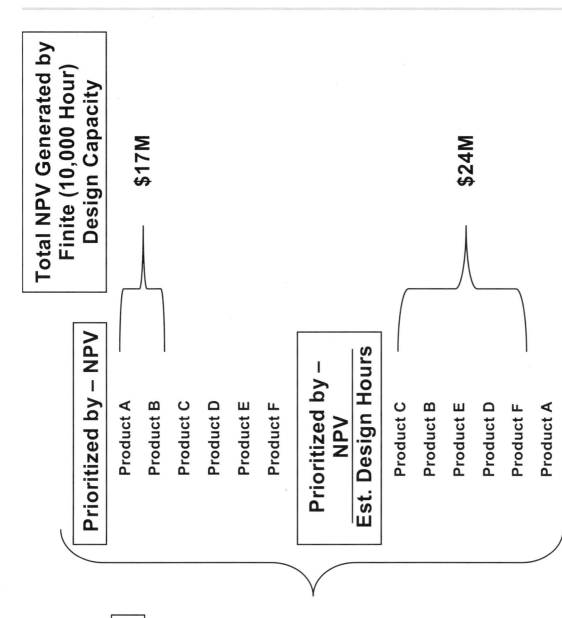

Total NPV Generated by Finite (10,000 Hour) Design Capacity

$17M

Prioritized by – NPV

Product A
Product B
Product C
Product D
Product E
Product F

Prioritized by – NPV Est. Design Hours

Product C
Product B
Product E
Product D
Product F
Product A

$24M

Possible New Products

Product A –
NPV = $10M
Est. Design Hours = 7000

Product B –
NPV = $7M
Est. Design Hours = 3000

Product C –
NPV = $6M
Est. Design Hours = 2000

Product D –
NPV = $5M
Est. Design Hours = 2500

Product E –
NPV = $3.5M
Est. Design Hours = 1500

Product F –
NPV = $2.5M
Est. Design Hours = 1500

Figure 2.4: An example that illustrates two ways of creating a priority list for new product opportunities. The use of net present value (NPV) alone to set priorities fails to consider the demands on finite development resources. By taking this factor into account, a firm can make better use of designers' and developers' time, resulting in higher total profits.

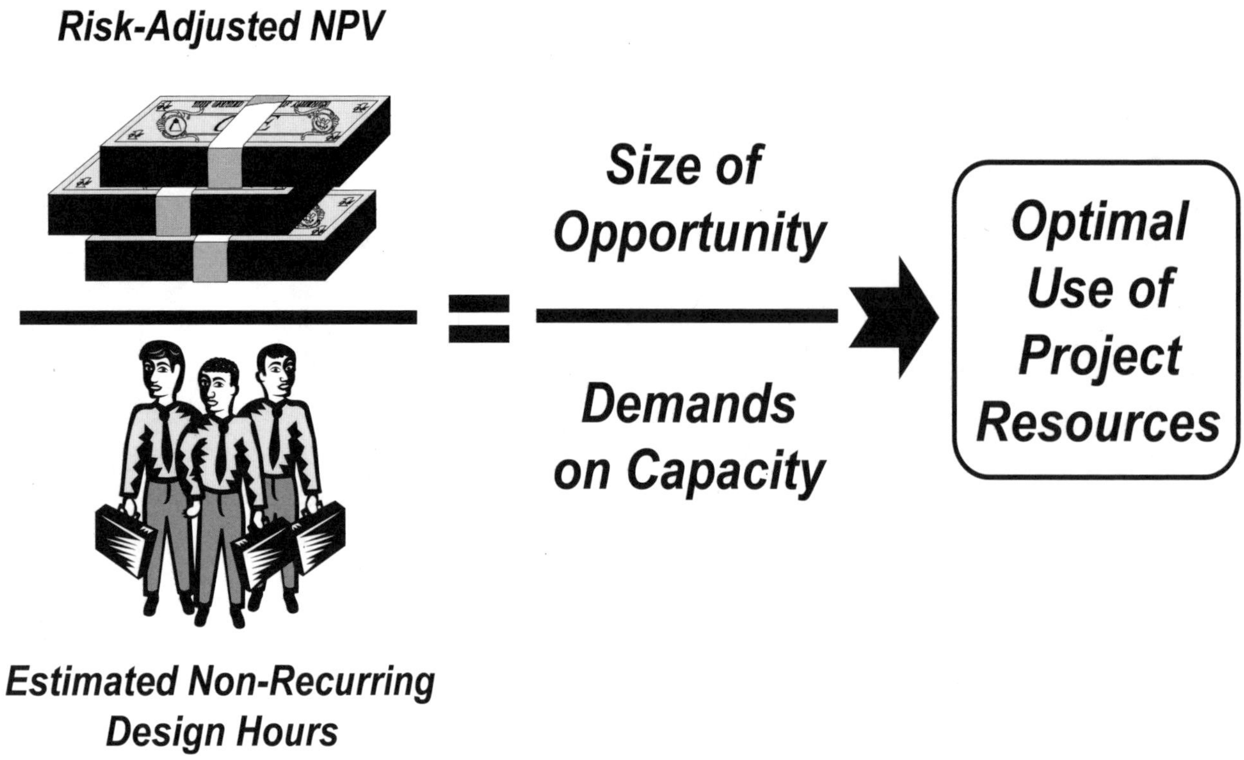

Risk-Adjusted NPV

Size of Opportunity

=

Demands on Capacity

Optimal Use of Project Resources

Estimated Non-Recurring Design Hours

Figure 2.5: A summary of the author's proposed metric for prioritizing new product development opportunities.

available capacity. Product development is not like a flexible bladder that can expand if enough force is applied. Driving an organization to work on far more projects than can be handled by its available capacity creates more waste than benefit. If you're frustrated with the number of new products your firm can create, why not expand capacity? No, you don't have to hire people (although that might be the best long-term solution for chronic capacity bottlenecks). Just put your shoulder behind implementing the lean methods described in this guidebook, and your firm's capacity will grow significantly without having to add any cubicles.

Strategic Products – Real and Imagined

The term "strategic product" is thrown around a lot in marketing circles as a justification for elevating the priority of a new product opportunity beyond its financial worth. In principle at least, a strategic product is one that creates long-term value and / or competitive advantage for a company. Often this type of product can have an impact far greater than its own (often paltry) revenues and profits. In these cases, strategic importance is assumed to outweigh mundane goals such as making money. While there is no question that such opportunities exist, for every truly strategic new product there is a plethora of imposters. In fact, it has become a common joke in the product development community that calling something a strategic product is really just another way of saying "money loser".

Several legitimate reasons for elevating the priority of a project above its financial value are given in Figure 2.6. This is certainly not a comprehensive list, but these factors are both typical and important. The first potentially valid justification is that the proposed new product will ensure retention of existing customers. As an example, consider a subsystem supplier to the commercial aerospace industry. There are really only two major customers in this sector, Boeing and Airbus, along with a few relatively minor players such as Bombardier and Embrear. If the subsystem supplier decides not to bid on a new contract with Boeing, for example, due to poor projected financial returns, they may find themselves in disfavor when competing for future contracts. In the commercial aerospace industry, the importance of keeping Boeing and Airbus happy can easily outweigh short-term profitability.

Likewise, it may make sense for a firm to pursue a new product opportunity that could enable significant growth of their market share, even if the net present value is marginal. Gaining a dominant foothold in a market can allow for a highly profitable back end, meaning that related products can be sold to the same customers in the future at a substantial profit. Typically this is referred to as the "razor and blades" strategy, wherein a firm offers a loss-leader product to penetrate a new market, and follows with a stream of highly profitable add-ons, parts, refills, etc. This same situation could apply to the

Strategic Factor	Subjective "Score" (1-10 scale)
Retention of existing customers –	
Growth of market share –	
Development of new markets –	
Increased "mindshare" among customers –	
Implementation of new technology –	
Total Strategic Score –	

Multiply total score by 2 to create a "strategic-importance" metric that is normalized to 100.

Figure 2.6: Several examples of legitimate strategic considerations that might elevate the priority of a proposed new product. A subjective scoring system is used to create a simple metric that represents "strategic importance".

development of new markets (the third justification identified in the figure). Although an initial product entry might not be profitable, it could pave the way for future cash cows.

The concept of "mindshare" is really just technospeak jargon for public relations. A firm can often create a powerful buzz within its customer community by introducing something exotic, highly advanced, or just plain clever. If done properly, the market awareness generated from this type of strategic product can put small firms on the map, and elevate larger firms to market dominance. A good example of this strategy is Microsoft's initial introduction of the Xbox gaming platform. It was well-publicized that they lost money on their first production version, but no one was playing the sad violin for Bill Gates. The relatively low introductory price of the Xbox (below their cost for the initial production runs) enabled Microsoft to successfully penetrate a highly competitive market. Once a substantial market share was established, the profits started rolling in from license fees, internally developed games, future upgrades to the platform, and so on.

Finally, the implementation of an exciting new technology may be justification for creating a product that is not highly profitable. Identifying a product to serve as a test bed for a new technology can be an effective way to work out the bugs, while simultaneously educating the market as to the advantages of the new approach. The first flat-screen televisions, for example, were priced well above the pain threshold of most customers; a fact that was clearly evidenced by miniscule initial sales. By releasing these early, high-priced models, however, firms like Sharp, Samsung, and Phillips, were able to create a market pull for lower-cost models, while establishing the technical expertise and production capability necessary to address a huge future market.

Clearly these and other firm-specific justifications should be considered when determining which new product opportunities to pursue. But how can we incorporate strategic factors into our prioritization scheme in a realistic and objective way? I've proposed a qualitative scoring approach in Figure 2.6 that can allow strategic considerations to enter into your decision process. For each strategic factor (the list will vary based on the nature of your industry and firm), a 1-to-10 score is assigned by a consensus of the product selection team. The scores are added together and normalized to one hundred (this is easy to do if you have five factors – just multiply the total score by two). The normalized score is representative of the strategic importance of the proposed new product.

To display this new metric, I suggest a two-dimensional diagram such as the one shown in Figure 2.7. On the vertical axis, the normalized score for strategic importance is displayed. The "risk-adjusted-NPV-per-non-recurring-design-hour" metric is shown along the horizontal axis. The goal when selecting new products for development should be to find opportunities that have both a strong business case (horizontal axis) and solid alignment with a firm's strategic objectives (vertical axis). Hence, the "sweet spot" shown in the upper-right quadrant of the graph. All development projects need not fall within the sweet spot, but for every highly strategic (aka, money-losing) product, we should endeavor to find a cash cow to compensate. Essentially, we should strive for a mean that falls within the sweet spot. The two-dimensional graph presented in the figure is often referred to as a portfolio planning tool; an essential part of every executive team's arsenal.

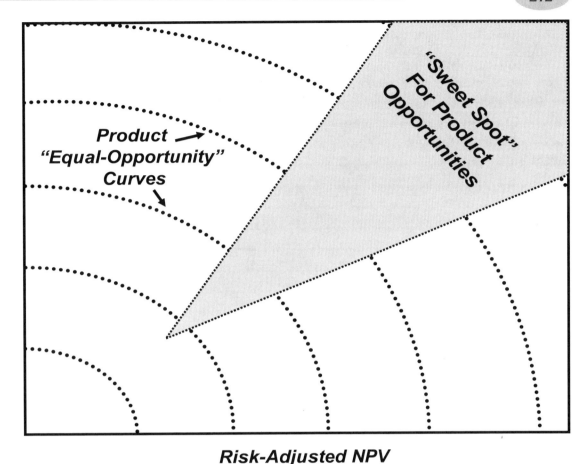

Strategic Importance (Normalized Scale)

Product
"Equal-Opportunity"
Curves

"Sweet Spot"
For Product
Opportunities

Risk-Adjusted NPV
Non-Recurring Design Hours

Figure 2.7: A two-dimensional portfolio planning tool that incorporates both
financial and strategic considerations. The "risk-adjusted-NPV-
per-design-hour" financial metric is plotted along the horizontal axis,
while a qualitative strategic-importance assessment is represented
on the vertical axis. New product opportunities that fall within the
"sweet spot" in the upper-right quadrant represent an excellent
balance between acceptable profitability and good alignment with
a firm's strategic objectives.

Yes, we've finally arrived at an effective method for selecting and prioritizing new
product development opportunities. Was the journey worth it? If you're thinking that all
of this financial and strategic rigor is way over the top, consider this: The vast majority of
failed new product introductions *could have been predicted and killed before the first hour of
design time was invested.* The best time to filter out weak opportunities is as early as
possible. Your organization shouldn't open the starting gate for a development project
until a reasonable effort has been made to justify your commitment of time and money.

Notes

A Simple Way to Manage Technical Risk

Section

It is rare these days to find a product that has not been dramatically transformed by recent technological advances. Even if the product design itself has not been affected by new technology, surely the manufacturing processes used to produce it have undergone revolutionary changes. From the customer's perspective, technology-rich products offer the prospect of higher performance, enhanced ease of use, broader capabilities, and often, lower cost. Yet for every new breakthrough in product or process technology, there is a company somewhere that is cursing the day they decided to be first. How can a balance be struck between the market benefits of implementing new technology (in some cases, bordering on a market mandate), and the inherent risks associated with anything new? As you will soon see, the key to achieving this balance is to deal with higher than acceptable risk *up front* during the design process. Often these risks can be mitigated through a front-end feasibility study. Ultimately, however, when it comes to new technology, firms need to know when to hold 'em and when to fold 'em.

The Technical Feasibility Review

First let me emphasize that incorporating new technology into a new product just for technology's sake can have disastrous consequences. Firms should avoid a knee-jerk reaction to changing markets; the choice of which technologies to use in your new products should be based on customer benefits, not paranoia. There are many fine examples of products that have achieved market greatness by using "old" ideas and methods. If you are a tool person, for example, pick up a recent Sears catalog and take a look at the Craftsman line of hand tools. Over the past decade, Sears Craftsman has introduced a steady stream of highly innovative devices to grab, turn, cut, and shape materials. Having made extensive use of several of these little gems, I can tell you from personal experience that they represent significant breakthroughs in functionality and ease of use. Yet, not a single one of them requires technology that wasn't available *prior to World War II*. While I'm sure that computer-aided design (CAD) systems helped their designers work out the details, and that computer numerically controlled (CNC) machines enabled tighter tolerances and lower costs, the basic designs could have been found in the Da Vinci manuscripts.

Now consider a contrasting example. Sony announced in Spring 2006 that they were delaying delivery of their much-anticipated PlayStation 3 gaming system for at least six months due to problems with a new copyright protection technology. It seems that the new technology was so deeply embedded in the structure of their system that it could not be either repaired or replaced by a lower risk approach without a major redesign of the product. Try to imagine what this delay has cost Sony. Although I am loath to criticize the decisions of such an amazingly successful and innovative company, in this case they really stepped in it. While effective copyright protection is critical to appropriating returns from their monumental R&D investment, the potential losses resulting from piracy cannot compare to the cost of a half-year launch delay in an incredibly competitive and fickle market.

If we assume for the moment that new technology is both necessary and appropriate for your next new product, how can your firm best manage the risks involved? The key is to *assess technology risk during the project selection and prioritization phase, before development resources are committed.* Based on this early assessment, a small-team feasibility study might be launched for a new product opportunity to bring the risk down to an acceptable level. Once the study is complete, the results would be fed back to the product selection team, which would then decide to either kill the project or begin full-scale development. A straightforward process to implement this risk-reduction strategy is shown in Figure 2.8.

As the figure illustrates, once the product-selection team has prioritized new opportunities (either by using the two-dimensional method described in Section 2.2, or any other approach that works for you), there is still one more step that should be completed before the development process begins. A technical feasibility review should be held for each high-priority project, unless the technical risks are well-understood and extremely low. During this review, the potential pitfalls of the proposed project are assessed, and a recommendation is made regarding its future development path. New opportunities that appear to have acceptable risk are assigned a fully staffed development team and given the green light (note that the level of acceptable risk is a strategic decision and can vary dramatically from industry to industry). Projects for which the risk is considered to be either unknown or unacceptably high, however, can follow two possible paths to redemption. If the risk level is truly hair-raising, the opportunity is sent back to the prioritization / planning stage and reserved for possible future development. If the risks are well-understood and not completely horrifying, a small team is selected to perform a feasibility study. The goal of this study is to more precisely quantify the risk level of the proposed project, and to reduce that risk wherever possible. Upon completion of the study, the newly fleshed-out project is resubmitted to the feasibility review team, and reassessed. Assuming that the risks are now manageable, the project moves forward into development. If the feasibility study yields a negative recommendation (risks cannot be easily mitigated), the project may be relegated to the bone yard.

The details of how to execute a technical feasibility review and feasibility study are discussed in the next subsection. From a high-altitude perspective, however, the goal is to equalize the risk of all projects that enter the development process. By applying minimal resources at this early stage, firms can avoid the catastrophic waste of time and money often associated with high-risk opportunities. Launching a lean product development process should be like pulling the trigger on a gun; once the team is given the go-ahead, it should be a straight shot to the factory, with all known obstacles to success either reduced or eliminated.

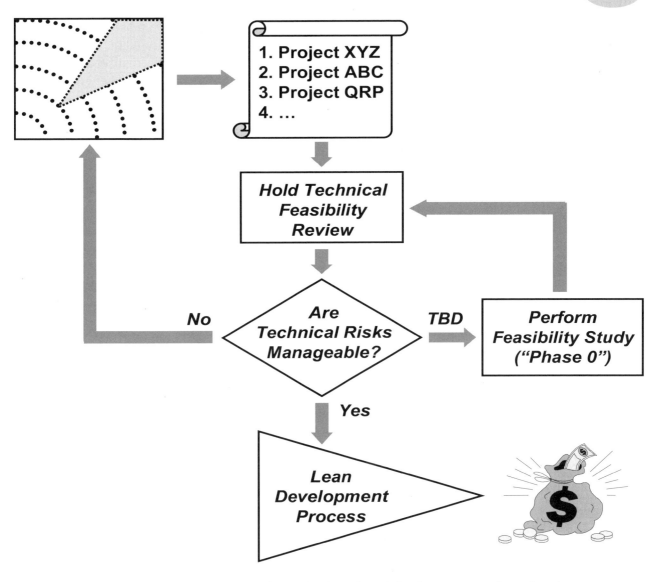

Figure 2.8: A simple process for reducing the risk of a new product development project to a level that is manageable. Risk can never be completely eliminated, but the use of a technical feasibility review and small-team feasibility study can filter out projects with excessive risk, and reduce the risk of the remaining projects to acceptable levels.

Turning a Crapshoot Into a Sure Thing

Unfortunately, there are no sure things in new product development (despite the hyperbole in the title above). Unforeseen problems can always arise, even after the most rigorous of initial risk reduction efforts. We can, however, address known risks before they cause major damage. A technical feasibility review need not be a formal (i.e., regularly scheduled) meeting. It can be invoked on an ad-hoc basis whenever a proposed new product is recognized to have serious risk issues. The attendees at this review should include members of your firm's product selection team, plus any additional technical experts that might be needed to identify and quantify the technical risks involved. If most of your projects are technically challenging, you might consider appending this type of review to your product selection process so that all new product opportunities are put through this screening process.

Once the meeting has convened, an agenda such as the one shown in Figure 2.9 should be presented to the group. In essence, this agenda is simply a series of questions that must be answered, with the final question being, "What are our recommendations for this new product?" I won't take the reader's time discussing each question individually; their meanings should be self-explanatory. As always, you may need to include additional questions, or rephrase the ones that I've suggested, to meet your firm's specific needs. Since it is the *output* of the feasibility review that is of the greatest interest, I will spend some time describing how to arrive at a valid recommendation.

The output from a technical feasibility review can come in three forms. The first possible recommendation is to kill the project altogether (or relegate it to an archive for future consideration). If, after ample discussion, the technical risks appear to be insurmountable, killing a project may be the best alternative. Valid reasons to sideline a promising idea include: a) your firm's internal competency is just not up to the challenge, b) it would be very expensive and time-consuming to mitigate all of the known risks, c) there are unknown or suspected risks that cannot be nailed down but appear to be pretty scary, and d) there is no data to support the compatibility of the new technology with a production environment. As hard as it is to be a killjoy, it is in the best interests of your company to make optimal use of finite development resources. Better to kill now than to kill later, after time, money, and emotional energy have been wasted.

On a brighter note, you might find at the conclusion of your feasibility review that the technical risks associated with a proposed product are manageable. Keep in mind that there is a tendency to fool ourselves about such things, so be sure that your review team has been as objective as possible. That being said, if the risks are acceptable, it's time to start the development process. At this point the unacceptably chancy projects have been sent to the dustbin and the pussycats have been given the go-ahead. What about those new product ideas that fall somewhere in the middle? In reality, these moderate-risk opportunities could prove to be winners, provided that technical concerns can be sufficiently mitigated. Hence, rather than simply making a "go / no-go" decision, I suggest that the feasibility review team be allowed a third option: the formation of a small team to specifically address the feasibility of the proposed project. The duration of this feasibility study effort should be kept short; generally no more than a month (remember that time still equals money). The study's objective would be to address a list of action items generated by the technical feasibility review team. These action items might include, for example, performing a literature or patent search, fabricating a rough prototype, conducting a design-of-experiment (DOE), or doing some environmental testing. Once these risk-mitigating tasks are complete, a follow-up feasibility review would be held and a final go / no-go recommendation would be made.

Before we leave this topic, I'd like to highlight some variations on the theme of risk mitigation. The strategy described above works great if your firm has some inkling that the

Key Questions for a "Technical Feasibility Review"

▶ **Do we have the <u>internal competency</u> to implement the new technology?**

▶ **If not, have we identified external consultants, suppliers, or partners that have <u>proven capabilities</u>?**

▶ **Has the new technology been <u>tested</u> under similar conditions, environments, performance demands, etc., to those expected for our products?**

▶ **Have working <u>prototypes</u> (or at least close analogies) been fabricated? If so, is the data acceptable?**

▶ **Has the <u>producibility</u> of the new technology been proven (e.g., yields, tolerances, variability)?**

▶ **Is the <u>cost</u> of the new technology both understood and within the target cost of the new product?**

▶ **And finally – Is the risk of implementing this new technology <u>acceptable</u>? If not, then what specifically should be done to reduce the risk to acceptable levels?**

Figure 2.9: A suggested agenda for a technical feasibility review. This type of meeting would be held on an ad-hoc basis, whenever a new product opportunity appears to have a higher than acceptable risk. The possible recommendations of the review team include: kill the project, proceed to full-scale development, or "more study needed".

risks associated with a proposed new product are high. What if a project turns out to be a wolf in pussycat's clothing (sorry about the mangled metaphor)? Keep in mind that product risk should be considered both at the inception of a new project, *and also on a continuous basis throughout product development* (see Section 3.3 for a specific method). Often, it is not until a project is well underway that some horrible "gotcha" is identified. Should the development team slog dutifully ahead, even when progress slows to a snail's pace? Not surprisingly, there is a better option. If a significant technical risk is identified mid-project, it may make sense to put the full-scale development effort on hold while a "tiger team" deals with the issue at hand. The rest of the team could be redirected toward other projects, or could work on unrelated activities within the same project. Again, the time to deal with a risk issue is *as soon as it is detected*.

Finally, is there a single, straightforward way to reduce the risk of every project that enters development? The answer is absolutely, but it doesn't come for free. I'll share a personal example to illustrate this technique. For many years, I worked on the development of advanced semiconductor devices for military and scientific applications. During the design process, we were often faced with technical risks that literally challenged the laws of physics. Although our customers were demanding unheard-of performance, it was well-understood that if we could achieve eighty percent of their needs, they would be reasonably satisfied. Hence, for every advanced device design that my team created, *there was always a second, lower-risk backup design*. Creating this low-risk backup took time and money, but the rewards were undeniable. In retrospect, I estimate that the low-risk backup design was selected for delivery roughly sixty percent of the time! Although the cost was not insignificant, carrying this second design saved six projects in ten from utter disaster. Something to consider the next time your firm commits to a risky, high-stakes development project.

Project Sensitivity Analysis

Here's something that I bet has happened to you. You are sitting in a long, boring meeting, and as your mind begins to drift, you look around the room and wonder, "How much is all of these people's time costing our company?" Interesting question; let's do the calculation. First we'll make an optimistic estimate: we'll assume that none of the attendees at your meeting have anything better to do with their time. For this rosy scenario, the cost to your firm would simply be the number of attendees times their fully burdened salaries (i.e., including fringe benefits and any overhead that is typically applied to the labor categories involved). In round numbers, let's say ten people times fifty dollars per hour base rate, which turns into about one-hundred dollars per hour fully burdened...you can do the math. It's costing your firm a grand an hour to bore its employees until they've lost all will to live.

Ah, but that was the "optimistic" case. Assuming that at least some of the attendees have useful work to do elsewhere, we now have to consider opportunity cost. The quality manager, for example, might have spent her wasted hour solving a costly defect issue on the factory floor, while the sales director may have used his time to make an important customer call. When lost opportunity is considered, the bill for your tedious meeting will certainly go way up. Clearly we have a powerful motivation here for avoiding wasteful meetings, and indeed this topic will be discussed in great detail in Section 5.5. Improving the way we run meetings, however, is *not* the subject of this section.

Actually, we are not done with our calculation. We haven't considered the worst possible scenario for your meeting. Suppose that just one attendee, perhaps that quiet, thoughtful-looking type in the corner, is on the *critical path* of an important new product development project. The "critical path" is the sequence of tasks or activities that directly drives a project's schedule; if you slip a day along the critical path, *the entire project will slip at least one day.* If that innocuous person in the corner chair happens to be a design engineer working on a critical-path task, the cost of all the other attendees' time will be rendered insignificant. We now must ask, "How much does an hour of schedule slip on a major project cost your company?"

What a Difference a Day Makes

The idea of "project sensitivity" was first brought to prominence in the incredibly valuable book, *Developing Products in Half the Time* by Preston Smith and Don Reinertsen (see References section, and note that the authors have published a significantly updated second edition). How much does an incremental change in project schedule cost your firm?

In other words, how *sensitive* is a given product development project to a slip in schedule? The answer will almost certainly shock you. Before we dig into the details, let's consider a real-world example. Suppose that a certain medical products company is developing a new life-saving device. The market for medical products is intensely competitive; typically the first mover will gain the lion's share of revenues and profits, since the life of a product generation is often just a few short years. In this particular case, the company actually calculated the cost of a delay in the introduction of their breakthrough new product. The result was truly staggering: A single day of schedule slip could conceivably cost this firm *over a million dollars in lost revenue!* To this company, a working-level design engineer in the middle of a schedule-critical task is worth as much per hour as a star athlete.

The book cited above states that the primary motivation for determining project sensitivity is to generate a set of "decision rules". These rules can then be used to perform intelligent tradeoffs during the planning and execution of a project. Should a new feature be added to a product, even though it will delay shipment by three months? Will an extra month spent on cost-reduction efforts yield a net increase in profits? Questions such as these should be answered by something other than seat-of-the-pants guesswork. While I am wholeheartedly in favor of developing decision rules for these types of tradeoffs, a thorough discussion of this process is provided in Smith and Reinertsen's book. Hence, I will approach this critical subject from a slightly different angle. My focus will be on schedule sensitivity alone (sensitivity to changes in production cost, performance, yield, etc., can also be calculated), and my purpose will be to create a tool for prioritizing team members' time, as well as establishing an unequivocal mandate for avoiding the "hour wasted in a boring meeting" syndrome described above.

As with any financial modeling activity, the calculation of project sensitivity can range from a simple estimate to a complex analysis. Guess which one we are going to pursue? As you may have noticed by now, I am a firm believer in the "80/20" rule, which states that "you can get eighty percent of the benefit from an activity in the first twenty percent of the time". Therefore, we will consider three basic cases that span the range of possible product / market situations. Hopefully, one of these scenarios will closely resemble your firm's business conditions. If not, you may have to dust off an MBA or two to create a more firm-specific sensitivity model.

To determine a development project's sensitivity to schedule slips, we must first decide how a delay will impact its net present value (NPV). As I'm sure you recall from Section 1.1, there are several factors that might be affected by a change in launch date. If we assume that a schedule slip does not result in the product being improved in any way (i.e., performance, quality, and manufacturing costs stay the same), the most important factors to consider include:

  1) A loss in total sales volume over the life of the product.
  2) A reduction in the price of the product throughout its market life.
  3) An increase in the cost of non-recurring development.

To illustrate the three basic cases that we will consider, I've reprised the lower portion of Figure 1.2 and modified it as shown in Figure 2.10. Suppose that a new product's launch date is delayed by one month. How much profit will be lost? The answer will depend heavily on how the product relates to the market clock. During the first-mover period ("Region A" in the figure), the profit implications of a schedule slip could be huge. In the absence of competition, the attainable price for a product will likely be higher than at any subsequent point in its market life. Moreover, the ability of a product to build and retain market share is greatest during this early period. Hence, the total sales volume that a first-to-market product might achieve throughout its years of production can be disproportionately affected by a relatively minor launch delay. If a first-mover product is entering a mature, relatively static market sector (e.g., farm equipment, machine tools, mechanical fittings, etc.), most of those lost sales might be made up later through aggressive promotions. For a relatively fast-moving, highly competitive market sector, however, the chance of recovering lost sales diminishes. Delays can often result in an unrecoverable loss of market standing; once competitors enter the market, prices will typically drop, and lost initial sales will be carved up among other contenders. Consider once again the example of Sony's Playstation III gaming platform. If a dramatic schedule slip causes Sony to miss even a fraction of its holiday sales, for example, those potential customers (and the profits they represent) will simply move to a competitive platform, never to be seen again.

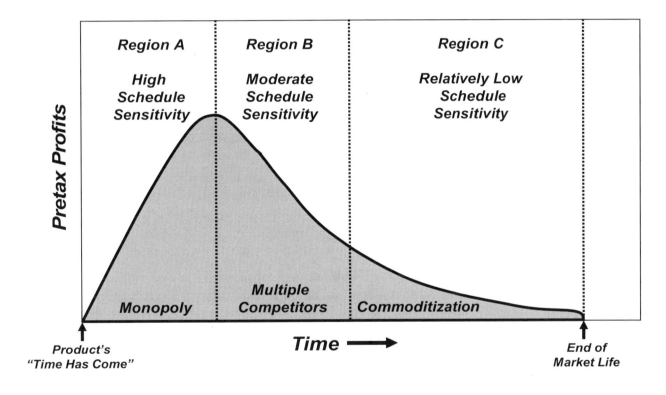

Figure 2.10: A graph showing the typical behavior of pretax profits as a function of time, from the point at which a product is accepted by its market to the end of its profitable life (i.e., the market clock). The sensitivity of a new product to slips in development schedule is generally a function of its position relative to the market clock: products that are launched within Region A, for example, are usually far more time sensitive than those that enter within Region C.

The impact of a schedule slip is typically less severe for products that enter the market within "Region B" of Figure 2.10. In a sense, the existence of even a small number of competitors has a damping effect on schedule sensitivity. In this region, the competitive environment shifts from a sprint to more of a long-distance race, with sales and promotional strategies eventually dominating over an early head start. Again, in a highly dynamic market the cost of a launch delay within this region can still be significant, particularly if the delay causes your product to miss being the "fast second" and end up being a sloppy third or fourth.

As additional competitors enter the market ("Region C" in the figure), the long-distance race morphs into a marathon, with a horde of competitors slugging it out for market share. Within this commoditizing region of market life, incremental changes in price and features will cause slow, pendulum-like shifts in profits and market share. In the land of the "me-too" product, time dilates and the logic of competition is turned upside down. Whereas in Region A the need for an aggressive launch schedule will typically outweigh the benefits of minor cost-cutting initiatives, in Region C a lower production cost translates into a critical competitive advantage. In this latter region, time spent squeezing every penny of cost out of a new product might be an excellent investment, even if the product's launch date is significantly delayed. Again, the development of relatively accurate *decision rules* to perform this type of tradeoff makes good sense for virtually any category of product.

Obviously, the three cases described above represent superficial generalities, but they illustrate a fundamental point. What really matters from a time-sensitivity standpoint is how a new product's launch date relates to the market clock in its market sector. While the strength of this effect will vary by orders of magnitude from industry to industry, in relative terms the cost of a schedule slip will be much greater for highly differentiated, breakthrough products than for more commoditized entrants. We will use this fact later in this section to prioritize the activities of designers and developers, but first we must crunch some numbers.

Estimating the Money Value of Time

As I've mentioned several times, simplicity is king when it comes to lean product development. Yet for some reason, it seems to be human nature to overcomplicate things. Taking a simple approach to calculating the schedule sensitivity of a new development project encourages everyday use. If this metric can be quickly generated from data that is readily available or easily obtained, then the chances of it becoming a standard operating procedure for every project are greatly improved. On the other hand, by including additional factors in our calculation, we can significantly increase its accuracy (provided that these factors are added *carefully*). Since I intend to use project sensitivity as a short-term prioritization tool requiring only modest accuracy, the simple end of the spectrum will serve us well.

A basic approach to calculating project schedule sensitivity is shown in Figure 2.11. Essentially we are comparing the NPV of a project that stays on schedule ($NPV_{T=0}$) to the estimated NPV if the project is delayed ($NPV_{T=DELAY}$). The difference between these terms represents the financial loss associated with a schedule slip. By dividing this loss number by the duration of the delay, we achieve our goal: a metric for the "money value of time" for a specific development project, in units of *dollars per day*. My choice of using such a short increment of time (days as opposed to weeks or months) is intentional, but any time-based units can be employed. The good news about this calculation is that we already know, or at least *should* know, the NPV at T=0. We also control the duration of the delay that is input to this calculation: it is the independent variable in the equation. Hence, the generation of a project-sensitivity metric really comes down to estimating the NPV at T = DELAY.

As mentioned previously, there are three primary factors that could cause a decrease in NPV if the launch date of a new product slips (keep in mind we are assuming that the product does not benefit from the delay). We will discuss each of these in turn, saving the trickiest for last. First the easy one: a delay in project schedule will cause an increase in *non-recurring investment*. Design costs will almost certainly grow, since presumably your firm won't fire the development team as a result of their missing the scheduled launch date. This added cost can be estimated with reasonable accuracy by determining the "burn rate" of the project and multiplying it by the duration of the delay. The burn rate is simply the number of people directly working on the project, times their fully burdened salaries. Typically the burn rate doesn't change as a result of a schedule slip; the same team just keeps working away. If this assumption holds, you can scale the non-recurring design cost used to calculate $NPV_{T=0}$ to the new (longer) project duration. (Note that the assumption of *linearity* is a cornerstone of this relatively simple approach, and is typically valid for small deviations from the original schedule.)

$$P_S = \left(\frac{NPV_{T=0} - NPV_{T=DELAY}}{T_{DELAY}} \right)$$

P_S = Project Sensitivity (in units of lost profit dollars per unit time)
$NPV_{T=0}$ = Original estimate of Net Present Value (NPV) for product
$NPV_{T=DELAY}$ = Estimate of NPV for product if launch date is slipped by T_{DELAY}
T_{DELAY} = Anticipated delay to product launch

Figure 2.11: Calculation of the sensitivity of a specific project to a slip in scheduled launch date. Since we should already know $NPV_{T=0}$, and the duration of the delay is the independent variable in the equation, the real challenge is to estimate $NPV_{T=DELAY}$.

Now things become more challenging. The second factor that we must consider is the effect of a delayed launch date on the *price* that the product can achieve throughout its market life. The easiest way to handle this term is to assume that the price trends that were used to calculate $NPV_{T=0}$ will not be altered by the delay. Certainly if the slip in schedule is relatively short (e.g., a few days or weeks), there should be little impact on the product's long-term pricing power in the marketplace. If the delay is significant, however, say greater than ten percent of the product's market life, the story could be quite different. In this case, while your promising product is languishing, new competitors might enter the market, or existing ones might introduce their own new products. The degree to which these events will impact pricing depends heavily on timing; in general, the earlier you are on the market clock, the greater the price impact of a major schedule slip. If a delay causes you to lose first-mover advantage to a competitor, for example, your pricing power could be significantly undermined both now and forever.

This is also true if a significant delay results in your product's launch date missing some critical milestone. For example, if you sell products to Wal-Mart and miss one of their rigid market windows, you might be forced to modify your entire pricing strategy to enable rapid penetration of other retail channels. The same might be true if you failed to show up at an important trade show. These discontinuities invalidate our assumption of linearity, and can have a major and often unpredictable effect on pricing. In fact, if you are looking at a schedule slip so dramatic that your new product may miss such a critical market window, it might make sense to reevaluate the priority of the entire project. Perhaps it would be better to stop the current development effort and do some soul-searching.

Once we have a sense of how price will be impacted by a slip in schedule, we come to the final factor that we must consider: the impact of a delay on *sales volume* over the life of the product. Here is where complexity can run rampant. There are myriad factors that could be considered when determining how a delay will affect sales. To make matters worse, even for relatively short slips an assumption of linearity is not always valid. Let's say, for example, that your product will be released into a commodity market (Region C in Figure 2.10). In this situation, the long-term sales volume may not be affected at all by a launch delay. The ramp rate for initial sales might change slightly, but this effect would likely be insignificant over the life of the product. Hence, for the case of true commodities, the simplest assumption is that there would be no loss of net sales unless the duration of the schedule delay is a significant percentage of the market life of the product. At the other end of the spectrum, if your new product is intended to be a first mover, then *every day of schedule slip could cost your firm unrecoverable sales*. In truth, if a product's launch timing relative to competitors is important, the market analysis upon which the $NPV_{T=0}$ calculation is based should be completely rethought before estimating $NPV_{T=DELAY}$.

A list of typical factors that should be considered when analyzing the impact of a schedule slip on sales volume is shown in Figure 2.12. Remember that our goal is to keep our calculation simple, so try to focus on only a few heavy-hitters. You should also recognize that several of the considerations that I've listed are dependant upon each other: "high degree of differentiation," for example, is usually strongly correlated to "inclusion of new technology". The best way to estimate the impact of a schedule slip on sales volume is to select the "modeling factor" on the list that best applies to your new product. If it is

Modeling Factor	Typical Impact of a Schedule Delay on Sales Volume	Comments
1) Intended to be a first-mover product	Ranges from extremely high for first-mover products to negligible for commodity products.	The greater the importance of competitors' actions in your market, the greater the impact a delay will have on sales volume. If a market window is missed, competitors may move to fill the void, resulting in unrecoverable lost sales.
2) High degree of differentiation	Increases with degree of differentiation.	The more differentiated a product, the more it looks like a first-mover in its market sector. Both the sales ramp rate and downstream market share can be dramatically affected by a schedule slip.
3) Inclusion of new technology	Advanced technology products tend to be more sensitive to delays than those using mature technologies.	This effect is strongest when the technology directly results in valuable differentiation. High-technology markets generally move faster than mature markets.
4) Long / short product life	Products with long market lives generally are less sensitive to delays than those with shorter lives.	The longer the product's expected market life, the longer a firm will have to make up lost initial sales.
5) High / low degree of market saturation	Unsaturated markets are typically more sensitive to delays than saturated markets.	A saturated market moves relatively slowly. Unsaturated markets offer a greater opportunity to build market share and customer loyalty by being earlier to market than your competitors.
6) High switching costs for customers	Products with high switching costs are less sensitive than those with low or no switching costs.	Switching costs tend to lock-in customers. They may be willing to wait through a significant delay in product launch to avoid the cost of switching to a competitor's product.

Figure 2.12: Several factors that might be considered when determining the impact of a schedule slip on a product's projected sales volume. Note that there can be overlap among these factors; the key is to select the few that best describe your product and use those considerations in your modeling efforts.

clearly intended to be a first mover, then that attribute will likely dominate over others from the standpoint of schedule sensitivity. Likewise, a technology-intensive product that depends for its market success on state-of-the-art innovation would likely be dominated by that factor, and so on.

The last entry in the figure deserves special attention. The term "switching cost" refers to the degree to which your customers are locked into your firm's products. This situation often occurs when a product is a component of a larger, more complex system. Industry sectors for which switching costs are typically high include aerospace and defense, telecommunications, and information technology. Yet even in less technology-intensive industries, the cost of changing suppliers can be prohibitive. If a firm produces toys, for example, and depends on a particular type of child-safe adhesive to fabricate their products, a change of adhesive supplier could be both expensive and risky. In fact, in almost any industry, the first mover in a market can often seduce customers into adopting their proprietary products. Once this dependency is established, the firm gains a degree of sustainable competitive advantage.

A special case of switching costs involves something that economists call "network externalities". If your computer uses Microsoft Windows software, for example, you live (and, no doubt, will continue to live) with extremely high switching costs. As tempting as it might be at times to throw your PC out the window (pardon the pun), changing over to the Macintosh or Linux operating system would require the purchase of new hardware, probably the replacement of application software, retraining of personnel, ensuring compatibility with existing IT infrastructure, and so on. Perhaps even more important, however, is the fact that virtually everyone on the planet knows how to use Windows, and has systems set up to interface with it (the "network" in network externalities). You might decide to bite the bullet within your own firm, but are you willing to deal with the continual frustrations of being different from the rest of the world? Anytime the value of a product depends on its degree of broad market acceptance (e.g., cell phones, DVD recorders, digital media in general, power transmission components, construction materials), the effects of network externalities can be felt. It's good to be the standard in an industry; the more that a standard becomes accepted, the less likely it is that a usurper will come along and unseat the leader. Yet another benefit of being first into a newly forming market.

Becoming "Sensitive" to Wasted Time

Finally we've arrived at the payoff. Assuming that we have chugged our way through the calculation of project schedule sensitivity, how can we make it worth the effort? In this final subsection, I'll describe three typical situations for which knowing the dollar value of time would be a significant advantage. In reality, these are just three of many, but they illustrate the broad range of benefits that can be gained through the use of project sensitivity analysis.

Situation #1 – "Let's squeeze in one more feature."

One of the greatest bones of contention between product designers and marketing types is over something called "scope creep". Despite the diligent efforts of the development team to hit their scheduled delivery date for a new product, those creative folks in marketing keep moving the finish line. An added feature here, a little more performance there, more versions, more customization, more, more, more! This desire to stuff ten pounds of (expletive deleted) into a five-pound bag is often poorly justified; just some hand waving about sales increases and price advantages. How might knowing a project's sensitivity to schedule delays assist in this timeless struggle?

Actually, it can turn an emotional and subjective debate into an objective tradeoff. Suppose, for example, that a certain development project has a sensitivity to schedule slips of $100K per day of delay. Although this may seem like an unrealistic number, it is well within the range of values that I've observed for highly innovative, first-mover products. Now suppose that marketing has asked to add just one more feature to the product. How might the design team respond? Well, their first response should be, "Show us the money!" What will the impact be on sales volume if the new feature is included? How much will the price increase? In essence, *what is the sensitivity of the proposed product to changes in features or performance*? (Note that this represents a different type of sensitivity analysis, which is effectively described in the reference by Smith and Reinertsen mentioned earlier in this section.)

Assuming that the marketers get their act together, the development team would be faced with the tradeoff described in Figure 2.13. Suppose that the added feature is projected to increase sales volume over the life of the product by six percent, and that each percent of sales growth would increase total pretax profits by $500K (we are assuming for this example that profit margin and other factors remain constant). How much of a schedule slip should be accommodated to capture this potential gain? In other words, *where is the breakeven point between additional sales and the cost of a schedule delay*? As you can see in the figure, the decision of whether to include the additional feature can now be made objectively. If the delay that would result from adding the feature is greater than thirty days, it is not in the best interest of the company to include it. If it could be done in a couple of weeks, however, it would positively impact the NPV of the product. No emotions, no pulling of hair or gnashing of teeth. Kind of takes the fun out of it, don't you think?

Situation #2 – "The project tug-of-war."

Here is a situation that is even closer to my heart. A firm has two major development projects underway, with each representing a significant contribution to its future balance sheet. Unfortunately, as is often the case, the two projects frequently compete for the same resources. Assuming that the firm has done its preliminary homework (see Section 2.2), the overall priority of the projects should be clear. So does the higher-priority project always win the contest for resources? Although this simplistic approach to resource prioritization is certainly better than letting the team leaders fight it out *mano-a-mano*, it is not the optimal solution. High-level prioritization of projects is an important

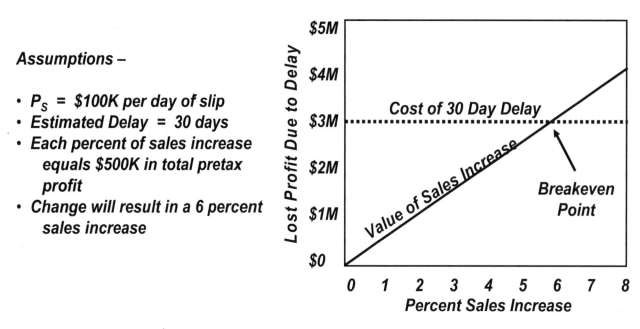

Assumptions –

- P_S = *$100K per day of slip*
- *Estimated Delay = 30 days*
- *Each percent of sales increase equals $500K in total pretax profit*
- *Change will result in a 6 percent sales increase*

➡ **Is this change worth the delay in schedule?**

Figure 2.13: Knowledge of a project's sensitivity to schedule slips can enable better decisions. This example illustrates the tradeoff between project schedule and the projected increase in sales that would result from inclusion of an added feature. For this case, inclusion of the new feature would make economic sense, provided that the additional work could be completed in less than thirty days.

guideline, but in certain situations priority decisions on where to apply shared resources should be based on *which project has the greater sensitivity to schedule delays*. Note that this subtlety should only be invoked when the shared resources are on the critical path of at least one of the projects. Remember that the critical path is the sequence of tasks on a project that directly determine the final delivery date. If a resource is working on non-critical-path activities, the high-level priority of the two projects should determine which work gets done first. If the shared resources are performing critical-path tasks, however, project sensitivity should (temporarily) override the high-level prioritization.

Just to make this point crystal clear, let's walk through a quick example. A key member of your quality organization is responsible for checking drawings on two major projects. Most of the time, there is little or no conflict: Project A is higher on the priority list than Project B, so it gets worked on first. However, as luck would have it, your quality engineer finds herself on the critical path for Project B. Should she still work on Project A drawings first? Just the fact that she is on the critical path of one of her two projects should cause management to reexamine her priorities. If she is not on the critical path for

Project A, the decision is easy; she should work on Project B drawings until she is no longer on the critical path. In fact, even if she is on the critical path for *both* projects, she should still work on Project B unless Project A has a higher schedule sensitivity.

This simplistic example can be extended to any multi-project environment. High-level prioritization works well for non-critical-path activities, however project sensitivity takes precedence for critical-path tasks. Of course this logic assumes that your firm's management understands the critical paths of all the projects involved, as well as any resource conflicts that might occur. This may well be true for project-intensive firms with well-established project management tools, but what about for the rest of us? Even a superficial understanding of project schedules is enough to identify the obvious critical-path tasks. With this rough knowledge, some of the major resource conflicts can be optimally resolved. When in doubt, simply ask the question, "Will the project's end-date slip if this resource does not work on their task?" If the answer is yes, compare sensitivities.

Situation #3 – "You've got to be kidding!"

Okay, we've finally reached my personal bull's-eye. This last example illustrates the most important reason for calculating project sensitivity: to avoid management (and team members themselves) from putting wasteful or low-urgency activities ahead of project work. I'll demonstrate this situation with a personal anecdote. I was recently teaching a workshop at an aerospace supplier's facility. During one of the breaks, an attendee came up to me with a desperate look in his eyes. After a brief chat, his dilemma became clear: he had been forced to attend my training despite being right in the middle of a critical-path activity on the firm's most important project. His human resource director had insisted that, "There is never a good time to go to training." As true as this statement is in most cases (my business depends on companies recognizing that important things must be accommodated), *it is not always the case.* There actually are better and worse times to do training, or perform improvement activities, or attend optional meetings, or even answer your voice and e-mail. Low-urgency interruptions should never cause an important project to slip schedule. If this sounds like a ubiquitous excuse for cutting out on training (i.e., "Sorry, but I'll be on the critical path for the next five years."), it really doesn't work that way. For many projects, the vast majority of activities are *not* on the critical path. Furthermore, I don't recommend that employees be given *carte blanche* regarding the use of this excuse. Being allowed at least one delay, however, as is the case with income taxes and jury duty, would make a great deal of sense.

All of this leads to my number one reason for calculating project schedule sensitivity: to put some sanity into the way employees' time is spent in the workplace. Simply knowing how big that number can be may be enough to cause a change of thinking. If you knew that having a certain employee attend one of your regularly scheduled meetings was costing your firm thousands of dollars per hour, would you still insist on their presence? Shouldn't we be putting critical-path team members under "cones of silence" to ensure their greatest productivity? This is not an overstatement, folks. The economic future of a company is based on how its employees use their time.

In closing, let me offer an analogy. Imagine that you come to work each morning with one-hundred dollars in your pocket. Throughout the day, your coworkers stop by your office and ask you to give them money. You happily empty your wallet, freely giving your peers and managers every cent you have by the close of business (no extortion involved, by the way). The very same thing occurs the next day, and so on. Every workday, your coworkers drain you of your cash, without offering anything in return, or even justifying their request.

Unless your generosity is bordering on sainthood, this situation should seem ridiculous to you. Why on earth would you give away your money without at least being offered a legitimate justification? Well, guess what: *You probably do exactly that with your time.* If project sensitivity analysis has taught us anything, it is that an individual's time can be extremely valuable to their firm. If you allow design team members' time to be drained away like the willing fellow shown in Figure 2.14, you're giving away a precious commodity. Time can neither be inventoried nor bought back. When it is gone, it is gone.

**Are you as free with your money
as you are with your time?**

Low-Priority Tasks

Standard Operating Procedures

Nuisance Interruptions

Noisy Work Environment

Low-Value Meetings

Unnecessary Documentation

E-mail Waste

Excessive Multitasking

Figure 2.14: It is not uncommon for critical members of a product development team to have their precious time wasted on low-value activities. Through the use of lean methods, much of this waste can be reduced or eliminated.

My goal is for developers (and every other employee in your firm) *to become frugal with their time*. I am not fomenting a rebellion here: naturally you wouldn't want employees to unilaterally boycott meetings or shut their (nonexistent) cubicle doors. However, an awareness of the cost of time, particularly with respect to critical-path project work, should be constantly on the minds of all who touch product development. Even if your firm calculates project sensitivity just once, for just one important project, the scale of that number should serve as a wakeup call. Every minute spent on low-value activities is a lost opportunity for your company.

<u>Notes</u>

Building a Lean Product Development Process

"*Coming together is a beginning,
keeping together is progress,
working together is success*"

Henry Ford

What's Your "Organization Number"?

Thus far, we have learned how a firm might go about selecting, prioritizing, and establishing the schedule sensitivity of new product development projects. In Part 3, we will discuss what a lean development process should look like. As always, we will begin at the highest level and work our way into the details. Therefore our first consideration will be the impact of your firm's organizational structure on timely project execution. Now I recognize that transforming the org chart of your company might be out of reach for many readers; my goal is simply to identify strengths and weaknesses, so we can capitalize on the former and mitigate the latter. Frankly, in most cases the structure of a firm is so deeply embedded in internal politics and executive predisposition, that anything more than a superficial change is next to impossible. I hope this is not the situation in your company, but one must accept reality. If you have both the clout and courage to affect organizational change, this first section will point you in the right direction. Even if your sphere of influence is defined by the walls of your cubicle, fear not. Just knowing the nature of your organization can enable significant and realistic improvements in product development speed and efficiency.

Traditional Organizations by the Numbers

From the earliest days of my career in aerospace, I recall hearing about the so-called "matrix" organization. The matrix was supposed to solve everything; functional managers would handle the development of core competencies and define long-term growth paths for the firm, while project leaders would deftly manage design projects and ensure cross-functional collaboration. It took me a few years to realize that, although the matrix approach seemed to work fairly well, it was, at best, a tense compromise. For the managers, it was a constant struggle to balance resources and priorities, while for the working-level designers, it meant having (at least) two bosses.

Once I struck out on my own, I began studying organizational theory, thinking that there must be some magical structure that would cure the weaknesses of the matrix. To my considerable disappointment, I found no new revelations. The literature speaks of many variations on the theme, but in reality they all stew down to the same matrix-like compromises. On the one extreme are "pure" functional organizations, in which employees are grouped by their technical disciplines with functional managers ruling the roost. At the other end of the spectrum are "fully projectized" organizations, wherein project managers form teams for specific contracts, and "own" those resources for the duration with little or

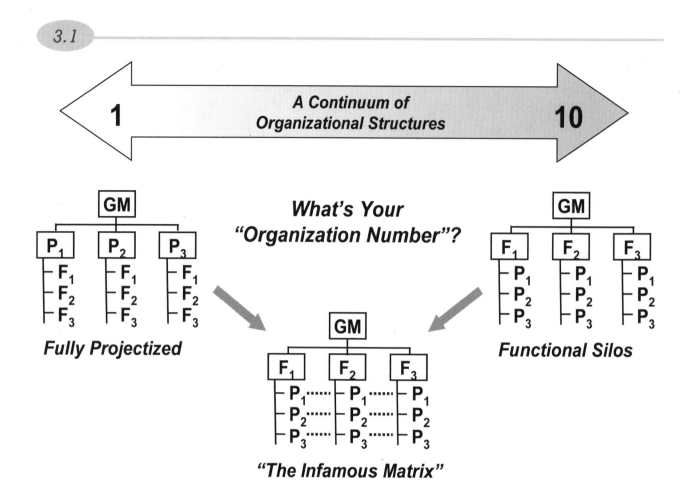

Figure 3.1: Traditional organizational structures can range from purely functional (at right) to fully projectized (at left). Between these two extremes is a continuum of possibilities that are all variations on the so-called "matrix" organization.

no interference from line management. Connecting these two extremes is a continuum of possible compromises, all of which represent a form of matrix structure, as shown in Figure 3.1.

Over the past decade, however, some light has appeared at the end of the tunnel. An organizational approach, known as the "value-stream organization," promises a modicum of relief from the ailments of the matrix, at least from the perspective of product development teams. Before I describe this innovative structure, however, we must first address traditional organizations, since it is a virtual certainty that your firm falls somewhere within the spectrum shown in the figure. As I previously indicated, it is rare for a firm to undertake a complete top-to-bottom reorganization. Even if such a decision were made, it can take years for a new structure to take hold and perform at optimal levels. Hence, we must, for the time being at least, make the best of what we have. Since the focus of this guidebook is on maximizing development-team productivity and speed, I will discuss traditional organizations from this perspective. Readers who are interested in looking beyond this simplified discussion should consult one of the references listed at the end of this section.

The pure functional organization is something of a dinosaur, having its roots in the first few decades of the twentieth century. Great innovators such as Henry Ford and Frederick Taylor recognized the benefits of specialization and division of labor within an enterprise. By segregating employees into areas of specialty, a high degree of efficiency could be gained in accomplishing routine, recurring tasks. Since in those days most manufacturing firms produced only a few products that changed little over periods of many years, new product development was a rare exception. The great majority of work involved simply turning the crank. From this period we have acquired such terms as "white-collar" and "blue-collar" workers. As the theory goes, the white-collar workers do all of the thinking, while the blue-collar workers take orders and perform the hands-on activities. In actuality, however, the white collars didn't do much thinking either, at least by today's standards. A sustaining organization is like a smoothly running machine; it trades off flexibility and agility for routine efficiency.

The idea of forming an organizational structure around the execution of unique, non-recurring projects didn't come into its own until after World War II. The Manhatten Project ushered in a new age of technology-based megaprojects. The dominant customers for such projects were governments, a situation that persists to this day. Indeed, the fully projectized organization evolved in response to the great post-war military and infra-structural buildup in both North America and Europe. Today, the best examples of project-based organizations occur in construction and defense contractors such as Fluor, Bechtel, Raytheon, Northrup Grumman, and so on. Although a functional line structure typically exists in firms such as these, the control of resources is largely in the hands of project managers. Projectized organizations (in diametric contrast to functional structures) are great at performing non-recurring, highly focused projects, but are not well-suited to recurring production. Indeed, defense contractors typically employ *both* structures; a project-focused organization for development work, and a function-driven structure for operations and sustaining support.

Although extreme examples do exist, the vast majority of manufacturing firms today fall within the grey region between numbers one and ten in Figure 3.1. Functional managers and project leaders coexist, and both non-recurring development work and sustaining operational activities are supported. Resources are often asked to respond to both a line manager and one or more team leaders, resulting in a matrix of authority. The key discriminator in this middle region (again, from the perspective of new product development) is the relative strength of project team leaders. If functional management holds the real power over resource allocation and project decision-making, team leaders are reduced to little more than liaisons among the functions. This is often referred to as a "weak matrix" organization. In contrast, a "strong matrix" organization implies that team leaders have significant influence over resource prioritization and project direction.

Where does your firm fall within this spectrum (i.e., what is your "organization number")? An interesting question to be sure, but your biggest concern should be whether your current organizational structure is well-suited to the type of product development work your company plans to perform. There is no right or wrong answer regarding the strength or weakness of development team leaders relative to functional managers. The optimal organization type for your firm (assuming you stay within this traditional matrix spectrum) is determined by the type and number of new products you wish to develop, as shown in Figure 3.2. If your firm's new product strategy primarily involves extensions of existing products, as is the case in many mature, commoditized industries, then a relatively strong functional structure makes good sense. This is particularly true if much of your design work is driven by special orders; basically a stream of quick-turn customization efforts in response to sales-order requests from customers. Smaller projects that involve riffing on existing designs require far less cross-functional collaboration than is necessary for entirely new products. A typical organization number for such firms should be in the range of seven through nine.

As the scale and differentiation of development projects increases, the need for a more projectized structure grows as well. A firm that depends on a few major new products for its future growth should empower its team leaders to a far greater extent, even to the point of creating dedicated teams that exist as entities unto themselves within the greater organization. Not surprisingly, an appropriate organization number for firms of

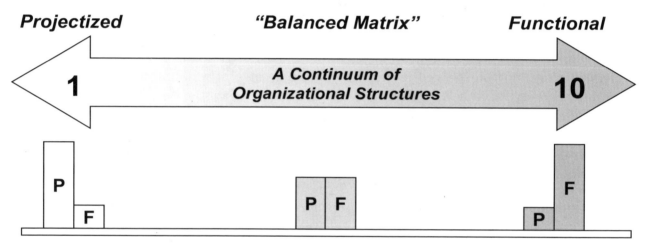

Relative Strength of Project Leader vs. Functional Manager

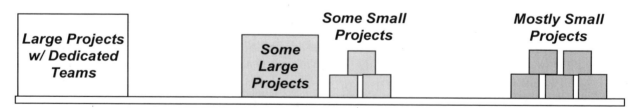

Typical Mix of Development Projects

Figure 3.2: The most important factor in aligning your organizational structure with an effective new product development process is the scale and number of development projects your firm wishes to execute. For smaller efforts involving minor modifications to existing products, a relatively strong functional structure may be appropriate (numbers seven through nine). On the other hand, if your company depends on major new product initiatives, project team leaders should be given significantly more control over resources and decision-making (numbers two through four).

this type would be at the other end of the spectrum, in the range from two through four. What about the middle ground (numbers four through six)? This is the most challenging region to be sure. With functional managers and team leaders having roughly equal control over resources and project decision-making, it often falls upon individual team members to sort out their priorities and keep everyone happy. In principle at least, a "balanced matrix" would be appropriate for firms that plan to execute a mix of large- and small-scale development projects. In actuality, however, a "number five" organization should never exist; decision-making would be severely diluted, and the constant compromises would sap the strength of the firm. A better solution would be to segregate larger projects from smaller ones, with major product development efforts having empowered team leaders and relatively dedicated teams, while the smaller, more routine projects would be handled under the auspices of department managers.

Compare your firm's organization number to the type and scale of products you typically develop. Are you properly aligned? If not, I'm willing to bet that your number is higher than it probably should be. I don't recall ever seeing a firm with team leaders that are *more* powerful than their types of projects require. In fact, I was recently asked what I thought was the single quickest way to increase the speed and efficiency of new product development. My answer in almost every case would be to *increase the empowerment and control of team leaders*. Taking this step can be politically challenging; functional managers are often loath to give up their authority. In the subsection that follows, I will describe some ways to finesse this obstacle that should placate all but the most self-interested line managers.

The Matrix...Reloaded

There are two variations on the matrix organization theme that deserve a brief mention. These adaptations are intended to ease the transition from strong functional silos to a more balanced, cross-functional approach to new product development. Let's begin with the most formal, and certainly the most controversial, option. In fact, from an organizational standpoint, there are few topics that will cause more emotional debate than the idea of establishing a project management office (PMO). The term "project management" has come to represent a well-defined set of skills and tools that enable effective execution of non-recurring project activities. The Project Management Institute (PMI) has famously published their *Project Management Body of Knowledge* (PMBOK), and many who are serious about leading projects (including Yours Truly) have become certified Project Management Professionals (PMPs).

First let's deal with the non-controversial part: There is no question that your firm would benefit from the use of some (but probably not all) of the tools and methods of project management. Books, software, and training programs on the subject abound, including a comprehensive set of resources provided by PMI (www.pmi.org). Despite its potential, however, opinions vary considerably about the value and benefits of utilizing "professional" project managers. The derogatory term "bean counter" is often used to describe these individuals, and frankly this is often an accurate assessment. Project management, as a discipline, is an *enabler* of efficient new product development, not a value-creating activity unto itself. If the right tools are used at the right times, a team leader with project management skills can be a powerful asset. However, if your project managers become obsessed with MS Project software, and begin chasing team members down the hallway asking for project performance indices and daily schedule updates, you are likely generating more waste than benefit.

The potential for this enabling skill-set to turn into a wasteful juggernaut is why the very suggestion of a PMO can cause fear and loathing among some executives. Yet if excesses are held in check, there can be significant advantages to an organizational structure such as that shown in Figure 3.3. The first advantage of creating a PMO is that it doesn't require a major change to the existing organization. Functional departments can generally remain the same, and even the day-to-day operation of the firm needn't change significantly. What *does* change is that there is an entity within the organization whose sole job is to get new products out the door. Unlike informal team leaders plucked from the lower ranks of the organization, the leaders who reside in a PMO have the same reporting structure and executive access as functional department managers. A second advantage is that the PMO can serve as a highly effective center of excellence for developing the team leaders of the future. Finally, a PMO can provide a credible and consistent interface with your external customers. In some industries, particularly those in which products are often developed under contract with customers, this can represent a competitive advantage.

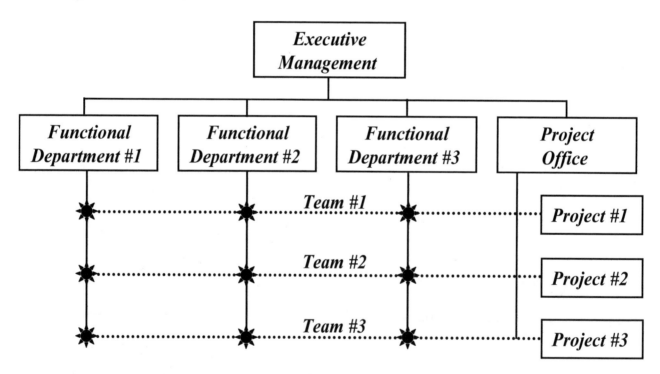

Figure 3.3: The addition of a Project Management Office (PMO) to a strong functional organization can help drive your firm toward a more balanced, team-based approach to new product development. However, unless your firm primarily works under contract with external customers, this structure may result in more waste than benefit.

So is a PMO the right answer for your firm? If contract work dominates your product development activities, this organizational structure deserves strong consideration. For firms that create products for the open market, however, the value and benefits of a PMO are not as clear. Whereas the training of team leaders in project management skills is an unequivocal positive, creating a bureaucratic superstructure to support those skills (and the people who possess them) may come at an unacceptable price. In truth, I've seen relatively few firms in non-contract industries make effective use of a PMO. Again, the problem tends to be an overemphasis on the tools, to the exclusion of both common sense and optimal efficiency. The benefits must be evaluated on a case-by-case basis, but be cautious; overshooting the appropriate use of project management methods may undermine the credibility of the entire skill-set. A failed PMO can create scar tissue that will last for years to come.

Is there another way that an organization can gradually move away from the strong functional end of the spectrum? I will offer an alternative that is simple to implement and has few if any negatives. The primary reason why functional managers might resist a move toward stronger team leadership is a perceived loss of their organizational power. No one wants to spend their career gaining influence within a firm, only to have that influence undermined by upstart team leaders. Even if the spirit is willing, the habitual actions of strong functional managers may nullify any "paper" shift in power. How can a firm finesse this very real issue? Why not allow functional managers to also serve as team leaders for major projects? I know this sounds blasphemous, but hear me out. First of all, I'm not suggesting that all projects be lead by functional managers. For those projects, however, that are either heavily weighted toward a single function or have significant importance to the organization, this might be your best alternative. Functional managers have all of the clout needed to ensure organizational focus, and frankly, they may well be the most talented leaders in your firm. Furthermore, much of their time is likely being spent overseeing the project work within their departments anyway, so the added responsibility may not be all that significant. Naturally, I am assuming here that your functional managers are not constantly at war with each other (if this is the case, strong team leadership is the least of your worries), and that the opportunity to run major projects is spread fairly among the functions.

You might think that I just pulled this idea out of the air, but in reality I spent most of my career serving duel roles as both a functional manager and project manager. And I was not alone; this was a relatively common occurence within Hughes Aircraft Company and many other defense contractors. Since leaving aerospace, I've seen this approach work well in many types of industries, provided that the firms involved maintain a culture that is reasonably flexible and focused on success. Allowing functional managers to serve as team leaders for selected projects can have a positive spillover effect on all teams within your firm. The sensibilities of cross-functional cooperation are reinforced, and the newly anointed functional / project managers can serve as mentors for future team leaders. You might even find that having functional managers walk a few miles in the shoes of a team leader will help break down some of those intractable barriers to cross-functional cooperation. At the very least, your firm's focus will be shifted in the right direction, toward a project-based, cross-functional approach to new product development.

A Promising Alternative: The Value-Stream Organization

The lore of the technological age is replete with stories of small start-up firms hitting the big time, often transporting their founding employees from working out of a garage to owning six-car garages in a few short years. Underlying many of these legends is a sense that smaller is better; start-ups appear to be single-minded in their goals, devoid of bureaucracy, and driven by a camaraderie that overcomes all barriers to collaboration and innovation. As these firms grow exponentially in size, however, it seems that something precious is often lost. Seasoned managers are brought in from other companies to establish order and structure, divisions are formed, cubicles are purchased, and employees are sorted and stacked like socks in a drawer. Soon those days of carefree collaboration fade into memory, replaced by the banal sameness of big-firm bureaucracy. Organizational barriers rise in proportion to share price, leaving the firm's original employees feeling deeply nostalgic for "the good old days," as they count their stock options.

Wouldn't it be wonderful if larger firms could somehow recapture the entrepreneurial efficiency and collaborative spirit of the start-up, while still maintaining their growth trajectory? Such is the promise of a value-stream-based organizational structure. In the parlance of lean, a value stream is the sequence of events or actions that enable value to be delivered to customers. On the factory floor, a value stream might take the form of work cells and feeder lines flowing like rivulets into a final-assembly flow line. A production value stream of this sort encompasses all that is needed for products to be fabricated and shipped, including both internal resources and the external supplier and distribution networks. Through the application of lean manufacturing principles, obstacles to the flow of value are reduced or eliminated, leaving behind a well-oiled and highly focused value-creating machine.

This same value-centric mentality can, at least in principle, be achieved in the world of new product development. Imagine assembling all of the employees of your firm on a large field. Now, just like in grade school, you start picking teams. Several team leaders are chosen, each of whom represents one of your major product lines. The leaders in turn select employees that they feel would be essential to developing and manufacturing the products within their respective lines. At first it would probably go fairly smoothly, until you reach those shared resources that are in demand by more than one team. Ultimately, after some bartering, the teams are settled. Each team has enough of the right people in the right disciplines to operate as a stand-alone, autonomous entity, with only the highest-level resources within the firm (e.g., finance, accounting, executive management, human resources) still spanning all product lines. It is likely that as time goes by, some teams would discover that they are understaffed, while others would find that their resources are more than adequate. After some additional shuffling, and perhaps some selective hiring, we have arrived at the key building-block of a value-stream organization; the *value-stream team*.

One form of a value-stream organization is shown in Figure 3.4. The value-stream team is situated in its rightful place at the core of the organization, reporting directly to executive management. The infrastructure of the organization is gathered under two key individuals: a *functional resource coordinator* and a *shared resource coordinator*. Reporting to each coordinator are centers that group together those functions and activities that cannot be effectively carved into product-line-sized chunks. Truth be told, the primary reason for creating these two powerful positions is to correct potential weaknesses of the value-stream concept.

The shared resource coordinator is responsible for allocating support personnel who are not needed by any one value-stream team on a full-time basis. Examples might include drafting, procurement, safety, regulatory administration, contracts, and so on. Providing these functions on a team-by-team basis could result in significant inefficiencies, not to mention a loss of shared knowledge. Instead, support functions are grouped into traditional functional departments, with the coordinator role serving as an intermediary to ensure that priorities are properly addressed, conflicts are optimally resolved, and that overall staffing is maintained at appropriate levels. In principle, the job of the shared resource coordinator is to manage exceptions; if adequate resources are available from all support functions, the coordinator need not be involved in day-to-day team operations.

The functional resource coordinator corrects a different kind of organizational weakness. If core functions such as engineering, marketing, quality, and manufacturing,

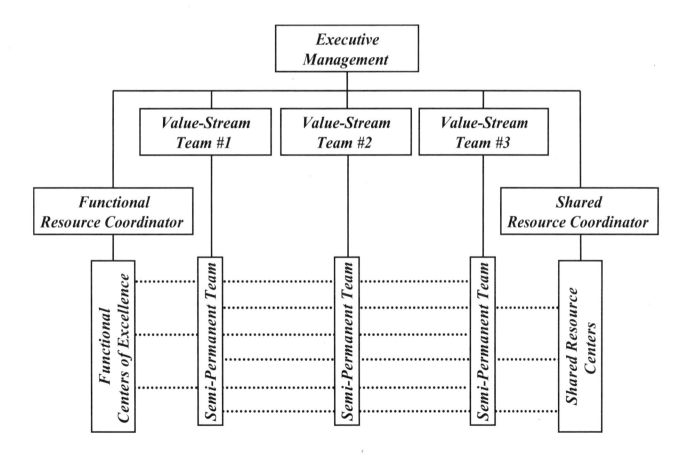

Figure 3.4: One vision of how a firm could organize around product-line-based value streams. Each value-stream team includes all of the core technical and operational resources required to produce a related line of products.

are divided up among value-stream teams, how can a firm build its core competencies in these fields over time? Specifically, issues such as selection of productivity tools (e.g., CAD hardware and software, test equipment, market research databases), sharing of lessons learned, and development of new technologies, require the involvement of all members of a functional group, regardless of which value-stream team they are on. Furthermore, if employees within these core functions are allowed to focus on a single product line for extended periods, there is a real danger that these individuals will become too narrow in their thinking, and may eventually stagnate. The functional resource coordinator is tasked with overseeing the centers of excellence for each core function. These centers would be chartered with selecting the best function-specific productivity tools, and would orchestrate the periodic rotation of value-stream team members to avoid intellectual stagnation.

At this point, you might be thinking that the value-stream organization is just too different to be a practical "future state" for your firm. Before I address your justifiable skepticism, however, let's suspend disbelief for a moment longer and consider the pros and cons of such a structure, as listed in Figure 3.5. At the highest level, the value-stream organization sacrifices optimal resource utilization in return for better product focus and fewer time-consuming distractions. Higher levels of synergy are achieved by creating semi-permanent value-stream teams that retain past development history and can easily identify common elements among new product initiatives. In contrast, however, there is a real potential for suboptimal resource utilization, particularly if the firm that has implemented this structure is relatively small. A larger firm will typically have significant redundancy within each of its core functions (i.e., a "deep bench," so to speak). In this case, allocating sufficient resources to each of several value-stream teams is made possible by having a large pool of individuals to pull from. As the size of the firm diminishes, this redundancy disappears; in smaller firms there will often be only one or two individuals who possess certain critical competencies. Unless sharing of these individuals among value-stream teams is permitted, there is a high probability that some teams will be missing key players. Realistically, if a firm or business unit has fewer than one-hundred employees, the disbenefits of a value-stream structure may outweigh the benefits. There is no hard and fast rule, however. What really matters is that each value-stream team represents a sensible, reasonably autonomous entity.

Now to our most pressing problem: how can your firm capture some of the benefits of a value-stream organization without completely scrambling your org chart? The first step is to determine how best to segment your product development activities to achieve the greatest synergy. In the discussion provided above, I have assumed that the value-stream teams are created based on product lines. This is not the only way that such a structure can be formed, however. Teams could be established based on market segments, distribution channels, common technologies, geographic regions, and so on. A firm whose products are differentiated based on the type of customer being serviced, for example, might choose to form value streams around specific customer categories (i.e., occasional users, advanced users, industrial applications, etc.). Selecting the best way to group your capabilities is key to avoiding resource conflicts and reducing barriers to the value-stream concept.

A second step might be to gradually shift your product development activities into semi-permanent teams, beginning with major new product initiatives. Why not keep

Criteria for Success	Advantages	Disadvantages
Effective Team Communication	Value-stream teams are inherently cross-functional, with members working together over several years and on multiple projects.	Communication among the value-stream teams may be problematic. A functional co-ordinator can mitigate this issue.
Optimal Use of Resources	Within each value stream, resources are highly focused on product-line-specific tasks and issues. External distractions are reduced or eliminated.	Balancing the workload among team members may be difficult, since work does not typically cross value-stream boundaries.
Building of Core Competencies	Within the context of each product line, core competencies will grow faster and more consistently than within a typical functional organization.	Company-wide competency development may be sacrificed in favor of more narrow, product-focused skill development.
Speed and Efficiency	Many of the obstacles to the flow of value are eliminated by assembling a product-line focused team. This can be significantly faster than alternative organizational structures.	Few disadvantages with respect to speed, provided that shared resources are efficiently allocated and prioritized. A shared resource coordinator will help achieve success.
Flexibility and Agility	More flexibility within each product line than with a strong functional management structure. More closely resembles the "start-up" model.	Few disadvantages from the perspective of new product development.

Figure 3.5: A summary of the advantages and disadvantages of a value-stream organization. In general, the value-stream structure benefits from higher levels of focus and synergy, but may suffer from suboptimal resource utilization, particularly if a firm is relatively small.

successful teams together for a series of projects, instead of constantly disbanding and reconstituting teams for each new generation of product? If these semi-permanent teams can then be linked directly to appropriate value streams within your factory, you will have the beginnings of a value-stream organization. Shared resources within your company are most likely already grouped into functional departments, which can gradually be transitioned into centers that allocate resources on a priority basis to all of the semi-permanent teams. Ultimately, your goal is to create as much independence among the teams as possible.

The gradual process identified above was successfully employed by one of the world's leading manufacturers of hydraulic and pneumatic equipment. The move toward a value-stream organization was initiated by a corporate mandate, but the deployment details were left to each business unit within the corporation to work out. Since this firm's business units span a broad range of product types, from mature commodities to cutting-edge high technology, this flexible approach to implementation made good sense. As is often the case with complex, multinational firms, the results of this reorganization initiative were mixed. Those divisions whose profiles fit the mold for a value-stream organization have been highly successful, while other business units have shown little or no progress. In particular, those units with several hundred employees, fast-moving markets, products with relatively high technology content, and a diverse product mix, found the transition to a value-stream organization to be a worthwhile and achievable goal. Conversely, smaller divisions in mature, commoditized markets didn't really see the applicability or benefits.

If you and your firm are serious about implementing a value-stream organization, either in gradual steps or as one big upheaval, several useful lean improvement tools are provided for you in Part 6 of this guidebook. In my experience, I've found that gradual but consistent movement toward a desired future state (in this case, a value-stream structure) is far more likely to be successful than attempting to achieve all of your goals in one big jump. Recall the old (and somewhat disturbing) adage on how one might go about boiling a frog. If you put the frog immediately into boiling water, it will jump out of the pot. If, on the other hand, you put the frog into cool water and gradually heat it, the poor thing will be cooked before it has a chance to object. Keeping persistent "heat" on your organization to move in a desired direction will eventually achieve lasting results, and all of those concrete heads in your firm who refuse to change will hardly know they are getting their gooses cooked.

Suggested Reading

The following books offer a broad range of perspectives on the topic of organizational structures *vis-à-vis* new product development.

Clark, K.B., and S. C. Wheelwright, 1993, *Managing New Product and Process Development,* The Free Press.

Cusumano, M.A., and K. Nobeoka, 1998, *Thinking Beyond Lean,* The Free Press.

Dimancescu, D., Hines, P., and N. Rich, 1997, *The Lean Enterprise,* American Management Association.

Leonard-Barton, D., 1995, *Wellsprings of Knowledge,* Harvard Business School Press.

Liker, J.K., 2004, *The Toyota Way,* McGraw Hill.

Mascitelli, R.O., 1999, *The Growth Warriors: Creating Sustainable Global Advantage for America's Technology Companies,* Technology Perspectives.

McLeod, T., 1988, *The Management of Research, Development, and Design in Industry,* Gower Technical Press.

Nonaka, I., and H. Takeuchi, 1995, *The Knowledge-Creating Company*, Oxford University Press.

Wheelwright, S.C., and K.B. Clark, 1995, *Leading Product Development*, The Free Press.

Womack, J.P., and D.T. Jones, 1996, *Lean Thinking*, Simon & Schuster.

Womack, J.P., and D.T. Jones, 2005, *Lean Solutions*, The Free Press.

<u>Notes</u>

From Silos to Gates to Continuous Flow

If your company happens to have a fully projectized organization, there is little need to establish a formalized product development process. Rigorous application of project management tools and methods should provide all the structure needed to ensure speed and efficiency. For the vast majority of manufacturing firms, however, this will not be the case. The very existence of functional departments within a firm mandates that some "artificial" structure be implemented to manage risk and facilitate cross-functional collaboration and coordination. An institutionalized product development process serves as both a catalyst and a roadmap for design teams. However, as we discussed in Part 1, this structure is simply an enabler. Value is not directly created by the process itself, but its existence is essential to efficient value creation. In this section, we will consider several traditional development process alternatives, ultimately arriving at a model for an advanced and highly efficient future state. This so-called "continuous-flow" process embodies the best attributes of more traditional approaches, while eliminating some important obstacles to the efficient flow of value.

A Brief History of Time-to-Market

What fills the vacuum in the absence of a well-defined product development process? Unfortunately, the answer is not very satisfying. Without the benefit of clear guidance and structure, most firms will resort to the lowest common denominator; the "over-the-wall" approach shown in Figure 3.6. The story goes something like this. Marketing comes up with a new product concept, jots down a rough description, and hands it over to the design department with little more than an admonishment to "get this done ASAP". The design group reviews the vague specification they have been given and takes their best shot at interpreting what is expected of them. The resulting prototype looks nothing like what marketing had envisioned, so its back to the drawing board (or CAD terminal as the case may be) for a second, and often a third, iteration. After several tosses back and forth over the wall between marketing and design engineering, an acceptable prototype is finally developed. The manufacturing organization, however, has been completely unaware of these proceedings. After taking a close look at the prototype, they pronounce it unproducible. Again, it is back to the drawing board, this time to address excessive cost and unachievable quality. Back and forth it goes until yet another compromise is reached. The resulting product is late, uninspired, and at best, only marginally profitable.

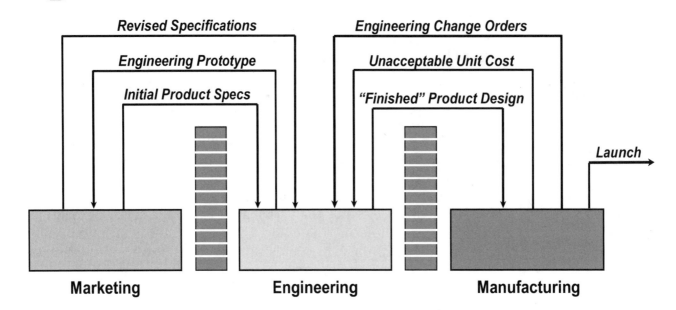

Revised Specifications

Engineering Prototype

Initial Product Specs

Engineering Change Orders

Unacceptable Unit Cost

"Finished" Product Design

Launch

Marketing   **Engineering**   **Manufacturing**

Figure 3.6: A diagram of the "over-the-wall" product development process. This approach tends to fill the void when no formal process is institutionalized within a manufacturing firm. Its drawbacks include slow execution, shifting priorities, poor compromises, and in many cases, suboptimal, lowest-common-denominator products.

Clearly the biggest problem with an over-the-wall approach to new product development is the lack of collaborative design. By working together cooperatively, marketing, engineering, and manufacturing can collectively identify the best possible tradeoffs. Innovative solutions supplant mediocre compromises, while the entire process is accelerated by eliminating unnecessary design iterations, and through the parallel co-development of the product and its manufacturing processes. A preferable alternative to be sure, but what about those imposing walls still separating the functions? This is where the need for a structured product development process comes into play. An effective development process essentially forces cross-functional cooperation, while providing a proven pathway to success. Initially, a firm with high functional walls may require a rigid, possibly even draconian structure. As the barriers to collaboration begin to soften, the process can be relaxed somewhat. Ultimately, the goal should be to eliminate the artificial aspects of the development process, leaving behind only those key elements that protect the firm against unacceptable risk, and ensure a timely and profitable product launch.

For most companies, the first step along this journey toward optimal new product development is the implementation of a phase / gate process, such as the one shown in Figure 3.7. Despite what some well-known consultancies will tell you, the origins of the phase / gate structure predate these modern upstarts by decades. Shortly after World War II, the United States government recognized the need for a formal structure to manage an increasing number of defense "megaprojects". With a pantheon of subcontactors contributing to such complex development efforts as the Polaris Missile System, a method for synchronizing work and managing risk was essential. As products in the commercial sector grew in both physical and technological complexity, it was natural to look toward government contractors for an appropriate development methodology. Since that time, many versions of the phase / gate approach have been promulgated. General Electric, for example, is famous for their "toll-gate" process, while the PRTM consultancy has contributed their PACE version. All share common elements, similar advantages, and a few significant disadvantages.

Although many of my readers are already familiar with the phase / gate approach, it is worth a brief description to ensure that we are all on the same page. A phase / gate process achieves cross-functional collaboration by creating a defined set of tasks that must be performed within successive phases of a development effort. These tasks require the participation of all core disciplines, and usually include risk-reduction activities and other essential considerations to ensure a positive project outcome. Once the tasks within each phase are completed, a "gate review" is held, in which the project's status is reviewed by upper management, the completeness of phase deliverables is verified, and the risks are assessed. If all is well with both the technical and business-case aspects of the project, the gate reviewers authorize the project team to proceed on to the next phase. And so it goes until the product is either ready for commercialization, or is killed due to unacceptable risk or a diminishing business case. The phases typically represent a logical flow of effort, from initial concept and planning, through detailed design, and finally to qualification testing and production readiness verification.

The primary advantages of a phase / gate process are forced collaboration and risk reduction, as described in Figure 3.8. The collaborative part reminds me of training wheels on a bicycle; they are needed at first to safely gain the requisite skills, but are something of an encumbrance once the rider knows what she is doing. The risk-reduction part is more important, in my opinion. In rapidly changing markets, a new product development project may look good in the beginning, but may lose its luster as time passes and market needs

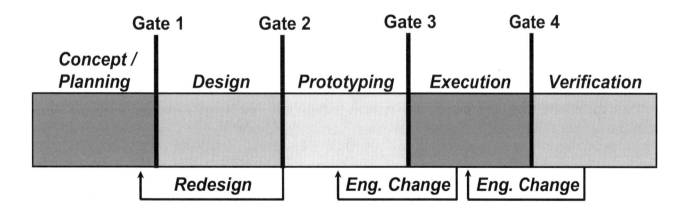

Figure 3.7: An archetypical phase / gate process is shown above. While five phases and four gates is a common implementation, there is no limit to the number and granularity of phases. While this process structure achieves considerable risk control, and can successfully mandate cross-functional collaboration, it is relatively slow, and doesn't follow the natural flow of value within a product development project.

change. This could also be the case when either technological or manufacturability risks are greater than expected. The gate reviews within a phase / gate process offer several opportunities to reassess the status of a project, and provide an institutionalized mechanism for killing those efforts which no longer appear to be worth the investment in time and money. A final advantage of the phase / gate structure is the somewhat methodical sequence of events. If a firm is relatively new to the cross-functional development game, spelling out each step in great detail can help all involved parties avoid missing something important. On the negative side, however, many firms that I have worked with have adopted the phase / gate structure, only to find that their time-to-market has actually gotten worse. True, the products that do reach the finish line are often better, more complete, and generally of higher quality. But is it necessary to give up optimal speed and efficiency to gain these positive results?

Let me state unequivocally that there is nothing fundamentally wrong with a phase / gate development process. In fact, I believe that virtually every firm should use this approach as a transitional step away from the over-the-wall, functional-silo mentality. That being said, I rail at those who refer to it as a "best practice". It is not necessary to give up time-to-market in return for managed risk and professional, high-quality execution. Once a phase / gate process has taught your firm the ropes, you can move beyond this artificial structure to one that is far more lean, efficient, and *natural*. In the next subsection, I will describe an evolutionary next step, one that has seen considerable success in firms representing several different industry sectors. It is called the *continuous-flow process*, and it is not the *best* practice (since the philosophy of continuous improvement precludes such nonsensical dogma); it is simply better than the process your firm is probably using today.

Continuous-Flow Development – An Ideal Worth Pursuing

When I was in college, I decided to take lessons in disco dancing (as you now know, I went to school in prehistoric times). The dance instructor taught us various steps using little painted "feet" on the floor which we were told to follow in sequence: one-two-three, one-two-three, etc. With the confidence gained through this learning mechanism, I ventured out to my first nightclub, only to find that the proprietors had neglected to paint feet on the dance floor. To my great surprise, however, I discovered that the painted feet were no longer necessary; I knew where to move next, and was able to recreate the same patterns without an artificial structure. Of course, I was still counting "one-two-three" in my head for a while thereafter, but even this artifice was gradually abandoned. Eventually, I learned to respond to the rhythms of the music with natural, flexible, and even improvisational dance moves. Only at this point could I actually say that I was a competent dancer, rather than a novice-in-training.

A competent design organization has no need for "feet on the floor" or the rigid counting of steps. Once the critical needs, tasks, and risk-reduction activities of new product development become embedded in a firm's collective subconscious, much of the unnecessary (and wasteful) structure of a phase / gate process can be relaxed or even eliminated, as shown in Figure 3.9. The transition described in the figure is presented in a logical order, but there is nothing wrong with jumping around somewhat as you progress

Evaluation of a Formal Phase / Gate Development Process

Required Attribute	Advantages	Disadvantages
Cross-Functional Collaboration	Excellent way to break down functional walls and encourage concurrent and coordinated efforts among key functions.	Once cross-functional collaboration is established, the formal structure of phases and gates can limit natural team development.
Risk Management	Highly effective at identifying missed steps, and determining weaknesses or threats to a project. Provides several points at which a weak project can be killed.	Risk management is achieved artificially, and may be overkill for more straightforward projects. Can cause organizations to become risk-averse and lose confidence.
Understandability	Although process documentation is often fairly complex, the general structure is easy to visualize and follow for all functions.	The detailed nature of the process can cause wasted effort, particularly if rigid adherence is mandated.
Comprehensiveness	Depending on the degree of detail embedded in the process description, it can be made as comprehensive as desired.	Can be very comprehensive, but it is often hard to avoid excessive and redundant work. Scaling of the process is not easily achieved.
Flexibility	If implemented with a "light touch," a phase / gate process can evolve into a reasonably flexible approach.	Intentionally somewhat inflexible. The "artificial" nature of the process restricts its ability to scale and conform to the real needs of a project.
Speed and Efficiency	Often better than the alternative: the "over-the-wall" non-process.	The serial nature of workflow and the "barriers to flow" caused by gate reviews can significantly limit time-to-market.

Figure 3.8: The phase / gate product development process offers some significant advantages, particularly for firms who are transitioning away from strong functional silos into a more cross-functional, team-based approach. Once this important step is achieved, however, the artificial structure of phases and gates can become a limitation to further improvement. In particular, gates represent obstacles to the flow of value, while serial, structured phases restrict project work and can significantly distort the optimized critical path for the project.

toward a more advanced approach. The key to success is taking gradual steps, evaluating results, and then proceeding farther as your firm's competency grows. An organization that begins this journey with a successful phase / gate approach could conceivably make the transition to continuous flow in a year, provided that its typical development times are relatively short. A longer period would be necessary for firms whose products require one or more years to design and commercialize. I've seen the best outcomes when companies select a showcase project team to lead the way. This team is asked to execute their project with a new, leaner process. After success is verified (and often a few tweaks are made), this more efficient process is deployed across the organization, and a new showcase team is selected to move the agenda farther along. Using this approach, only a few iterations would typically be needed to fully transition to the future state described below.

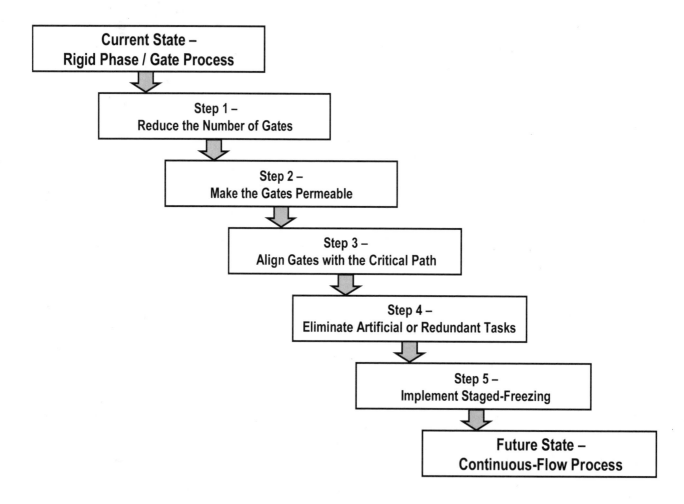

Figure 3.9: It is possible to evolve your current phase / gate development process into a far more efficient and time-sensitive approach. The five steps described above can be applied in the order provided, or in any other sequence that makes sense for your firm. Note that making the full transition from a rigid phase / gate process to a future-state, continuous-flow process can take several years, and a few generations of development projects.

Step 1: Reduce the Number of Gates

Let's go through each step in sequence. We will assume for this discussion that your firm has a relatively rigid phase / gate process in place. The first and most obvious step toward a leaner process is to reduce the number of phases and gates. A typical phase / gate process employs five phases and four gates, but I've seen some unbelievably cumbersome implementations that have as many as *eleven* formal decision points. Keeping in mind that gate reviews represent an obstacle to the flow of value, what would be an optimal number? In the absence of risk, the answer would be zero. Recognizing that technical, market, and manufacturability risks must be managed, I believe that once a product has passed feasibility screening (see Section 2.3), three gates are more than adequate. The first might carry the title of "Preliminary Design Gate," and would focus on the verification of the proposed conceptual product design *vis-à-vis* marketing requirements. The second gate might be called the "Detailed Design Gate," and would provide an opportunity to review modeling results, prototype test data, software compliance, drawing packages, etc. The final gate would validate the production design in all its glory, and might carry the title of "Production Readiness Gate". This sequence of decision points will be discussed in more detail in the next section, but the generic titles that I've proposed should give you a high-level perspective.

Reducing the number of gates within your existing process should be relatively straightforward; simply lump together phase deliverables and checklists as needed to reorganize your more numerous gates into the three bins I've described above. In principle at least, having more phases and gates gives you tighter control over risk, but in reality the financial risk associated with being late to market may far outweigh the benefits of maintaining more than three critical decision points. If feasibility screening is properly employed, every product that enters the "executable" portion of the development process should be a winner-in-waiting. Don't let risk-aversion cause your company to miss opportunities for increased market share and profits.

Step 2: Make Your Gates Permeable

Once your firm has rationalized the number of gates in its development process, the next step toward continuous flow should be to make your gates permeable. A number of years ago I worked with a leading telecommunications company that had recently implemented a rigid phase / gate structure. At each gate, the design team would stop all project work and spend up to two weeks preparing for the upcoming management review. If an important issue was raised at the review, a "tiger team" would go off and address the problem, leaving the rest of the team to essentially sit on their hands. Once the gate was passed, it would take another several weeks to get back in the groove, only to come to a screeching halt at the next major review point. This "hurry up and wait" mentality (combined with a rancorous relationship among the functional managers) caused this company to lose its leadership role in an important market segment.

How might this catastrophic result have been avoided? Very simple: *Let the design team continue working before, during, and after the gate review.* Although preparation for a gate review might sap some resources away from project work, the permeable-gate approach would allow the continuity of the effort to be maintained. Ah, but what if a problem is identified? The worst that could happen is that the team would continue working in the wrong direction for a few weeks, but the benefits (yet again) would most likely outweigh the risks. I suppose it comes down to making a presumption of success rather than a presumption of failure. If a development project is ultimately killed, the few extra weeks of wasted effort is probably insignificant relative to the sunk costs already accrued. On the other hand, if the project ends up being approved to proceed, weeks or even months of wasted time can be saved.

Step 3: Align Gates with the Critical Path

Assuming that your firm has now reached this enlightened point in its transition toward continuous flow, the next logical step would be to align your gate reviews with the *critical path* of the project. Theoretically, the critical path is the shortest duration achievable on a project, given the resources available. In other words, it is the sequence of dependant tasks that drive project schedule; if you slip one day along the critical path, your project would slip (at least) one day in its overall duration. I will cover the critical path in more detail in Section 5.4, but for now we can think in terms of schedule-critical tasks and non-schedule-critical tasks. If an activity on a development project does not directly impact the overall project schedule (i.e., there is some *slack time* in the execution of the activity), it is not on the critical path. If, however, an activity directly drives schedule (e.g., ordering long lead-time tooling, fabricating a prototype, completing a key suite of tests, etc.), that task is embedded in the critical path.

How can this concept of the critical path impact the timing of gate reviews? In virtually every project, there are several logical "pinch points" during development at which project work transitions from one level to the next. The first typically occurs when a conceptual design has emerged and been validated, and detailed design work is about to commence. This point in time is not necessarily dictated by a checklist of gate deliverables or by management fiat, but rather by the natural flow of the project (and it could be somewhat different for each new product you develop). At this point, the Preliminary Design Gate would be scheduled. As the project proceeds through detailed design, another logical point is reached just prior to the fabrication of production prototypes and the initiation of qualification testing. Here the second gate review, which I call the Detailed Design Gate, would be scheduled. Finally, after production prototypes have been qualified and all materials, tooling, and manufacturing documentation has been completed, a final Production Readiness Gate would be scheduled. By aligning these three permeable gate reviews with the natural junctures that occur within product development, the gates become an integral part of the critical path, rather than a wasteful distortion to the flow of value.

Step 4: Eliminate Artificial or Redundant Tasks

As you've moved away from a rigid phase / gate process, you might have noticed that a number of previously required tasks and deliverables no longer seem to be necessary.

This is a result of the artificial structure imposed by the phase / gate process; checklists for each phase often include activities whose sole purpose is to service the process itself. Eliminating these superfluous items can free up valuable resources and save considerable time. Look for documents or tasks, for example, with titles that include terms like "preliminary" or "Phase X," or are mandated as "gate deliverables" with no other obvious purpose. If you need to identify which phase or gate a document or deliverable applies to, it is probably redundant. In the next section, I will describe a simple way to scrub your process for unnecessary deliverables and activities, using something that I call a deliverables roadmap. This tool allows a design team to visualize all tangible deliverables within a project and clearly identify their dependencies (or in some cases, their lack thereof). If two activities or outputs can be combined with no loss of clarity, then do it. If the same information is generated or documented in two places, eliminate one of those places. And so it goes, until you have streamlined your effort to its value-creating core.

At this point it is worth mentioning that the lean improvement philosophy provides us with several additional tools for accomplishing the above goal in a straightforward and systematic manner. For example, your design organization might consider holding a "mini-*kaizen*" event to strip the waste from a specific aspect of project work (see Section 6.1). If an activity must be performed on virtually every development project, you might create a small improvement team and utilize value-stream mapping to identify a leaner future state for that recurring task (also covered in Section 6.1). These and other lean improvement tools have proven their worth time and time again in the context of recurring manufacturing, and apply equally well (with a few modifications) in the non-recurring world of new product development. However you accomplish the goal, it is important to get rid of unnecessary effort; after all, there is little enough time available to do the *real* work.

Step 5: Implement Staged Freezing

Finally, we have arrived at the final step in transitioning to a continuous-flow development process. To illustrate this last critical enhancement, I will walk you through the diagram shown in Figure 3.10. I've presented continuous-flow development as a "narrowing funnel". This shape is reflective of the way that ideas should flow within product development. At the onset of a project, a wide range of design possibilities should be considered. This early stage is often referred to as the "fuzzy front end," and is depicted in the diagram as the wiggly portion of the funnel on the left. As the project progresses, initial prospects are narrowed down, first to a rough conceptual design, and finally to a highly refined production design. Rather than jumping to a final solution, however, it is important that this transition from fuzzy to final occurs systematically and gradually (for a discussion of how Toyota Motor Company accomplishes this systematic transition, see the discussion of Set-Based Design provided in Section 4.3).

Although the idea of a narrowing-funnel approach to product development has been around for awhile, you will notice that the funnel I've presented in the figure has some "kinks" in it. These kinks represent the three gate reviews described in Step 3 above. However, unlike traditional gate reviews, my version of a continuous-flow process utilizes these three points to control requirements changes, using a process known as *staged freezing*. A detailed description of the staged-freeze methodology is provided in the next section, but here is the essence. Rather than holding gate reviews solely as risk-reduction checkpoints, why not put some teeth into them? At each of the three gate reviews (which I've suggestively titled *freeze gates*), the design team proposes a list of items that must remain unchanged for the duration of the project if the planned product launch date is to be achieved. This list might include performance parameters, material choices, physical specifications, environmental considerations, features, user interfaces, and so on. The goal of staged freezing is to force all parties involved in the design process (including upper management) into a disciplined approach to change control. By creating this so-called *freeze list*, the design team is drawing a line in the sand; any scope changes (aka, scope creep) that occur after this freeze list has been approved almost certainly will cause a slip in project schedule. In this way, changes can be corralled into less invasive portions of the project, and the critical path can be maintained.

As with several of the other steps described above, there is much more detail that needs to be discussed. In the next section, we will flesh out some of the key attributes of the continuous-flow process. Please note, however, that even if you are not up to the significant challenge of totally revamping your product development process, you can implement just one or two of the attributes that will be discussed and gain considerable benefits in resource utilization and time-to-market. Again, we are reminded of the ancient Sufi parable about eating elephants (a delicacy which I'm sure was not actually on their menu); small bites can eventually overcome huge challenges.

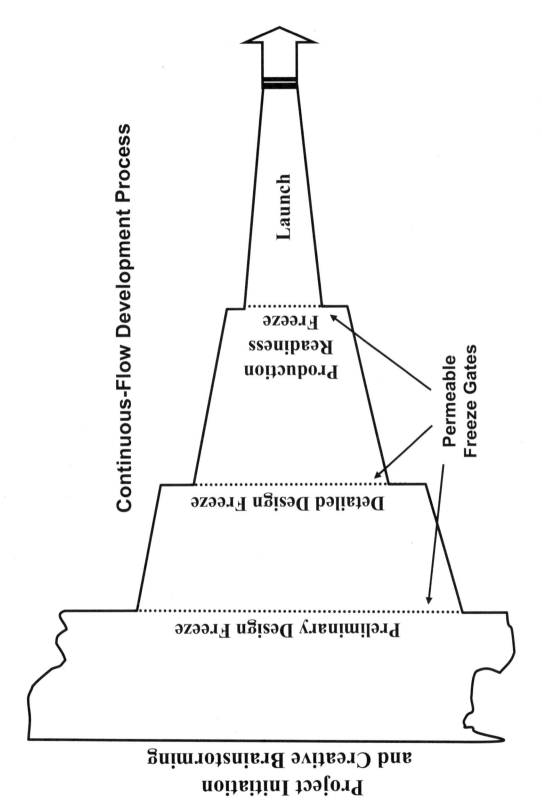

Figure 3.10: A graphical depiction of the continuous-flow development process. The narrowing-funnel shape represents the essential evolution of a product design from soft (i.e., fuzzy) form, to hard (i.e., production-ready) form. The three "kinks" in the funnel are representative of three freeze gates that serve both as a review point for the project's business case, and as a means for controlling invasive scope / requirement changes. The freeze gates are aligned with the critical path of the project so as to minimize any distortion that could negatively impact time-to-market.

Notes

3.3

Section

Managing Quality,
Risk, and Change

Now that you've been exposed to the big picture of lean product development, it is time to start taking action. In this section, several key aspects of the continuous-flow development process are described in practical, deployable detail. From this point forward, I will use the term "lean method" to describe proven and easily implemented techniques for solving specific waste problems within the development cycle. Each lean method can be used independently of the others; there is no "all or nothing at all" restriction. That being said, you will discover that there are some natural groupings of techniques that offer synergistic benefits. The lean methods described in this section are perfect examples of this synergy. Each technique is useful and important on its own, but collectively they take the conceptual view of continuous-flow development described in the previous section and give it legs. The true benefits of lean product development can only be gained if waste-slashing ideas can be implemented in real firms, with real teams, working on real projects.

Lean Method: The Integrated Product Team

What should an ideal product development team look like? As always, a precise answer would depend on the firm, the market, and the product involved. We can, however, identify some absolutely essential attributes of a lean design team. These include:

1) Representation of all critical functions involved in commercialization.
2) A relatively strong and empowered team leader.
3) Continuous participation in the development process by all "core" functions.
4) The availability and active participation of "extended" functions when their contributions are required.

The first two attributes have been thoroughly discussed both in the previous sections of this book, and in many other works on concurrent engineering and team-based development. The latter two criteria, however, are worth delving into more deeply. In a perfect world, team members from every discipline under the sun would be dedicated to a single project, with no other responsibilities. Experts would be just standing in the wings, awaiting their chance to move the project forward. Unfortunately, a more realistic situation finds designers and engineers spread among several projects, and those unfortunate members of support functions such as purchasing, drafting, and testing, potentially servicing *dozens* of active development efforts. How can our ideal view of the design team be reconciled with this multi-project, limited-resource reality?

Well, the answer is that it can't. Except in those rare industries in which major, complex products are produced for well-defined markets, the idea of the dedicated team is just not realistic. The best we can do is try to mitigate the potential damage associated with a heavily multitasked environment. The diagram shown in Figure 3.11 illustrates two important steps in that direction. The first is the differentiation between *core* and *extended* team members. Core team members represent functions that should (indeed must) be involved in the development process from cradle to launch. These typically include design / engineering, marketing, manufacturing, and possibly other functions, depending on the product involved. Although these core functions may not be actively creating value at every moment in the process, their inputs and oversight are needed on a continuous basis. Even if their attention is divided among several projects, core team members should allocate a well-defined fraction of their time (e.g., half-time, quarter-time) to every project to which they are assigned. Moreover, the membership of the core team should not change from start to finish; having warm bodies sitting in chairs at meetings is not the same as a truly integrated product team. I know, I know; it's really hard to allocate resources consistently, maintain continuity, and frankly, just keep all the balls in the air. I will offer several lean methods to help your firm conquer the very real problem of resource allocation and management in Section 5.6. For now, please suspend disbelief and accept the possibility of continuous participation by all core functions.

Now what about the extended team? While there are tremendous advantages associated with continuity of participation, there are some functions within a manufacturing firm that simply don't need to be involved at the same level as core team members. This does not imply that these disciplines (e.g., purchasing, regulatory, tooling fabrication, etc.) are second-class citizens. Far from it. In fact, their time is typically in such short supply that it simply doesn't make sense to demand high-level participation at times when their contribution is not essential. Certainly extended team members should be assigned at the inception of a project, and they should be kept involved in all key activities, meetings, reviews, etc. The primary distinction between core and extended team members is the nature of their participation; core team members are in for the duration, whereas extended team members become directly involved only when their contributions are on or near the critical path. Frankly, this is a tradeoff. There are certainly benefits to having extended functions involved at every point in the process, yet this is clearly not an optimal use of their limited capacity. So we make a difficult choice; a compromise between risk, speed, and product development capacity. This is one of many compromises that we must make in this regard: If you are an idealist, you will find new product development to be a very disquieting place.

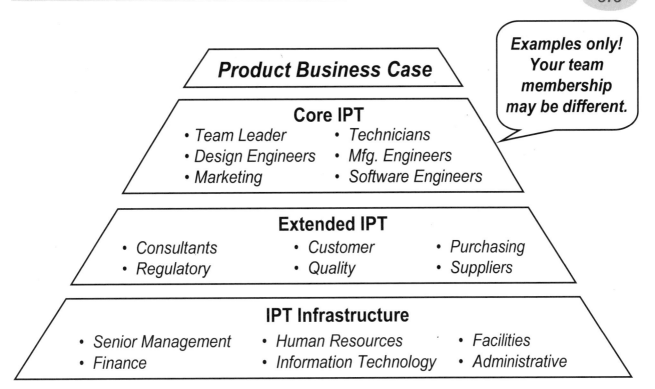

Figure 3.11: The structure of an integrated product team (IPT) consists of both *core* and *extended* members. Core team members should be involved in the development of a new product from cradle to launch, whereas extended team members become actively involved in a project during periods when their contributions are needed.

Lean Method: The Deliverables Roadmap

One of the mainstays of the lean improvement philosophy is the use of visual communication to reduce ambiguity, improve speed, and enfranchise a larger audience for information. I will introduce several visual product development tools throughout the remainder of this guidebook, culminating in the *visual project board* described in Section 5.2. The first of these tools should be employed at the earliest stage of the planning process for a new development project. Imagine being able to capture all of the important elements of a project on a single sheet of paper: key schedule milestones, dependencies, responsibilities, gate reviews, the critical path, and most vital of all, project deliverables. This can be achieved through a graphical planning method that I call the *deliverables roadmap*. Before exploring this extremely useful tool, however, we must first define one of the terms in its title.

A *deliverable* is any tangible and transferable item that contributes to the commercialization of a new product, as shown in Figure 3.12. A deliverable can be a document, a drawing, a decision, a report, a prototype, a piece of hardware or software, literally anything that can be passed from one individual to another. Deliverables are the outcomes of tasks and activities; they are what remains standing after the work of a project is complete. More important, these tangible outcomes provide us with an unambiguous way of sorting waste from value within the product development process: *All of the value generated by a design team is embodied in the deliverables they create.* Recall our definition of value from Section 1.3; transforming deliverables is the goal of product development. Hence, it makes sense to begin the project planning process by enumerating all of the essential deliverables that the design team must create.

The deliverables roadmap shown in Figure 3.13 accomplishes this objective and then some. I will describe this tool by taking you through the process that an integrated product team might use to kick off a new development project. Picture a typical project kickoff meeting; lots of energy and exuberance (the fatigue and disillusionment come later), representatives from all key functions, a freshly anointed team leader, and perhaps a few curious executives. The meeting is called to order, doughnuts are consumed, personal anecdotes are shared, and lots of "storming and norming" takes place. The team leader

A "Deliverable" is any item that is tangible and transferable:

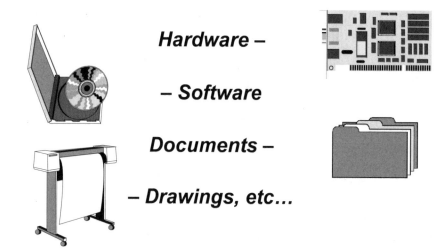

Hardware –

– Software

Documents –

– Drawings, etc...

> **Key Principle of Lean Product Development:**
> **ALL PROJECT VALUE IS EMBODIED IN ITS DELIVERABLES**
> **(For a task to be value-added, it must have a deliverable and a customer who needs it!)**

Figure 3.12: A deliverable is anything that is both tangible and transferable from one person or group to another. Deliverables are critically important; all value that is created by a product development team is embodied in the deliverables they generate.

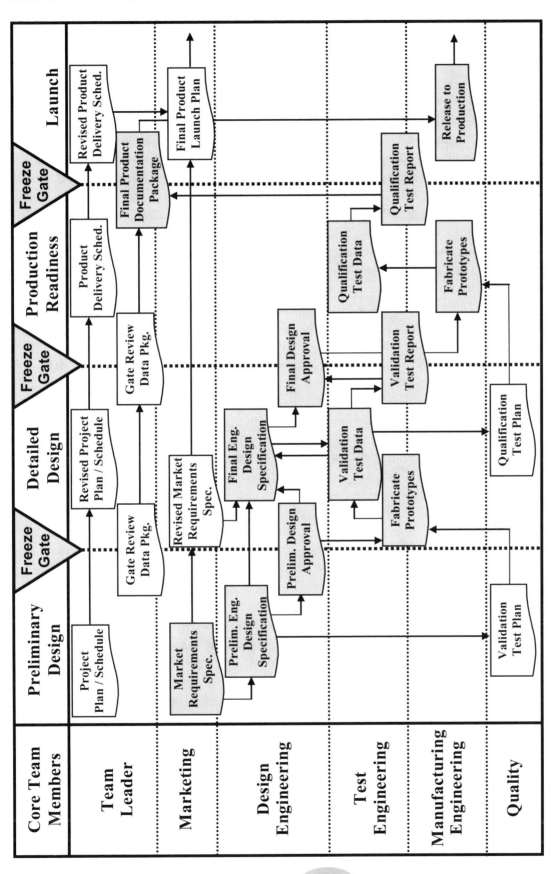

Figure 3.13: The deliverables roadmap provides a high-level overview of a development project in a simple visual format. All project deliverables are assigned to specific team members, and completion dates, dependencies, gate reviews, and other important information are graphically represented. Note that the simplified set of deliverables shown here is typical of a "waterfall-style" development project.

takes the floor and begins facilitating the creation of a deliverables roadmap for the project. She hands out a pad of sticky notes to each attendee, and asks them to write down any deliverable that they think is essential to project execution and completion (sorry about the gender-specific pronouns by the way – until our language matures, fair-minded authors are forced to alternate between he, she, he, she...). The sticky notes start flooding in, and as they arrive, the team leader places them on a large white board or flip chart. Once the flow reduces to a trickle, she begins rationalizing all of the inputs and arranging them into rough chronological order. Some inputs are combined, redundancies are eliminated, and most important, questionable items are either refined or rejected. Keep in mind that we are not interested in tasks here, but rather the *outputs of tasks*. Hence, in some cases the inputs might need to be reworded to focus on the tangible outcome, rather than the activity itself. With the team's support, it doesn't take long for the team leader to create a visual representation of all project work, albeit in rough form.

Next, she lists all of the core team members along the vertical axis of the emerging roadmap. Not every discipline needs to be represented, but it is better to be inclusive rather than exclusive. Once the individual names are identified, the team leader assigns each deliverable to one of the core team members. Assuming that they agree to take on the responsibility, the sticky note representing that deliverable is placed in the horizontal row associated with the responsible individual. So it goes until all deliverables are assigned to an individual, with no shared responsibilities, and no "team deliverables". This is not to say that cross-functional collaboration won't be involved. In fact, for large-scale projects, a deliverable may represent an entire mini-project unto itself, requiring considerable collaborative effort. The reason for assigning a single name to each deliverable should be obvious; the team leader (or overseeing manager, for that matter), needs to have an earlobe to tug on if a deliverable is late or incorrect. Having the team be responsible for a deliverable is the same thing as having no one responsible.

Once the deliverables are divvied up, the group begins assigning a process structure to the roadmap. Where should freeze gates be positioned? What are the dependencies among the deliverables? Note that much of this structure could be standardized, particularly if your firm's development projects are relatively similar. For example, a roadmap template could be created for each category of project (e.g., minor product modifications, major new platforms, etc.). This would allow a new integrated product team to easily modify the template, rather than being forced to start from scratch. Likewise, a standardized list of project deliverables would greatly facilitate the initial brainstorming session described above. It is critical, however, to keep this standardization process *flexible*. It should be expected that each newly formed team should be allowed to make whatever changes they believe are necessary to conform to the practical realities of their specific project.

At this point in the kickoff meeting, the team is most likely exhausted, and unless a very enticing platter of cookies shows up, it is probably time to adjourn. The team leader will take the rough roadmap created by the group and generate a strawman final version using the format shown in Figure 3.13. A graphical tool such as Visio works well to capture this type of roadmap, and don't be afraid to print it out as a D-sized drawing; you want this to be a visual tool, not an eye chart. If the number of deliverables is just too great, consider merging several items into higher-level deliverables with multiple elements. The team leader might also assign some tentative completion dates to each deliverable, as the first step in developing a sane and achievable master schedule (more on project scheduling in Section 5.4).

Hopefully you recall the concept of the *critical path* of a project from Section 3.2. This all-important sequence of schedule-critical tasks can be easily visualized (at least at the highest level) through the use of the deliverables roadmap. In Figure 3.13, the critical path of a simplified development project is highlighted in grey. In this case we are focusing on deliverables rather than tasks, but the dependencies and flow of work should be representative of what drives the schedule on a particular project. You will notice that some of the deliverables feed the critical path but are not themselves schedule-critical, while others are right in the thick of things. Although the roadmap only provides a top-level perspective, it is useful as a starting point for more detailed planning, and as a way to visually communicate the critical path to the uninitiated. (Note to project management aficionados: The actual critical path must be determined using a Gantt-chart-type schedule rather than a roadmap, since tasks may not depend on each other in a start-to-finish relationship.)

In actual use, the deliverables roadmap can be either static or dynamic. The static form would not change beyond the initial planning of a project. It would serve as an intermediary step to ensure common thinking and completeness before creating a more detailed, "living" schedule. It can also, however, be used dynamically as a way to capture significant progress by the team, and to identify those deliverables that are ahead of (in your dreams) or behind schedule. To accomplish this, simply update the roadmap for your project on a regular basis using a "current-date" line that crosses the diagram from top to bottom. Deliverables that have been successfully completed can be colored green. Those that are on the line but not yet complete could be made yellow, while any deliverable to the left of the line that is incomplete could be colored red. A nice way to get a 10,000 foot perspective on the status of a project.

One final point is worth mentioning. There is a very important relationship between the deliverables roadmap and what is referred to in the lean community as the value stream. In Part 6 of this guidebook I will describe an improvement tool known as *value-stream mapping*, in which a sequence of tasks within a process are systematically graphed and analyzed for wasted time. The good news is that once you've created a deliverables roadmap for your project, you will already have some experience in generating a value-stream map, because from the perspective of product development, *they are essentially the same thing.* Since all value in a project is embodied in its deliverables, I have found great success in mapping deliverables rather than tasks when performing a value-stream-mapping improvement exercise. However, this only works up to a point; once it becomes necessary to dig deeply into a process to seek root causes for waste, a more task / schedule oriented value-stream map is often needed.

Lean Method: Permeable Freeze Gates

I've previously used the term *freeze gate* to describe my vision of an all-encompassing decision point within the continuous-flow development process. In principle at least, a freeze gate manages all categories of project risk: profitability risk, schedule risk, technical risk, and scope-change risk. How is this possible within a single gate review? The answer is that it isn't possible in the same review, but it *is* possible at about the same *time*. The freeze-gate review is not a single meeting, but rather several meetings that take place at about the same point in the project schedule, and are synchronized with the critical path of the development project. My recommended structure for a freeze-gate review is described in Figure 3.14. Basically, it consists of three separate meetings: a technical design review, a project-plan review, and finally a business-case review. These meetings can be held in any order, but it makes the most sense to hold the technical review first (to understand the risks to cost, performance, and schedule), followed by the project-plan review. After a revised and sensible project plan has been developed, the final checkpoint would be the business-case review. In a sense, these three meetings ask the questions: "How are we doing?", "What will it take to finish?", and "Is it worth it to continue?"

From a logistical standpoint, I suggest that a week be identified within the project schedule during which all three meetings would be held. Standardized agendas could be created for each meeting, along with a standard matrix of attendees, such as the one shown in Figure 3.15. Keeping in mind the design team's workload, the formality of these meetings should be kept to a minimum. These reviews need to be comprehensive, but not necessarily pretty (unless external customers will be attending). They certainly should not be redundant; each meeting should cover a different aspect of the project, with no repeats or rehashing. The duration of each meeting should scale with the complexity of the product, with smaller projects requiring only a few hours per review, while sophisticated, system-type products potentially requiring a full month to complete all three freeze-gate meetings.

The technical design review should focus on both risks and opportunities. Are all customer requirements being met? Can the product be made to perform better? Is the projected manufacturing cost (see Section 3.4) acceptable, and if not, can it be improved? Are environmental and quality standards understood, and can they be achieved? What are the major technical risks as the project moves forward? Finally, which requirements or other product attributes can be frozen to avoid time-consuming changes later in development? (This is a reference to the staged-freezing process described at the end of this section. Note that a simple technique for facilitating an effective technical design review is presented in the next subsection, but any sensible approach will get the job done.) The attendees at this first freeze-gate meeting should include all technical contributors to the project, the team leader, and key members of senior functional management, particularly from design / engineering. It is important to recognize that if any of the key players are not present at a freeze-gate meeting, the risk to the project increases. Comprehensive risk mitigation demands comprehensive attendance and participation.

Assuming that no disasters are identified during the technical design review, the next meeting to be held would be the project plan review. This meeting provides an

---

Topics Covered in a Typical Freeze-Gate Review

Part 1 – Technical Design Review:

☐ Spec. Verification   ☐ Prototype Test Data

☐ Simulation Results   ☐ Software Design

☐ Manufacturability   ☐ Quality / Reliability

☐ "Freeze List"   ☐ Open Action Items

Part 2 – Project-Plan Review:

☐ Project Schedule   ☐ Resource Plan

☐ Development Cost   ☐ Risk Management

☐ Testing Plan   ☐ Launch Schedule

Part 3 – Business-Case Review:

☐ Cost Targets   ☐ Launch Date

☐ Revised NPV   ☐ Market Conditions

Figure 3.14: The author's interpretation of a *freeze-gate review* consists of three separate reviews that take place at roughly the same time within a development project. Collectively, the three reviews can successfully manage technical, schedule, and market risks.

opportunity to modify the schedule, scope, and resource allocation of the project to reflect the current reality. The attendee list shifts slightly from that of the technical design review, with more focus on functional management participation, and less need for attendance by the working-level team members. The output of this second meeting should be a new project plan that balances acceptable risk with aggressive time-to-completion.

Finally, the results of the previous two meetings are summarized and presented to executive management at the business-case review. The main focus of this gathering should be on exceptions; what has changed since the project was approved for development? It might turn out, for example, that several planned product features are too costly to include in the new product. What impact would that have on sales volumes and pricing strategy? Perhaps the launch date has slipped a few months. Will that cause the new product to miss a critical market window? If nothing of importance has changed since the

---

Recommended Attendees for a Typical Freeze-Gate Review

Meeting 1 – Technical Design Review:

Mandatory

- *Team Leader*
- *Core Team*
- *Design / Eng. Mgmt.*

Optional

- *Marketing*
- *Operations*
- *"Gurus"*
- *Consultants*
- *Other*

Meeting 2 – Project-Plan Review:

Mandatory

- *Team Leader*
- *Major Task Leaders*
- *Functional Mgmt.*

Optional

- *Executive Mgmt.*
- *Suppliers*
- *Purchasing*
- *Other*

Meeting 3 – Business-Case Review

Mandatory

- *Finance*
- *Executive Mgmt.*
- *Marketing*
- *Team Leader*

Optional

- *Operations*
- *Engineering / Design*
- *Other*

Figure 3.15: A recommended attendee list for the three meetings that constitute a product development freeze-gate review. Note that the "mandatory" individuals must attend their respective meetings to ensure adequate risk mitigation.

beginning of the project, either in the external competitive environment or in the scope of development, you could conceivably cancel the business-case review entirely. On the other hand, if the net present value has gone into the dumpster, it may be time to kill the project and reallocate those precious design resources.

In the interest of lean thinking, it is important to keep waste and value in mind throughout the freeze-gate activity. Remember that these gates are permeable; the team should continue to make progress before, during, and after a freeze-gate review. It's also important to recognize that excessive formality can be a tremendous time-waster, and can possibly represent an obstacle to effective communication. Presentations need to be neat and understandable, but they do not need to be long or artsy. Meetings should last only as long as necessary and no longer; try focusing on highlights and exceptions rather than on covering every bit of minutia. Lastly, let your intuition guide you regarding how much effort and attention is needed. If a project "seems to be going well," it probably requires somewhat less scrutiny than one that makes your skin crawl at the very thought of it. I've said it before and I'll say it again; one size doesn't fit all. Right-sizing your freeze-gate reviews can save considerable time and reduce these potential obstacles to the flow of value down to nothing more than speed bumps.

Lean Method: The "Waste-Free" Design Review

In the aerospace and defense sector where I cut my teeth, technical design reviews were so important, so much a part of the design process, that one couldn't imagine executing a development project without them. Much to my surprise, when I began working with commercial firms in other industries, I often found that design reviews were treated with grudging acceptance at best. Why the disconnect? Certainly the aerospace industry is far more contract and project focused than most commercial enterprises. Yet the fact that design reviews were a mandatory part of many government contracts was only a minor factor in their acceptance by development teams. These technical meetings provided an invaluable opportunity to expose a nascent design to a new set of informed eyes, and to harvest feedback that might avert a catastrophe (or at least a missed opportunity) downstream.

After much digging into the subject, I've discovered that the bad rep that design reviews have in many commercial firms is due both to a misunderstanding regarding their purpose and benefits, and to the way in which they are conducted. The purpose of a design review should be to give a proposed product design an aggressive wringing out. The desired output should be a list of possible risks, errors, manufacturability issues, and even opportunities to improve the performance of the design. Each of these factors can potentially impact a product design in ways that would benefit external customers. So why don't more commercial firms embrace this valuable tool? In some instances, design reviews have become no more than administrative check-boxes, often driven by an ISO 9000 (or similar) requirement. They are perceived as necessary evils; an intrusion into the business of the design team, with no technical benefit whatsoever. In other cases, design reviews have the proper intentions, but the execution is so wasteful and disruptive that the teams feel they would be better off without them.

Let's fix these problems once and for all. First, we must agree on the objectives of a technical design review; to reduce risk and improve a new product design. Second, let's get away from the check-box mentality. If your firm is going to hold a design review, why not make it a valuable and important activity? Take the administrative aspects out of your current review format and move them elsewhere (preferably to the trash can), *and let the design teams own these meetings.* A successful design review should not be a superficial tutorial, or worse yet, a fluffy "dog and pony show" intended to make everyone feel good about the upcoming product. A design review should be executed by and for technical peers, without the encumbrance of executives or external customers. If your firm must perform contract-mandated reviews, use the technique described below *first* to scrutinize the design, and then bring in the execs and contract customers for a fluffy, but technically sound, presentation. Finally, leave defensiveness at the door. There is a common defect in company cultures that goes by many names: the "not-invented-here" syndrome, the "ugly-baby" syndrome, and so on. These colorful terms imply that design teams are both insecure and insular. All of us who design products think that our "babies" are beautiful; we take great pride in developing a new design, and most of us are loath to hear criticism of it. Yet there has never been a design team that could guarantee that they haven't missed something important. Don't let misplaced pride get in the way of your firm producing the best possible products.

So how does a waste-free design review avoid the common traps mentioned above? Some of the important attributes of this approach are contrasted with a typical design review in Figures 3.16 and 3.17. (Incidentally, please pardon the hyperbole in the title of this lean method; it should really be called the "lower-waste" design review, but that doesn't have much of a ring to it.) The first step in executing a truly valuable design review is to select the right attendees. Naturally, the integrated product team should attend, including any key extended team members. More important, a group of outside partici-pants should be invited who can bring a fresh perspective to the meeting. We used to refer to these folks as "gurus," because they were often the most senior and expert members of our technical staff. You should be looking for individuals with extensive experience in products similar to the one under development, with a focus on any attributes of the product that are particularly high risk. Make no mistake about this; including gurus in your review can be a humbling experience. But in truth, learning in general is a humbling experience; you must first admit that you don't know something before you can begin to learn. There is nothing wrong with not knowing, but there is something very wrong with being afraid to learn.

Once the review attendees have been selected and their schedules coordinated, give each participant about a week to review pre-work materials (e.g., drawings, specifications, test results, etc.). In addition, each attendee should be given one more assignment; to bring to the design review *at least one suggestion for improving the product design*. This requirement ensures that most participants will at least briefly review the pre-work materials, and will encourage immediate contributions from everyone involved. On the day of the meeting, begin with just a brief question and answer period. I like to limit this to ten minutes or so; just enough time to clarify any misunderstandings about pre-work materials, and allow for some quick explanations if necessary. If a more extensive tutorial is required, you can hold an informal pre-meeting for those who need some brushing up. Don't bog down the design review with redundant and tedious details, unless a specific explanation is necessary to understand a potential design problem.

Once the Q & A session is over, the real meat of the review begins. From this point forward, brainstorming rules will apply: no bad ideas, no negative feedback, no defensive comments, etc. Begin at one side of the room and ask each attendee *individually* to provide the improvement idea that they brought to the meeting. This step is very important, since often the brightest people at your review will not be the most outspoken. By giving each attendee a turn to speak, you ensure that everyone's perspective will be heard. As each suggestion is received, write it down on a flip chart or white board. No discussing

A Typical Design Review

▶ Detailed "tutorial" presentations by the design team.

▶ Audience is expected to speak up if a problem or risk is identified...otherwise the design is assumed to be correct.

▶ Output of the review is a list of unprioritized action items that must be dispositioned, whether they make sense or not.

The "Waste-Free" Design Review

▶ A brief technical overview.

▶ "Systematic brainstorming" yields a list of problems, risks, and opportunities.

▶ Brainstorming list is ranked, based on _impact_ and _probability_ of _occurrence_.

▶ The product of these two rankings provides a priority-ordering of action items for disposition.

Figure 3.16: Attributes of a typical technical design review compared to those of a "waste-free" design review. The waste-free review methodology involves using a simple facilitation technique to gain the maximum number of valuable inputs from a review meeting in the minimum amount of time.

suggestions, other than a brief clarification if necessary. Continue this process for several rounds, first harvesting the attendees prepared suggestions, and then any additional inputs that might have been triggered by other participants' comments. If an attendee runs out of valuable inputs, he or she can simply say "pass". Once the number of new inputs reduces to a trickle, open the floor up to anyone with additional comments. Don't let this brainstorming go on forever; I like to keep these sessions to no more than an hour. For simple products, the entire design can be reviewed at one sitting. For more complex, system-type products you might consider holding several reviews that focus on different subsystems.

The final step in the waste-free design review is critical: you must filter and prioritize the feedback you've received. Since brainstorming doesn't allow for discussion, it is likely that many of the suggestions you've received just won't apply to the product design under review. Even if the suggestions do apply, they may not be important enough to the product's future to be worth implementing. How can you quickly establish which ideas are both applicable and of high impact? A simple group-scoring technique accomplishes this in short order, as shown in Figure 3.18. Ask the group to rank each suggestion on your list based on two subjective scoring criteria. The first criterion is "probability," meaning the probability that a suggestion is applicable to the product under review. I use a 1-to-5 scale,

▶ **No "dog and pony shows"**   ▶ **No "ugly-baby" syndrome**

▶ **No rubber stamp approvals**   ▶ **No wasted time and resources**

Figure 3.17: The waste-free review avoids some of the common traps of typical design reviews: unnecessary formality, defensive behavior, and poor participation of attendees.

and ask the members of the group to hold up the appropriate number of fingers. If there is a reasonably good consensus, just take the average and write it down next to the suggestion. If there is poor agreement, take a moment to discuss the reasons for the disparity, but if convergence cannot be achieved quickly (in just a few minutes), just pick a number that is close to the average and move on. Remember that this scoring process serves only as an advisory to the team; they can evaluate the suggestions on their own once the review is over. Before moving on to the next suggestion, ask the group to provide a second 1-to-5 score. This time, they should assess the impact that the idea might have on the product's future if it is implemented. In both cases, a higher score means greater probability and / or impact. By multiplying the two scores together for each suggestion, you arrive at a quick but useful prioritization metric, with twenty-five being the highest possible total and one being the lowest. A template such as that shown in Figure 3.19 is helpful in capturing both suggestions and their respective group rankings.

Whether you use the above facilitation technique or not, there are several rules that should be followed when executing any technical design review, as shown in Figure 3.20. First, be sure to hold your technical design reviews early enough in the development process to have a real impact on the new product. It is common to hear great suggestions for improvement waved off with a comment such as, "Good idea...but it's just too late to implement it." Second, always invite the gurus, even if you have to schedule the review around their busy calendars. Without these objective eyes, a technical design review is likely to become just a back-patting lovefest. These outsiders can help ensure that the next

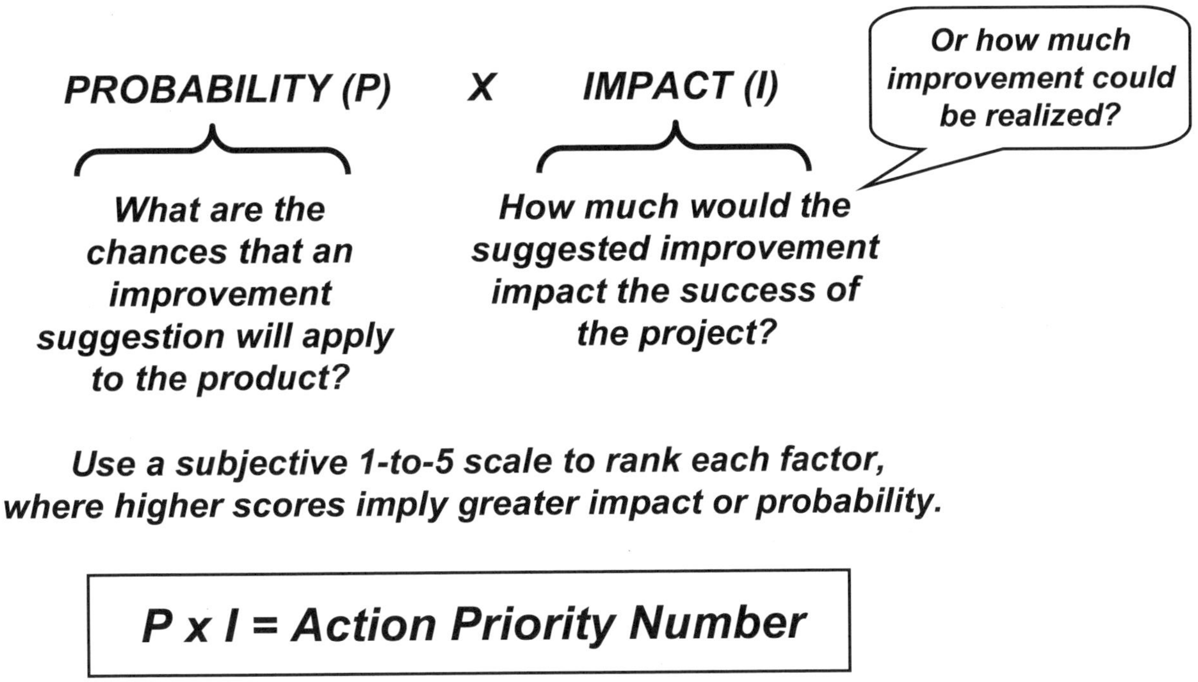

PROBABILITY (P)   X   IMPACT (I)

What are the chances that an improvement suggestion will apply to the product?

How much would the suggested improvement impact the success of the project?

Or how much improvement could be realized?

Use a subjective 1-to-5 scale to rank each factor, where higher scores imply greater impact or probability.

$$P \times I = \text{Action Priority Number}$$

Figure 3.18: The inputs gathered from review participants are filtered and prioritized using two 1-to-5 subjective ratings: the probability that a suggestion actually applies to the product under review, and the impact the suggestion would have on the product's success if it is implemented.

rule on the list is achieved: It is vital that the design team question their assumptions. An assumption is like a blind spot in your vision. Once it is made, it disappears from consciousness, but lurks in the background distorting your objectivity. The best way that I have found to break through these blind spots is to ask the design team, "What would you do if you couldn't do it that way?" This can apply to material choices, physical design, software structure, manufacturing process selection, really any aspect of a product's design and commercialization. By making design assumptions explicit, you have an opportunity to reevaluate their validity and potentially identify a better way.

The last two rules are equally important. Manufacturability issues are always in order. There is never a time during product development that we can ignore this topic, especially in the earliest stages of design. Make sure that operations is well-represented at your reviews, and give their suggestions special consideration; they are probably the most practical people in your meeting. Finally, be sure that your design teams follow up on design-review suggestions. It is not necessary that the teams report on the disposition of every idea, but some level of accountability should be maintained. In particular, the highest scoring improvements should be given active attention, and either accepted or rejected for good reasons. This final rule validates the entire process. If you have no way of ensuring that the suggestions generated by a design review will be given objective consideration, *don't bother holding the review.* There is no value in getting people together to scrutinize a design, only to have their valuable inputs fall on deaf ears.

Design Element Under Review	Suggestions for Product Improvement	Subjective Rating		Priority Ranking
		(P)	(I)	

Figure 3.19: A template for gathering inputs from design review participants and prioritizing them for future disposition by the integrated product team.

Lean Method: Staged Freezing of Requirements

One of the complaints that I hear most often from development teams is that the specification that they are designing to is constantly changing. Is this just a fact of life during product development, or is there something that can be done to minimize disruptive requirements changes? Unfortunately, it is impossible to eliminate this problem entirely, for a very good reason; some changes are actually *beneficial* to the future of a new product. During the course of development, events in the marketplace may occur that must be accommodated to avoid a market failure. A competitor might release a new product that undermines your business case. Market preferences may shift due to factors that are out of your control. Sometimes just the learning involved in the development process may uncover either risks or opportunities that could not be anticipated at the start of a project. In these cases, a change in direction by the design team may mean the difference between success and failure.

Of course, there is another side to this story. Unnecessary "scope creep" can be caused by poor decision-making, management insecurity, an overly zealous marketing group, or a denial of the impact that requirements changes can have on time-to-market.

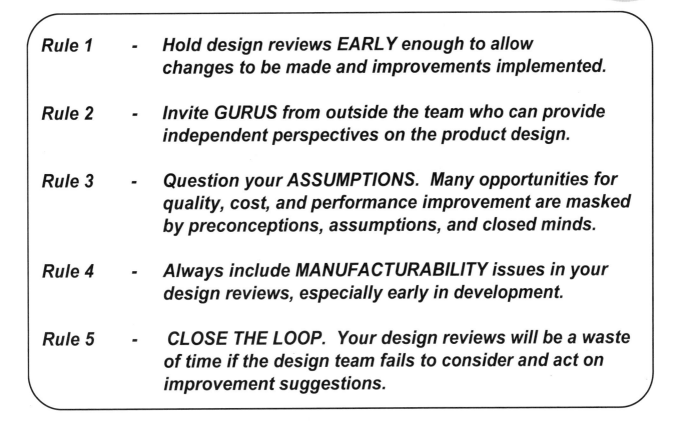

Rule 1 - *Hold design reviews EARLY enough to allow changes to be made and improvements implemented.*

Rule 2 - *Invite GURUS from outside the team who can provide independent perspectives on the product design.*

Rule 3 - *Question your ASSUMPTIONS. Many opportunities for quality, cost, and performance improvement are masked by preconceptions, assumptions, and closed minds.*

Rule 4 - *Always include MANUFACTURABILITY issues in your design reviews, especially early in development.*

Rule 5 - *CLOSE THE LOOP. Your design reviews will be a waste of time if the design team fails to consider and act on improvement suggestions.*

Figure 3.20: Five important rules that can help improve the value and efficiency of any design review.

Before I describe a method for reducing these disruptive and often frivolous changes to product requirements, it's time to face an important reality. Changes to product specifications during the execution of a project *will almost certainly result in a schedule slip*. To illustrate this point, consider the "three-legged stool" shown in Figure 3.21. This analogy is familiar to many who have been trained in project management. In a sense, it shows that there is no free lunch. If one of the legs of the stool (i.e., schedule, resources, or project scope) is changed, the other two legs must be adjusted for the stool to remain standing. More specifically, if scope is added to a project, schedule will almost certainly increase, and potentially the required resources may also grow. Occasionally a change may be noninvasive, but this is the exception, not the rule. It should be assumed that schedule will be impacted, so a tradeoff must be made between the benefits of a desired change and the costs associated with a longer development time and a delayed product launch.

How can we inject some discipline into the development process, so that necessary changes are accommodated and low value ones are rejected? We could put all design requirements under rigid configuration control from the very beginning of a project. This way, any requested change would be forced to go through a formal engineering change process, including a change review board. Although taking this step would reduce the number of trivial changes and add considerable discipline, it would also hamstring the design team and possibly restrict innovation and creativity. Fortunately, there is a middle ground between no control and draconian control, and that middle ground is referred to as *staged-freezing*. This is not a new concept. Boeing Company, for example, has achieved great success in using staged-freezing during the development of the 777 commercial aircraft, and more recently the 787 Dreamliner. The idea is to use an informal change-control process during the early stages of development that allows the design team to freeze specific requirements as the project progresses. The frozen items are selected based on their impact on project schedule. For example, if a piece of capital equipment is essential to the launch of a product, the lead time associated with ordering that item may force the design team to freeze a number of specifications well before product launch. Likewise, some design attributes such as feature sets, user interfaces, and so on, may be difficult to change once the detailed design of a product is underway. By allowing the design team to identify those specifications that must be frozen, the team is essentially saying to all functions within the firm (particularly marketing), "The door is closing on these attributes, so make up your mind and be prepared to stick with your decisions."

The "Three-Legged Stool" of Change Management

Project Schedule –
- **Key Milestones**
- **Delivery Dates**
- **Drop-Dead Dates**

Impact on Resources –
- **Team Members**
- **Factory Capacity**
- **Overhead Rates**
- **Return on Capital**

Project Scope –
- **Key Requirements**
- **Optional Features**
- **Customization**

Figure 3.21: The "three-legged stool" of change management. If the length of one of the legs of the stool is changed (such as by adding scope to a project), the length of the other two legs must also be changed for the stool to stay balanced. In other words, if additional work is added to a team's development project, it will almost certainly require additional resources and / or additional time-to-completion.

A "Major Freeze" –

- *Occurs only two or three times in a project*
- *Requires a "freeze review" with management, etc.*
- *Enables dependent work to begin with minimal risk*
- *Should be based on a team-defined "freeze list"*

A "Minor Freeze" –

- *Can occur at any time during a project*
- *Only requires team agreement*
- *Focuses on only a few specifications*
- *Can be used to accelerate downstream tasks*

Figure 3.22: Staged freezing can be implemented using a combination of major and minor freezes. Major freezes occur at the three freeze gates of the development process, wherein the design team submits a list of items that must be held constant for the project to stay on schedule. Minor freezes can be instituted at any time by agreement among the core development team, and are then added to the freeze list for the next freeze-gate review.

In actual use, the staged-freezing process can involve both "major freezes" and "minor freezes," as shown in Figure 3.22. A major freeze takes place at each of the aptly named freeze gates (described previously in this section). During the preparation for each gate, the design team would create a "freeze list" that includes any specification that they believe is schedule-critical. This list is then presented to management at both the technical design review and the project plan review. If there is agreement among all participants, these specs would be frozen at that time. If an item on the list is still up in the air, an action would be assigned to run it to ground in a timely manner. In addition to these major freeze points, the design team should be allowed to initiate minor freezes amongst themselves at any time during the project. These are just internal, team-level agreements not to change some attribute of the design, so that project work can continue without disruption or rework. For example, the interface between two subsystems might be frozen, so that each subsystem can be designed independently of the other, with assurance that they will integrate together properly at the end of development. The minor freezes during each phase would be gathered up and included on the freeze list for the next freeze-gate review. Again, the goal is not to eliminate specification changes, but rather to corral them into noninvasive periods within the project. Some additional advantages of the staged-freeze methodology are shown in Figure 3.23.

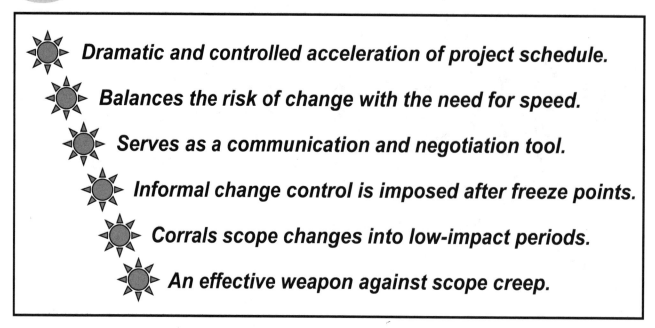

Figure 3.23: Several of the significant benefits of the staged-freeze approach to informal change control.

How does the design team keep track of which specifications are frozen? I suggest including the freeze status of each spec explicitly within the development specification document, as shown in Figure 3.24. At the start of a project, all project requirements are subject to change. As the development process progresses, the team would record frozen items and their freeze dates on the engineering specification. If an item must be defrosted, the thaw date would be recorded, along with the refreeze date whenever that occurs. In this way, there is no ambiguity among the core team and project stakeholders; specs are either frozen or open, there is no middle ground.

Finally, how do we control the defrosting and refreezing of specifications? We certainly don't want this process to be too easy; it would serve no purpose to freeze product specs if anyone can defrost them at their whim. Instead, I recommend that an informal change-review process be established that forces consideration of the impact and benefits of a change to any frozen item, as shown in Figure 3.25. This change control could be accomplished by an ad-hoc change review board that convenes only when a change to a frozen product spec is requested. Alternatively (and preferably in my opinion), a "change czar" could be empowered to arbitrate changes to frozen items for each development project. This role could be performed by the team leader in some cases, but it would more likely be a high-level manager or executive that has purview over the project. In either case, the change process should be quick but rigorous. You need a forum at which the pros and cons of a requested change can be weighed, and a prompt and intelligent decision made.

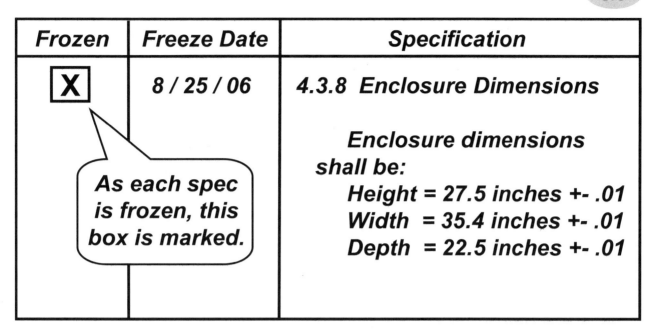

Frozen	Freeze Date	Specification
X	*8 / 25 / 06*	**4.3.8 Enclosure Dimensions** **Enclosure dimensions shall be:** **Height = 27.5 inches +- .01** **Width = 35.4 inches +- .01** **Depth = 22.5 inches +- .01**

As each spec is frozen, this box is marked.

Figure 3.24: Frozen requirements can be shown explicitly on the development specification document, along with when each item is frozen. If a spec needs to be defrosted, the date this occurs can also be recorded, along with the subsequent refreeze date.

The lean methods presented throughout this section represent the heart of a lean product development process. Two considerations remain, however, that are so important that I've set them apart as separate sections. In Section 3.4, we will discuss how manufacturability can become a primary focus of the product development team, particularly in the earliest stages of design. Finally, in Section 3.5, you will learn how Toyota and other great firms manage knowledge and learning within their product development process, so that each new design team can benefit from the past experiences of the entire firm.

Alternative #1 – An Informal Change-Review Board

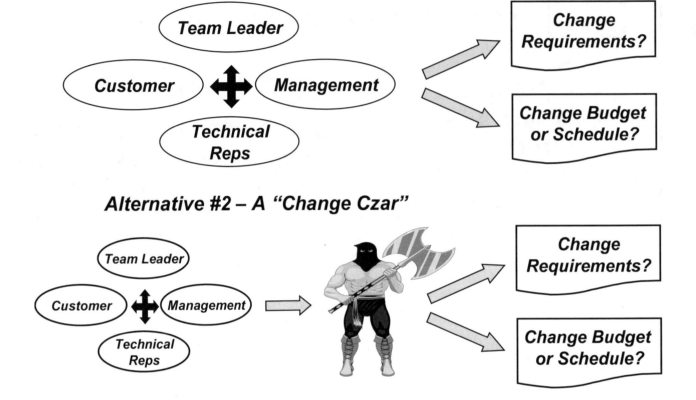

Alternative #2 – A "Change Czar"

Figure 3.25: A method must be established for arbitrating a request to defrost a frozen requirement or specification. This can be done either through an informal change review board, or by an individual (a "change czar") who is entrusted to make these decisions.

Manufacturability:
The "How's it Built?" Review

Manufacturability is not an optional consideration during new product development. Yet surprisingly few engineers and designers have taken even a single class in design for manufacturability. This is not the fault of the employees; many firms spend enormous sums on CAD tools and simulation software, but won't invest a nickel in either training or tools for product cost management. In fact, in some cases the *target cost* for a product (i.e., the unit manufacturing cost after production rampup) is barely discussed until a new design is approaching completion. How can a product development team be expected to hit their company's profitability goals *if they don't know what target to aim for?* To be truly successful at product design, teams must consider the material costs and manufacturability of a product from the very earliest stages of development.

In this section, I will describe several practical methods for injecting cost discipline into your firm's product development process. The relatively few pages dedicated to this topic are not a reflection of its importance; in fact, I've written an entire guidebook on the subject. Readers who are interested in delving deeper into manufacturing cost reduction should give *The Lean Design Guidebook* a read. For the rest of you, the concepts presented below will help your design teams to significantly improve the manufacturability of new products with only a small investment of time.

Start with the Basics – Target Costing

When should the manufacturing cost of a new product design be addressed? No, not once it reaches the factory; that's far too late to fix all but the most superficial cost problems. What about when the formal bill-of-materials is created? Still too late to truly optimize the production cost of a new design. In reality, most of the critical decisions relating to materials, product architecture, tolerances, complexity, and features are made *in the earliest stages of development,* as shown in Figure 3.26. The incurred cost of development may be relatively low during conceptual design, however a large percentage of the ultimate production cost of a product is already committed by the time the first design review is held. Clearly, the best way to optimize manufacturing cost is to address this challenge early and often.

The starting point for improving the cost focus of your design teams is to treat the target cost as a mandatory specification. Teams should be given a cost target at the inception of a development project, and should follow the logic tree shown in Figure 3.27 as

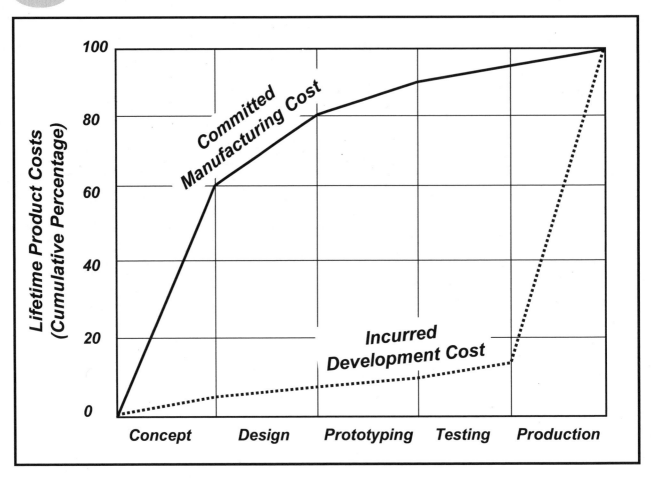

Figure 3.26: Virtually all of the opportunities to reduce the manufacturing cost of a new product occur during the earliest stages of design. Although the incurred cost of development may initially be quite low, the committed manufacturing cost of a product is largely determined by decisions made in the conceptual design stage.

the project progresses. At first, just a sanity check is all that's necessary. Is the target cost reasonable, based on the performance and features expected from the new product? This can be answered by looking at historical data from similar products that are already in production, and scaling the material and labor costs as necessary to correct for any significant differences. A rough calculation to be sure, but if this initial check shows that the new product will miss the target cost by fifty percent or more, some soul-searching may be necessary before the team takes another step.

What can be done if the target cost appears to be unreasonable? The first consideration should be whether the product's market price can be changed. The market price is driven by customer acceptance, but which customers? Often firms will aim a new product at the largest possible market segment. However, this may force the price of the product to be lower than necessary. By focusing on only those customers who will fully appreciate the capabilities and performance of a new product design, it may be possible to increase the market price. If this is still not sufficient to achieve the desired margin, it may be

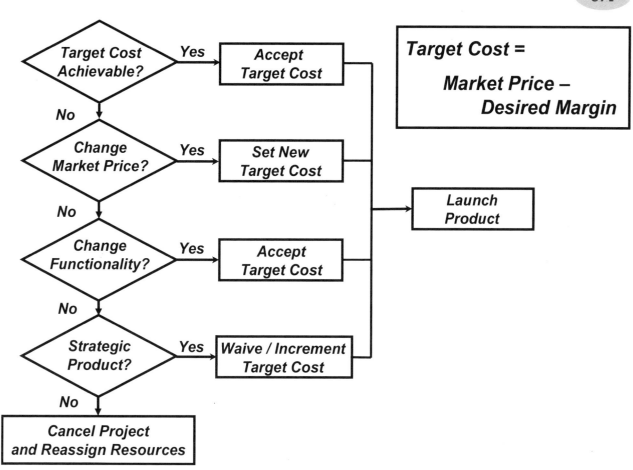

Figure 3.27: The target cost of a product is calculated by subtracting the desired margin for a new product from its projected market price. Design teams should use the target cost as a touchstone throughout development. If at any point the target cost appears unachievable, the logic tree shown above should be employed. Ultimately, it may make the most sense to cancel a product whose profits will not be sufficient to justify consuming valuable development and manufacturing resources.

necessary to modify the functionality of the product. Features that are of minimal importance might be trimmed, for example, to shave cost without adversely affecting price. This is a tricky game to play, but offering the right features and eliminating the low value ones can make the difference between profit and loss for a new product.

Finally, if all else fails, the design team should consider whether the product is strategic. As I mentioned (several times) in Section 2.2, labeling a product "strategic" is often used as a justification for pushing ahead with designs that are not strategic at all. I won't belabor this point, but keep in mind that only a small minority of products should be allowed to move forward based on their strategic value alone. Assuming that the design under consideration is not strategic, what should be done if the target cost still cannot be met? The painful answer is to kill the project and move on to more profitable opportunities. Admittedly, it might be premature to jump to this extreme conclusion at the very beginning of development. Instead it may make sense to perform some aggressive value engineering on the design to determine if a cost breakthrough can be found. If no breakthrough is identified, however, a mercy killing may be the most humane action your firm can take.

Assuming that an initial sanity check against the target cost goes well, the conceptual design of the product would begin. As the development process proceeds, the design team should repeatedly ask, "Is the estimated actual cost of the product still in line with the target cost?" The decision loop shown in Figure 3.28 should be executed whenever important new cost information becomes available, but certainly no less often than monthly. If actual and target costs are aligned, development continues unhindered. If the actual cost grows beyond its limit, the design team should take *immediate action* to reduce cost. Cost problems almost never improve over time; taking prompt action can save a design team from a far more time-consuming redesign later in the process.

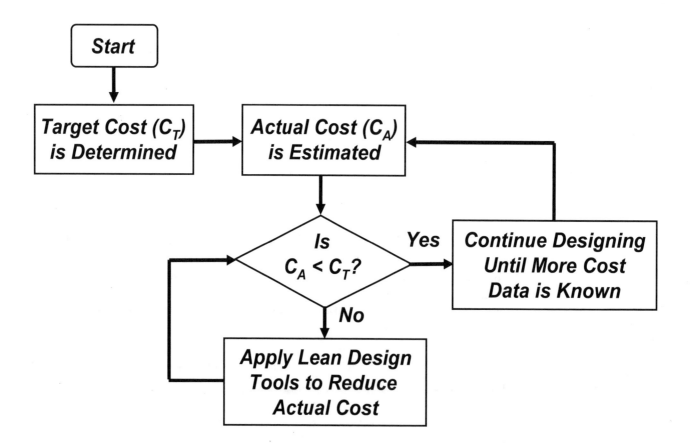

Figure 3.28: Cost problems must be dealt with as early as possible during development. Hence, it is important that design teams periodically compare the product's estimated actual manufacturing cost to the target cost. If the actual cost ever exceeds the target cost (after allowing some reasonable margin for error), the design team should immediately divert its efforts toward applying cost reduction tools.

One final note regarding target cost. A common excuse that I've heard for not providing designers with a target cost at the inception of a project, is that by doing so, the firm might be leaving some money on the table. What if the product could be designed to be even cheaper than the target that is given? Won't the design team just quit looking for cost reductions once they hit the desired mark? Yes, in fact that is exactly the point of providing a cost specification. In actuality, a target cost is no different than any other spec that is provided to the team. Perhaps more performance could be squeezed out of a product if the team wasn't given performance specifications, right? If time was not an issue, we might consider giving teams the challenge of improving *everything* about a product without limits. Once time-to-market becomes a driving consideration, specifications let a team know when it's time to stop designing and get that product into the factory. It's far better to have several new products out in the marketplace making money, rather than consuming excessive time and resources trying to squeeze every penny of unnecessary cost out of a single design.

The "How's it Built?" Review

Toyota Motor Company is famous for its pioneering work in product and process co-development. Not surprisingly, a number of scholars and consultants have attempted to document Toyota's so-called "3P" process (which stands for either "Production Preparation Process" or "Production Process Preparation," take your pick). Frankly, I believe that trying to distill Toyota's magic and repackage it neatly into a viewgraph presentation or journal paper is, for the most part, futile. Certainly there are elements of the Toyota Way that can be genericised, and there is much that we can learn from these manufacturing wizards. However, most of what makes the 3P process work for Toyota is the fact that it is being executed by Toyota employees within the Toyota culture. This is a company that has lived and breathed manufacturing process improvement for over thirty years. If you really want to emulate Toyota, you've got three decades of natural selection and acculturation ahead of you, so you'd better get started.

While the above may be true, there are still some gems that we can glean from the masters; consider the methods that I'm about to describe as a first baby step down the path. One of the most obvious attributes of Toyota's 3P is that the development of production processes is given essentially equal status to the design of the product itself. A process development team is formed at the inception of a new design, and runs in highly collaborative lockstep with the design team. It would not be an exaggeration to say that even the earliest, blue-sky concepts are screened and validated for their manufacturability, and that no design decision is made without parallel decisions occuring within the process team. Is there a way that an average firm can capture the essence of this proactive philosophy?

A fully staffed process development team would be neither practical nor cost-effective for most firms, but even the smallest companies should be able to focus on manufacturability for at least one full day. The "How's it Built?" review described in Figure 3.29 provides an early opportunity to consider the cost and quality ramifications of a conceptual product design. The timing of this review is critical; it must take place prior to the solidification of a design concept, and certainly prior to the preliminary design freeze. The goal is to take advantage of the high leverage that exists at this early stage in development, and provide the design team with a prioritized list of considerations that should be incorporated into the detailed design of the product. I've suggested that this be a one-day meeting, but the duration should be scaled to the complexity of the product. For a relatively simple product, a few hours may be all that is necessary; for a sophisticated system product, a week or more might be needed. The facilitation of the review should be the responsibility of the manufacturing engineering group, with support from quality and operations.

As with any serious review meeting, some pre-work must be done. The host of the meeting should create a conceptual manufacturing plan that includes enough detail to paint a realistic picture. A key element of this plan should be an assessment of the impact that the proposed product would have on the factory. How much floor space will be needed for storage, production, packaging, etc.? Can the product fit within existing flow lines or

Product XYZ
"How's it Built?" Review
August 32, 2036

Proposed Agenda –

8:00 – 8:30	**Overview of Conceptual Product Design**
8:30 – 9:00	**Brainstorming on Critical Cost / Quality Factors**
9:00 – 11:00	**Proposed Manufacturing Plan**
	• **Factory Layout Model**
	• **Capital Equipment List**
	• **Capacity and *TAKT*-Time Calculations**
	• **Critical-to-Cost / Critical-to-Quality Issues**
	• **"Seven-Alternatives" Process**
11:30 – 12:00	**Factory Walk-Through (Optional)**
12:00 – 1:00	**Lunch – Discussion of Proposed Manufacturing Plan**
1:00 – 3:00	**Structured Brainstorming on Improvements**
3:00 – 4:00	**Ranking of Improvement Opportunities**
4:00 – 4:30	**Assignment of Action Items**

Figure 3.29: A sample agenda for the "How's it Built?" review. This highly focused event is simply a one-day conceptual manufacturability review, based on the conceptual product design proposed by the design team. The key to making this review successful is to hold it as early as possible in the development process.

work cells, or will an entirely new layout be required? Are there any incompatibilities that might cause excessive launch costs? For example, the use of materials that require special storage and handling might be disruptive if they are new to the factory environment. It may make sense to create a "before and after" representation of the factory layout that highlights any significant changes that would be mandated by the proposed product design.

Another key area of pre-work would be to identify any required capital equipment, as well as important outsource suppliers. Whenever necessary, a make-vs.-buy tradeoff should be done for critical or expensive parts. Are there process alternatives that might be considered? Can existing capital equipment be used, and if not, what would have to change in the product design to allow reuse of existing equipment or tooling? Keep in mind that even though an investment in capital equipment is most likely buried in your overhead rate, it still directly impacts the profitability of your new product. The degree of automation should be carefully considered, as well as any product-specific tooling, fixtures, or process equipment.

Assuming that all preparations are complete, your team is ready for its "How's it Built?" review. Attendees should include all members of the core team and any key members of the extended team, along with selected "outsiders" that have insight into manufacturability issues. In general, I suggest leaving senior managers and executives out of the discussion (unless it would be career-limiting to do so). Peer reviews are far more productive than those that are skewed by the presence of bosses. The meeting begins with a brief overview of the proposed conceptual product design. Once everyone is clear on what is being proposed, an initial brainstorming session is held to harvest some first thoughts on both critical-to-quality and critical-to-cost issues. This preliminary session is intended to get the juices flowing and stimulate conversation, rather than to generate a formal list of actions. Therefore, I recommend keeping it informal and fast paced; the group will have a more structured opportunity to propose suggestions later in the day.

The "meat" of the review is a presentation of the conceptual manufacturing plan, followed, if possible, by a factory walk-through. This is an important step, since it is likely that your designers and engineers don't spend as much time as they should on the shop floor. Ask some of the folks on the line to be prepared to describe the key process steps, and in particular, any critical issues with respect to yield, ease of assembly, and so on. It is surprising how much knowledge is held in the heads of people whose opinions never see the light of day. Opening up some lines of communication here can have long-term benefits that transcend just one product and one review meeting. If your factory is not collocated with the design team, consider creating a video walk-through, provided that the new product is important enough to your firm to warrant the time and trouble.

Now for the payoff. Reassemble your review team and begin a more formal brainstorming process. I like to focus first on critical-to-quality issues, and then move on to critical-to-cost suggestions after the initial topic runs out of steam. Some typical considerations are listed in Figure 3.30. As always with brainstorming, just write down the ideas as they come in, without commentary or discussion. The one criterion that should be imposed on the reviewers is that their suggestions be detailed and specific enough to be of practical value. Although it is certainly true that "the product should be easier to assemble," this suggestion is worthless to the design team. A more specific recommendation, such as "you should redesign the pump housing to allow for bottom-up assembly," is both informative and actionable. Once you have mined the team for great ideas, you might wish to revisit the informal brainstorming that took place earlier in the day to see if any suggestions were missed.

The final step in your "How's it Built?" review is to prioritize the suggestions, and in the process, filter out the less useful or non-applicable ones. The template shown in Figure 3.31 can be used to rank the harvested ideas, based on two criteria. The first reflects the probability that a specific suggestion is applicable to the product under review. A 1-to-5 scoring system works well, with a high score implying almost certain applicability, and a low score indicating that the idea is a *non sequitur*. The second metric reflects the impact that the idea would have if implemented; the higher the score, the greater the potential impact on either cost or quality. Use the entire group to assess these metrics and then take the average of the attendees' scores. By multiplying the two scores together, you can prioritize the suggestions, and weed out those that would be of little value to the design

---

Examples of Critical-to-Cost and Critical-to-Quality Considerations

Critical-to-Quality –

- Tolerance stack-up
- Ratio of product tolerances to process accuracy / precision (C_p)
- Delicate assembly steps
- Surface treatments
- Raw material variability
- Extremes of use environment
- Reliability issues

Critical-to-Cost –

- Unique / once-used parts
- Tight-tolerance parts
- Exotic raw materials
- Assembly steps requiring high skill level
- Capital-intensive process steps
- Low-yielding process steps
- Excessive complexity
- Incompatibility with existing flow lines or work cells

Figure 3.30: Some examples of critical-to-quality and critical-to-cost considerations that might be discussed during a "How's it Built?" review.

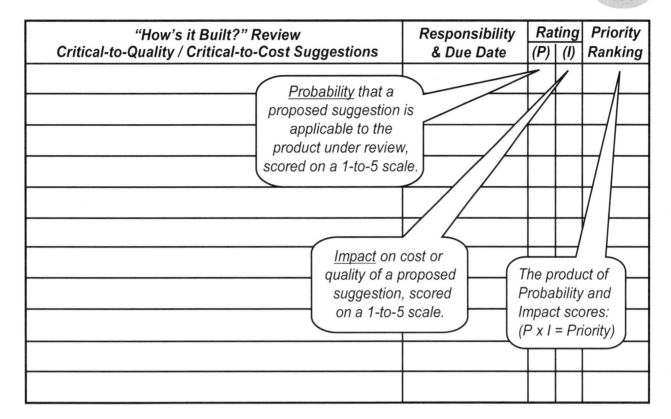

Figure 3.31: The desired output from a "How's it Built?" review is a prioritized list of critical-to-quality and critical-to-cost issues. The simple template shown above allows efficient gathering of ideas, and provides a quick way to rank-order them for the design team.

team. At this point, you could pass along the prioritized suggestions to the core team leader and end the meeting. Personally, I like to go one step further and assign action items to investigate the highest ranking recommendations. Either way, it is important that the team follows through with the suggestions derived from the meeting or the time spent was wasted.

The "How's it Built?" review described above has little to do with the way Toyota actually does business, but the underlying principle is the same; an early focus on manufacturability. There is one methodology used by Toyota, however, that deserves special attention. This method can be embedded in your "How's it Built?" review, or can stand alone as a separate project activity. The so-called "Seven-Alternatives" process is the subject of the next subsection.

The Toyota Way – Consider Seven Process Alternatives

One of the greatest causes of excessive product cost is a failure to select optimal manufacturing processes during new product development. In many instances, a firm's industrial and manufacturing engineers are stretched so thin that they have precious little time to perform the upfront tradeoffs needed to make the best possible choices. As a result, yields suffer, quality may be compromised, and capital investment can be squandered. The effectiveness of lean manufacturing depends heavily on process selection. But rather than spending time up front considering alternatives and weighing options, many design teams assume that a new product will require the same types of equipment and processes that have always been used. Ultimately, it is left to the operations group to hold *kaizen* events (i.e., intensive process improvement efforts) after a new product is already in production.

Toyota Motor Company recognizes that the selection of optimal manufacturing processes must be an integral part of product development. To that end, they have adopted a methodology that mandates consideration of seven alternative process options for every major step in the manufacture of a new product. Why seven? I suspect this is one of those "lucky number" situations, and truthfully, seven alternatives may be a bit over the top. That being said, I have yet to find a manufacturing operation for which seven different options could not be identified. Try a little thought experiment. Pick a typical process that is used to manufacture one of your firm's products and start listing alternatives. Begin with the traditional ones: for a plastic part, for example, these might include injection molding, vacuum forming, extrusion, etc. Didn't make it to seven? Now add in the degree of automation of the process: manual, automated cassette loading, robotic handling, and so on. If you are still short on options, pull out the appropriate *Tool and Manufacturing Engineers Handbook*, published by the Society of Manufacturing Engineers (www.sme.org), and do some research. Examples of seven process alternatives for some common design elements are shown in Figure 3.32.

What are the benefits of performing this exercise? Let's continue with our thought experiment. Now that you have identified seven alternatives, ask yourself the following questions: Which process option would produce the highest quality? Which would require the lowest tooling cost, consistent with the production volumes required? Which would result in the smallest batch size? What about error-proofing, setup and changeover, training, and maintenance? My guess is that none of the alternatives on your list would be ranked as number one for all of these important considerations. Hence, it is safe to say that there is no obvious best choice. Given the fact that your design team probably considered only one or two alternatives, what are the chances that the processes you are currently using are truly optimal for the products in your factory?

From a practical standpoint, it wouldn't make much sense to perform this exercise on every trivial step in the production flow of a new product. I recommend focusing on those steps that require significant capital investment, such as tooling, fixturing, new equipment, and so on. By concentrating on these heavy-hitters, you are assured that the time spent will have significant leverage on the profitability of the product. Alternatively, you could go after any process step that is known to have yield or quality issues. Either way, select only a handful of options at first, and move down the priority list if time permits. The template shown in Figure 3.33 can be helpful for rank-ordering your selections, based on "must-have" criteria chosen by your process designers. The criteria respresented in the figure are based on Toyota's methodology, but feel free to change, add, or subtract as needed to tailor the list for each new product under development.

Design Element	Process Alternatives						
	1	2	3	4	5	6	7
Metal Cylinder with Bottom	Deep Drawn	Cut from Tube Stock & Welded	Milled from Solid Bar Stock	Rolled from Sheet Stock & Welded	Liquid Metal Injection Molded	Sand Cast	Die Cast
Plastic Enclosure	Injection Molded	Compression Molded	Vacuum Formed	Structural Foam Molded	Welded from Sheet Stock	Milled from Solid Stock	Extruded and Machined
Electronic Circuit	Single-Layer Printed Circuit Board (PCB)	Multilayer PCB	Flexible PCB	Wirewrap Circuit Board	Multi-chip Module	Surface Mount vs. Through-Hole	Application Specific Integrated Circuit (ASIC)
Mechanical Fastener for Final Assembly	Screws	Pins	Clips	Barbs	Captive-Nut Fasteners	Rivets	Velcro

Figure 3.32: Examples of seven process alternatives for some common product design elements. In addition to the type of process to be used, you should also consider variations in the degree of automation.

Any subjective scoring system will work fine, but I often use a "10-5-0" scale, with a ten implying very high support of a process criterion and a zero indicating little or no compatibility. Although this is a nice way to quickly filter out the unacceptable choices, a more quantitative analysis is required to home in on the optimal alternative. The most important factors to consider, of course, are quality and cost. The quality aspect can be analyzed using six-sigma-type process capability calculations, while the cost aspect should focus on both non-recurring (capital investment) costs as well as recurring (direct labor and scrap) costs. One of the most common reasons for suboptimal process choices by a design team is that the new product has some attribute that is markedly different from other products in the factory. For example, a firm might produce mostly high-volume products, but the new product under development has a substantially lower projected volume. Choosing a high-volume process, in this situation, could cause a huge waste of capital investment.

To illustrate this point, as well as the power of the seven-alternatives methodology, I'll share a true story. Several years ago, one of the companies that I work with was embarking on the development of a new transmission for a piece of earth-moving equipment. As a key supplier to firms like Caterpillar and John Deere, they had designed similar products many times before. Hence, when it came time to select manufacturing processes, the choices seemed like no-brainers. After adding up the capital investment

Selection Criteria	Weighting Factor	Process Alternative						
		1	2	3	4	5	6	7
1. Suitable for estimated volumes								
2. Supports one-piece flow								
3. Minimal operator involvement								
4. Poke-Yoke (error proofing)								
5. Minimizes capital investment								
6. 100% gauging (measurement)								
7. Minimizes process downtime								
8. Rapid setup and changeover								
9. Low tool-room maintenance								
10. Minimal tool replacement cost								
11. Not dangerous, dirty, or difficult								
12. Minimal operator training								
13. Equipment is readily available								
14. Process is low risk / known								
15. Maintenance is minimal								
16. Requires minimal time to develop								
WEIGHTED SCORE								
RANKING OF ALTERNATIVES								

Figure 3.33: A template that can be used to evaluate seven alternative processes for each major step in the manufacture of a new product. A "10-5-0" scoring system works well, and weighting "multipliers" can be used to equalize the importance of various "must-have" criteria. The criteria you choose should be based on the type of product involved, and may be different from the Toyota-based list shown here.

required to get this new design into production, however, they were horrified to discover a $2.2M total non-recurring bill. This unacceptable investment drove them to employ the seven-alternatives methodology to see if anything could be done to drive down the required capital. A two-day event was held, at which it became apparent that the excessive capital cost was related to the projected volumes of the new transmission. Although most of this firm's products sold dozens, if not hundreds, of units per month, this new product was intended for some of the world's largest earth-moving equipment, at production volumes of less than ten units per month. Once this disconnect was identified, previous assumptions collapsed and some substantial rethinking was in order. After challenging virtually every item on the capital equipment list, it was found that about half of the total investment cost was being directed toward unnecessary automation, and another substantial portion was being spent on tooling that was intended for high-rate manufacturing. Some creative solutions were found, including reworking of old tools and using CNC machines to mill parts that would have traditionally been cast. The net result was a *$2 million reduction in required capital*, leaving only a $200K investment needed to go into production. Not a bad return for two days of effort.

Knowledge Management and Organizational Learning

In Jeffrey Liker's fine book, *The Toyota Way*, the author highlights fourteen principles that distinguish the Toyota Motor Company from other successful manufacturing enterprises. Among these principles is one that stands out as being seriously neglected by many Western firms:

> "Become a learning organization through relentless reflection (*hansei*) and continuous improvement (*kaizen*)."

The concept of a learning organization is not some academic ideal that is devoid of practical application. In fact, learning from the collective experiences of your product development teams represents a critical competitive mandate. A firm can't survive if its designers continue to make the same mistakes over and over again. It is only through organizational learning that a company can hope to remain successful as markets change, technologies evolve, and competitors rise to challenge their position.

In this section, I will survey some of the most valuable and straightforward methods for harnessing internal knowledge within your design organization. Before we begin, however, it is important to recognize that the learning process requires three essential elements:

1) A commitment of time. Even the leanest of methods for knowledge capture and organizational learning will take time away from product development activities.

2) A strong motivation. Learning is hard work, so there must be a substantial benefit to be gained for designers to invest the required effort.

3) A humble attitude. Your teams can't begin to learn until they recognize that they don't already know everything.

These are not insignificant considerations when one is dealing with product development teams. Time is always in short supply, and learning initiatives may be regarded as optional "enablers" rather than essential activities. Furthermore, understanding the motivation for organizational learning requires a long-term, strategic perspective; something that may be hard to come by among already overworked team members. Finally, designers and engineers are not known for their humility (present company excepted, of course). Each of these issues must be dealt with before your firm can become an effective learning organization. Fortunately, the tools and methods that follow will require minimal time to implement, and will yield significant and highly visible benefits, thereby mitigating two of the three concerns. Convincing your design teams to open their minds and be willing to learn from the experiences of others...well, that will be left as an exercise for the reader. You can't expect me to do *all* of the hard work for you.

Capturing Knowledge Through Standard Work

One of the reasons why the lean improvement philosophy has met with some resistance in the product development environment is its strong emphasis on standard work. In the factory, where lean cut its teeth, the idea of standardizing all aspects of production makes sound sense. Since variability is the enemy of quality in the manufacturing arena, creating standard work instructions can have a substantial positive impact on defect rates, production costs, and customer satisfaction. Now rotate your thinking ninety degrees and consider how standard work might impact new product development. In this domain, variability (in the form of creativity and innovation) is essential to success. You can't develop a winning product by doing exactly the same thing as you did on the last development project. Moreover, unlike factory workers, engineers and designers can achieve high-value outputs using a variety of approaches. Some design team members may prefer to spend hours simulating the performance of a new design on a CAD system, while others might choose to build working prototypes and run extensive tests. In short, *you can't standardize the work of product developers in the same way as factory workers without destroying the development process itself.* It is the fear of this kind of overbearing standardization that has given lean a bad name among some design and engineering groups.

On the other hand, this does not mean that a healthy level of conformity cannot be achieved. Nor must we miss out on the error-reducing and risk-mitigating benefits of standardization. Instead, we will take a more flexible approach to standardization by embracing adaptable templates, guidelines, and checklists, as opposed to rigid recipes. Even with this caveat, standard work should only be employed when one or both of the following conditions are met:

1) Standardizing the work saves significant time.
2) Standardizing the work reduces risk of errors or avoids missed opportunities.

In my opinion, these are the only two legitimate reasons to standardize; all other justifications are specious. Wanting every document or presentation to look alike, for example, is not a valid reason to standardize, unless errors are likely to occur as a result of the difference in formats. Likewise, cramming projects into rigid process structures that needlessly constrain design teams is misguided. Every project team should be encouraged to customize all product development standards, including their approach to executing the development process itself. Naturally, an appropriate level of review and approval for this "scaled plan" is essential, but once the plan is approved, the development team should be free to move within their allowed space as freely as possible.

The place to begin capturing product development knowledge is where all value in a project resides; in the deliverables themselves. Typically, most intermediate and final deliverables will not change from project to project, with some deliverables being essential to every new product launch. Begin your organizational learning endeavor by creating a standard approach for each of these essential items. The first step should be to establish a common definition for each deliverable, as shown in Figure 3.34. This must not be a tome; just a few paragraphs that define the format that should be used, and the content that must be present. Once these basic definitions are in place, your next step should be to create either a template or a guideline for each critical deliverable. Templates and guidelines represent a ripe opportunity for firms to capture knowledge by embodying the current "best way" of doing things. Be sure to harvest inputs for each deliverable from both internal and external customers before releasing your initial draft of a template. As project teams begin using this standard format, gather feedback (i.e., lessons learned) and capture all valuable improvements in a revised version of the template. By developing a suite of templates and guidelines, you are establishing a repository for knowledge. The number of mistakes and omissions will decrease, and you will save team members' time as well; having a well-defined starting point is far more efficient than creating each deliverable from scratch.

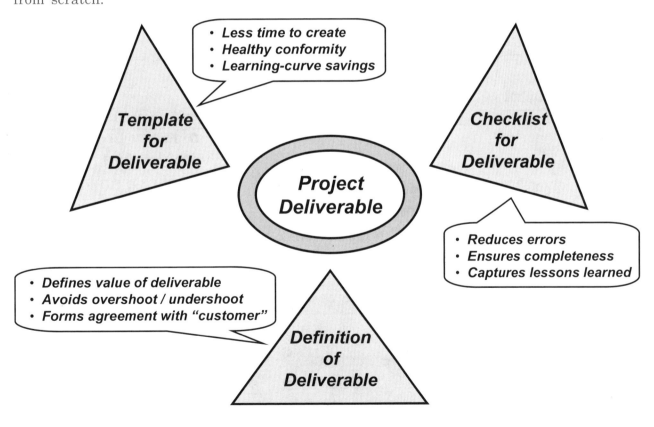

Figure 3.34: Any organizational learning initiative should include a focus on essential product development deliverables. Each key deliverable should be clearly defined, have an associated template or guideline, and a risk-reduction checklist that serves as a repository for lessons learned in previous projects.

There is another deliverables-based opportunity for capturing knowledge that is truly powerful. I've used standard checklists as a knowledge management tool almost from the first day that I began leading project teams. A checklist can be as simple as a list of "dos and don'ts," or as sophisticated as an "expert system" that automatically identifies potential errors or omissions. The key to using checklists effectively is to target specific deliverables, rather than creating a massive compendium of bullet points that spans the entire development process. Each essential deliverable should have an associated checklist that contains preventative warnings, and highlights any known risks and common omissions. As with templates and guidelines, your checklists should be "living documents" that are updated on a periodic basis. To ensure that organizational learning takes place, you might consider assigning a person to maintain each template or checklist. These individuals would be responsible for updating their documents several times per year, based on lessons-learned feedback from project teams, as shown in Figure 3.35. At last you will have an appropriate place to store all of those hard-won project experiences that are currently being sent into oblivion.

I will not belabor the topic of standard work, since I believe that effective organizational learning demands far more than a bundle of common practices. Before we move on, however, I will highlight an important consideration when deploying any form of

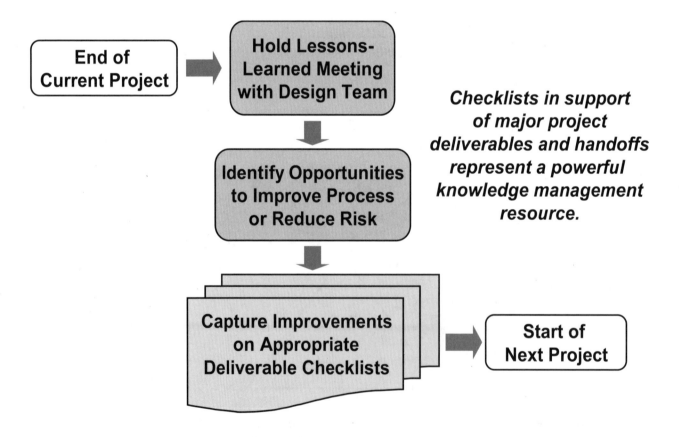

Figure 3.35: One of the best ways to harness the valuable experiences of project teams is through the use of deliverable-specific, risk-reduction checklists.

standardization. I once worked with a firm that consisted of a large number of semi-autonomous operating divisions. Their corporate headquarters was a completely separate entity that was loosely connected to the rest of the company through financial reports and an occasional strategic investment decision. The executive team of this company decided that a lean improvement initiative was essential to their continuing competitiveness. Rather than empowering each division to take the lead in defining a suitable approach for lean deployment, however, the corporation's staffers lobbied for centralized authority and control. An unwieldy team of representatives from selected divisions was identified as an "advisory group" to the corporate staff, and after a year of machinations, a "corporate standard" for lean new product development was released.

What followed was a classic example of "one size fits none". The corporate mandate was highly detailed and specific, with no latitude for adaptation to each division's unique markets, products, and culture. Not surprisingly, the general managers of the divisions took one look at the corporate standards and tossed them into the trash. Absolutely nothing happened. The divisions went on doing business as usual, paying only occasional lip-service to lean implementation whenever a corporate officer was on site. Soon the whole program evaporated, and a year had been wasted in a failed attempt at standardization.

This unfortunate situation could have been avoided by recognizing that standards within a firm must be "tiered and inclusive," as shown in Figure 3.36. I use an umbrella analogy to illustrate how broad corporate guidelines can span many different operating groups. Each division under the corporate umbrella is given latitude to tailor the corporate standards to meet their specific needs. Going even further, each product team within an operating division should be allowed to customize their division-level standards as necessary. At all times, the product- and division-level standards must align with the intent of the corporate mandates, but flexibility is paramount. If my umbrella example doesn't do it for you, consider the United States Constitution and Bill of Rights. Imagine just a few sheets of paper upon which every law in the U.S. is based. States have the freedom to interpret the federal constitution and to establish their own state constitutions. Even local municipalities can define unique laws to suit their constituents, but they must always be aligned with state and federal law. This tiered and inclusive approach makes far more sense than including thousands of highly specific local laws in the national code. Inalienable rights require centralized enforcement, but rules about not feeding the polar bears, for example, should be defined in Juneau, not Washington D.C.

Building a "Design History"

There are two categories of information that are essential to a product development organization: process knowledge and technical knowledge. The capture of process knowledge is best accomplished by using the tools described in the previous subsection, but what about the critical technical information that can be gleaned from the experiences of design teams? There are a number of software applications that specialize in logging and categorizing design data, but rather than leaping directly to canned software, let's consider how a technical learning initiative should be structured. First and foremost, the knowledge that is archived must be in a form that can be immediately used by future

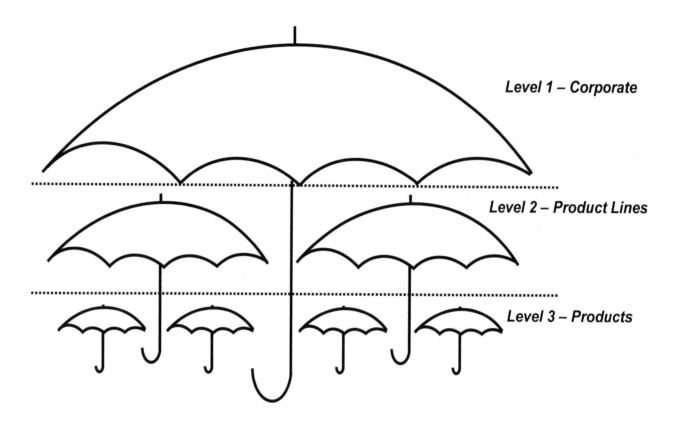

Level 1 – Corporate

Level 2 – Product Lines

Level 3 – Products

Figure 3.36: Company-wide "standards" should be tiered and inclusive. High-level corporate standards should be kept broad and general, while division- and product-level standards can be far more specific.

development teams. This factor is often neglected in the rush to automate, but it is critical to reaping long-term benefits from your precious design information. If designers and engineers experience even a modicum of resistance when searching for historical data, they will quickly give up and choose to reinvent the wheel. Before you begin creating any form of design-history database, make sure you have a clear understanding of how it will be used and by whom.

Some examples of the types of technical knowledge that might be included in a design-history archive are shown in Figure 3.37. Obviously, the choice of which data to gather will depend on your firm's core competencies and product mix. The main criterion should be *recurrence*; will a given category of information be useful on a significant proportion of future development projects? It may be worthwhile to document even the most mundane technical details if they will be reused on essentially every future project. However, you should avoid turning your technical learning initiative into a massive archiving of all design data; use the 80 / 20 rule to select those items that will be of the greatest long-term value to your organization.

Although design databases are a good thing, they don't go nearly far enough in capturing the insights and experiences of designers. I suggest establishing a separate

Figure 3.37: Some examples of technical knowledge that could be included in a company's learning plan. Each of these items can provide significant benefits to future projects, provided that the data is filtered for its long-term utility and organized in an easily accessible format.

library of "design best-practice guidelines" that will serve as a foundation for all future product development work. A guideline document such as the one shown in Figure 3.38, captures an archetypical example of how a specific product component should be designed, and could be originated by anyone within your technical departments. A library of such best-practices has been in use for several years at a major aerospace contractor in Southern California. This firm has established a policy of capturing design best practices as a routine part of each development project. At the end of a project, the entire core team "votes" for elements of their product design that represent the best of the best. The company then provides funding for the designers of those elements to document their contributions in the firm's best-practice library. The compendium of best-practice guidelines that has evolved thus far includes hundreds of detailed descriptions for future designers. Moreover, it is mandatory that design teams consult the design-history library before making any critical technical decisions.

A final opportunity to build a comprehensive design history involves documenting the performance tradeoffs that commonly occur within a firm's new product development projects. I'll illustrate this technique with an example. Suppose that you are the engineering director of a world-class automobile manufacturer (with a name that starts with a "T" and ends with an "a"). Every time your organization designs a new car, they must go through a very similar set of performance tradeoffs. A heavier car, for example, will be more stable and have a smoother ride, but will accelerate more slowly given the same horsepower. A lighter car will zip along like the wind, but without the glass-smooth ride. Increasing the horsepower will increase acceleration, but at the expense of both manufacturing cost and gas mileage. What is the optimal combination of weight, horsepower, and acceleration that will delight your target customers?

A simple graphical tool, such as the one shown in Figure 3.39, can turn such complex, multivariable tradeoffs into a straightforward process. What is depicted is a three-parameter plot of performance curves that spans the design trade-space for a given category of automobile. Acceleration is graphed against vehicle weight along the traditional x and y axes, while a third parameter (in this example, I've selected horsepower) is presented as a set of "level curves" across the graph. By including the third parameter in this fashion, far more useful information can be derived from the plot. For example, if we knew that our target customers would not accept a 0 - 60 mph acceleration of greater than eight seconds, we could immediately decide which half of our trade-space to focus on. Furthermore, if market research tells us that our new car must weigh at least 3,000 pounds to have an acceptable ride, we can immediately determine what our horsepower specification must be (in this case, roughly four-hundred horsepower).

Although this is certainly a useful approach for performing design tradeoffs, it has additional, long-term value as a means of capturing knowledge for future use. Every new car that our firm designs represents an opportunity to validate our performance tradeoff curves, and perhaps expand the range of values they portray. Over time, such curves can help enable rapid, low-risk decision-making. Moreover, this approach to organizational learning requires almost no additional time investment by designers. Your design teams are probably already generating tradeoff data of this type during every project; you just need to have a way to capture and organize it for future use. As with the best-practice library, an archive of frequently used tradeoff curves can be established within your design group, along with a process for updating the appropriate curves at the end of each project. When combined with a practical design database and a library of design best-practice guidelines (both described above), this final element completes a comprehensive and powerful repository for your firm's vital technical knowledge.

Problem-Solving as a Learning Tool

Organizational learning doesn't always come from remembering successes. Some of the greatest opportunities for knowledge capture result from solving intractable problems. Suppose, for example, that your product development group has had difficulty in smoothly transitioning their designs to the factory. Each new design requires several months of engineering changes and process adjustments before reaching the quality and performance levels necessary to begin shipping products. How might you go about dealing with this

---

Design Best-Practice Guideline

Design Element Description: _____

Created by: _____   **Release Date:** _____

                                 Revision Number: _____

Potential Application(s):

Current Best Design Approach –
          (Include drawings wherever possible)

Reference Documents –

Benefits of Best-Practice Over Previous Design Approaches:

☐ **Performance Improvement**   ☐ **Cost Reduction**

☐ **Yield Enhancement**   ☐ **Quality Improvement**

          Suggestions for revision or improvement should be submitted to:

                      _____
                          Sponsor Signature
                      Sponsor Contact Information

Figure 3.38: A simplified template for a "design best-practice guideline". These documents capture successful design practices, and represent a baseline of technical knowledge that is not dependant on individual employees or tribal memory.

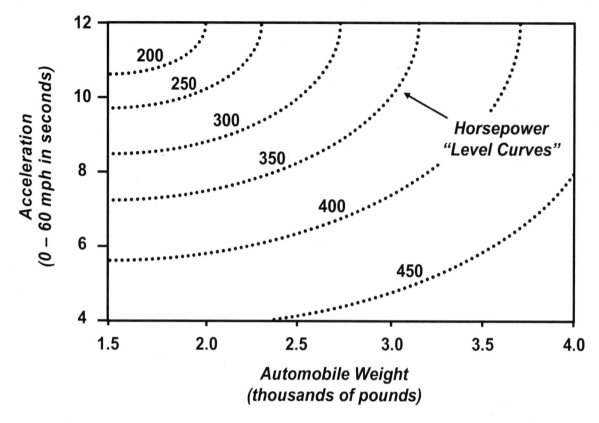

Figure 3.39: An example of a three-parameter performance tradeoff curve. In this case, the acceleration of an automobile is plotted against vehicle weight. Several "level curves" are shown, representing the behavior of the automobile at various horsepower levels.

issue? Before a problem of this sort can be solved, it is essential that the root cause(s) be understood. Otherwise, any solution that might be implemented will be like putting a band-aid on an infected wound. To that end, a methodology has evolved that can help uncover the hidden causes of organizational and technical problems. This technique is referred to as the "method of five 'whys'".

To illustrate how this approach might be applied to the challenge described above, consider the conversation presented in Figure 3.40. These questions might be asked by a senior manager, and directed toward a cross-functional development team. As you might expect, the initial response is not very satisfying; essentially a statement of the obvious. Hence, the manager must dig deeper. The second question (i.e., the second "why") converts the answer from the first question into a more specific question. Again, the answer does not illuminate a root cause, but we are getting closer to the truth. At least we now know that the launch delays result from a lack of quality and manufacturability considerations in new product designs. The third and fourth "why" questions bring us still closer. It appears that the design problems are being caused by a lack of attention by manufacturing engineers in the early stages of product development. But is this just a matter of poor discipline on the part of the MEs? The final "why" gives us a useful and actionable answer: The MEs are not participating in the design process because of a perception that their

---

Question #1: *Why* are we suffering from delays when launching new products?

Answer: Because we are having to make major changes to product designs after they reach the factory floor.

Question #2: *Why* are we having to make these significant changes?

Answer: The changes are needed to correct manufacturability and quality weaknesses in these new designs.

Question #3: *Why* are these issues not corrected during the design process?

Answer: We do not have enough manufacturing involvement in the early stages of the product development process.

Question #4: *Why* are the manufacturing engineers not getting involved? Aren't they included on all of our cross-functional development teams?

Answer: Yes, they are included on the membership list. But they rarely attend team meetings and don't seem to be interested in contributing.

Question #5: *Why* would they not get involved? Don't they have everything to gain by participating at every point in the design process?

Answer: The MEs don't think that their contributions are valued by the rest of the team. Besides, they are severely backlogged trying to fix the manufacturability and quality problems on our current set of new product launches.

Figure 3.40: The "method of five 'whys'" is a straightforward technique for identifying the root causes of waste, errors, or other obstacles to the flow of value.

inputs are unwanted, combined with a serious backlog of work. The irony of this root cause is that if the MEs had participated in the design process up front, they wouldn't be overwhelmed with fixing the problems that resulted from their lack of early involvement! At this point, the manager has enough information to begin addressing these two interrelated issues. As this situation improves, the organization becomes "smarter".

The method of five "whys" is not a panacea. In fact, it represents just the beginning of the problem-solving process in most cases. However, it is the logic behind this method that is critically important; you cannot solve something that you don't truly understand, and that understanding often requires far more insight and diligence than most people are typically willing to apply. Incidentally, the number "five" is clearly just a guideline. You should ask "why" as often as necessary to get to a root cause, or until you really start getting on people's nerves.

A Word About Product Data Management

I am frequently asked to recommend a software application that can help firms organize their design data and other forms of product development knowledge. My response is always the same: "First you must understand what your organization actually needs, both now and in the foreseeable future, and then choose a software package that does that, and nothing more." You would be correct in noting that my response avoids the question. Frankly, there are so many applications available, under titles such as product data management (PDM) and product life-cycle management (PLCM), that I would have to spend all of my time reviewing software products to offer a credible answer. More important, however, is the fact that I've seen such a poor success rate with this type of software, that I am uncomfortable with the entire topic.

Certainly some level of automation is essential to managing the massive amounts of design data that flow from any product development group. However, it seems to be an almost inescapable fact that whenever a PDM-type package is implemented, it creates at least as much waste and inefficiency as it eliminates. The main reason for this sad situation is that firms often purchase the most "powerful" package that they can afford, thinking that more is better. Instead, they find that these cumbersome and overblown products force their designers to become slaves to the tool, spending hours of their productive time feeding the PDM system, instead of benefiting from the automation. It is important to realize that software companies pack their products full of as many features as possible to create the impression of value, and that customers for these products are often swayed by such excessive features. It sounds so appealing to have customizable reports, data-mining capabilities, and so on. In fact, many firms believe that they would be missing something important by not using all of the functions provided by a PDM package. The result is that while some benefit is gained, a great deal of waste is generated as well.

Now that I've given you fair warning, I will also note that if a PDM-type tool is used properly and with discretion, it can be highly effective at managing organizational knowledge. Some of the information that can be captured by such software applications are shown in Figure 3.41. If you believe that your firm is ready for such a product, begin your selection process with some deep soul-searching about how the tool will be used, by whom, etc. Don't allow yourself to be swayed by sales people, or even by your own information technology group (which often has a vested interest in selecting the most sophisticated and administration-intensive products). Use the lean mentality you have developed while reading this guidebook to scale your requirements to an optimal level. Also keep in mind that despite what the "interested parties" might tell you, you can always upgrade software capabilities and add features later, when the need arises. A recent study by the Software Engineering Institute determined that of all of the productivity software purchased by firms in the U.S. over the past ten years, *only twenty-five percent of those products were successfully implemented and beneficially employed.* Your chances of being included in that twenty-five percent will greatly increase if you keep it lean, and focus on gaining the maximum value for the time and money spent.

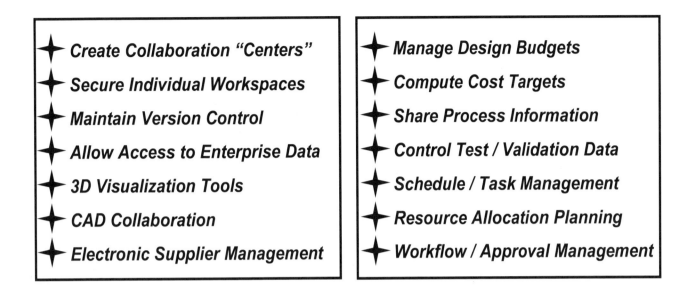

Figure 3.41: Some of the potential benefits of product data management (PDM, aka product life-cycle management) software.

<u>Notes</u>

Establishing Product Design Requirements

4.1 - Customer Perception and Product Value

4.2 - Must / Should / Could Prioritization

4.3 - An Overview of Set-Based Design

"Look beneath the surface;
let not the several qualities
of a thing, nor its worth
escape thee"

Marcus Aurelius Antoninus

Customer Perception
and Product Value

4.1

Section

In Part 4, we will make the transition from a 10,000 foot view of the lean product development process to skimming the treetops of daily team activities. Our goal will be to establish a comprehensive toolbox of waste-slashing methods and techniques that can be immediately applied to real projects in your very real firm. But where shall we start? Since product development is all about pleasing the customer, gaining an understanding of how customers perceive value seems like a logical place to begin. In this section, we will delve into the minds of consumers, and uncover some inconvenient truths about what really determines market winners and losers. If you're expecting some rational criteria for success, forget it. Consumers are driven by irrational considerations and emotional factors to a far greater extent than most of us would like to believe. I am not just referring to soccer moms and Generation X,Y,Zers; even the most technically savvy, business-to-business customers are influenced by considerations that go well beyond the product specification sheet.

When it Comes to Value, Perception is Everything

It is impossible to determine which products will become market winners by simply comparing performance. Our recent history is littered with examples of suboptimal products beating the pants off of superior competitors. A quick look around your home is all that is needed to validate this point. For example, there is a better than ninety percent chance that the personal computer on your desk upstairs is a Windows-based machine rather than a Macintosh. Yet the Mac has been, and probably continues to be, a more usable, reliable, and capable choice. While you're upstairs, consider that VCR you've relegated to the spare bedroom. It uses VHS format, rather than Betamax, right? In both of these examples, the winner in the marketplace was determined by force of numbers, not by objective comparison; most people just followed the herd, and wound up with a lesser product. The clothes in your bedroom closet are probably not the best made garments on the market, and those designer shoes that cost a week's salary will probably give you sore feet. From power tools to home appliances, your choices are most likely in discord with objective rankings based on performance tests (my apologies to the small minority of you who read Consumer Report). What about the car you drive? Were you influenced by styling, luxury, or prestige? Finally, take a look in your refrigerator. The bottled water you purchased for several dollars per liter is indistinguishable (based on chemical analyses and blind taste tests) from plain old filtered tap water. Ah, but *your* water is from Fiji, and that makes it better, right? In each of these instances, the buying decisions you made were driven by factors that go beyond (and may even fly in the face of) logic.

There are at least four dimensions to customers' perception of value, as shown in Figure 4.1, and all four of these factors are embodied in virtually every product. The first dimension of perceived value is, not surprisingly, its *performance*. This factor reflects a product's ability to perform its intended function; in other words, its use or utility. Business-to-business products, for example, tend to be dominated by this pragmatic consideration. Whether it be production materials, business software, or a new laser printer, it makes sense that these types of buying decisions are primarily based on practical concerns. Yet even in this domain, the other three dimensions of value come into play, as I will illustrate shortly.

For consumer products, performance is often important, but it may not be the primary consideration. Several centuries ago, Adam Smith proposed a paradox in his landmark book, *The Wealth of Nations*, that illustrates this point. He noted that if

Product Examples	Dimensions of Product Value				Relative Market Price
	Performance	Esteem	Scarcity	Retained Value	
Paper Clip	▆	▏	▏	▏	▏
Gold Tie Clasp	▅	▅	▅	▃	▇
Tap Water	▇	▏	▏	▏	▏
Imported Bottled Water	▇	▅	▃	▏	▅
Decorative Wall Poster	▏	▏	▏	▏	▏
Original Oil Painting	▏	▆	▆	▅	▇
Tickets to Local Movie Theater	▃	▏	▏	▏	▏
Tickets to See Bruce Springsteen	▃	▅	▆	▆	▇
Magnetic Compass	▃	▏	▏	▏	▏
Portable GPS Locator	▃	▏	▅	▏	▅
Generic Office Software	▃	▏	▏	▏	▏
Fully Customized Office Software	▅	▃	▆	▅	▇
Digital Alarm Clock	▃	▏	▏	▏	▏
Swiss Grandfather Clock	▃	▃	▃	▅	▇

Figure 4.1: Customers' perception of value is driven by at least four critical factors: the performance of the product, the impact that the product has on the customer's self-esteem, its scarcity in the marketplace, and its ability to retain value. All of these elements are present in virtually every product, and should be fostered by designers to achieve the highest possible market price.

performance was the only consideration in determining the desirability of a product, than why is it that water (which is essential to sustaining life) is free, and diamonds (which have no practical utility) are extremely expensive? Let's take this example a bit farther. These days, it is possible to possess all of the beauty, fire, and sparkle of a diamond for a fraction of the price. Yet try to convince most people that a cubic zirconia is equivalent to a diamond. It has the same crystal structure as a diamond, it can be made in any color, including perfectly clear, and even has more fire, due to a higher index of refraction. Few of us, however, would consider them as equals. One justification for this bias is that diamonds are rare...or so we have been led to believe. In actuality, diamonds are among the most common gemstones, and would be worth only pennies on the dollar if they were sold freely on the open market. If not for the artificial controls imposed by the DeBeers cartel, diamonds would be roughly the same price as topaz or garnet. Well, if *scarcity* (one of the other four dimensions of value presented in Figure 4.1) is not the reason for the high price of diamonds, maybe it is because they *retain their value*. The ability of a product to hold its value is a rational consideration to be sure, but in reality diamonds cannot typically be resold for anything close to their original purchase price, due to the very high markup between wholesale and retail. Let's face it; the primary reason for the dearness of diamonds is that they positively impact our *self-esteem*. It makes us feel good to own and wear these costly items, a feeling that has been manipulated by diamond sellers over decades to become embedded in our subconscious. After all, a diamond is forever.

Okay, so most of us may not be ready to embrace the cubic zirconia, but how are our other buying decisions influenced by the three dimensions listed in the figure that go beyond performance and utility? Let's first consider retained value. This factor can be translated into reliability, durability, use-life cost, and even trade-in or resale value. Car manufacturers such as BMW have promoted their products by claiming that they have a higher retained value. In fact many of us have been known to justify the purchase of a more expensive product by telling ourselves that it will "last a lifetime". If this rationale is valid, it represents a logical consideration when making a buying decision. Certainly for business-to-business products, value retention can be a major differentiating factor. Machine tools with a reputation for a long use-life and low maintenance costs, for example, are worth a higher price than those with a spotty past. For the average consumer, however, this dimension is often abused or misunderstood. Virtually every person who purchases something "collectable," for example, does so believing that it will go up in value. Collectors of all kinds use retained value to justify indulging in their passions, yet rarely do these artifacts actually hold their value, let alone make a profit for their owners.

This segues nicely to a third dimension of perceived value; the scarcity or rarity of a product. For some inexplicable reason, people are attracted to items that are one-of-a-kind, previously owned by someone famous, or in some other way unique. My brother-in-law, for example, has a pair of Babe Ruth's undergarments framed and on display in his living room. And let me assure you that owning a pair of the Bambino's underpants doesn't come cheap. I suppose that this distinctly human behavior stems from our desire to distinguish ourselves as individuals within a communal society. Whatever the reason, the more unique or customized a product appears to be, the greater the price it can garner. From a product strategy standpoint, this fact translates into a mandate for high levels of product differentiation, and whenever possible, patent protection. Customers perceive a customized product as satisfying their specific needs more fully, while at the same time enhancing their own individuality.

This brings us to the final dimension of value identified in the figure; the impact that a product can have on our self-esteem. Although the pride-of-ownership factor is certainly important to many consumers, I prefer to broaden this category to include any attribute that appeals directly to our emotions. If a product makes us feel safe and secure, for example, it is typically more desirable than one that leaves us feeling nervous. Products that evoke a nostalgic feeling can be disproportionately appealing, because they bring back warm memories of our youth. An item that reinforces our own self-image in any way will be coveted. Hobbyists will often indulge in grossly overpriced "toys" that make them feel good about their commitment to a chosen sport or pastime. I am an amateur pianist, for example, and although my musical skills warrant little more than a used piano with broken strings, I crave owning a Steinway.

The point of this discussion is to emphasize that if a design team fails to acknowledge and incorporate all four of these value dimensions into their new product, they may be leaving money on the table. For consumer products this is unquestionable, but what about those hard-nosed business-to-business customers I mentioned earlier? Even though they may not realize it, there is no escaping emotionality in buying decisions. Although the involved parties may deny it, I strongly suspect that the Department of Defense was influenced, at least in part, by aesthetics rather than performance when they selected the Lockheed-Martin version of the Joint Strike Fighter (JSF) over the Boeing version. Surely the capability of these machines was the dominant consideration, and both met the specifications of the military. But with all other things being nearly equal, the fact that the Boeing version looked a little like a flying frog, while the Lockheed-Martin plane was sleek and menacing, may have swayed the final decision. After all, how effective would a "shock and awe" campaign be if the enemy is being threatened by a squadron of Kermits?

The Dangers of Overshoot and Undershoot

How do customers respond when a manufacturer produces a product that falls short of their needs? The answer is simple...they look elsewhere. Any of us who purchased an American-made automobile in the 1970's knows firsthand what it is like to own a product that *undershoots* the needs of the market. In fact, it could be argued that the shockingly poor quality of cars from that era may have actually *enabled* Toyota and other Japanese auto manufacturers to aggressively pursue quality and efficiency improvements. In hindsight, we tend to think of Toyota as being visionary, but in reality if U.S. automakers had not left the market wide open for outside competition, it would have been far harder for Toyota and others to fund the huge investments required to develop and implement their breakthrough improvements. Undershooting customers' needs creates a vacuum into which new competitors are drawn. Even the *de facto* monopoly that Microsoft enjoys in computer operating systems is being threatened by open-source alternatives such as Linux. A dark-horse product such as this would not have been worth the time and effort to develop if it were not for the notoriously poor security and reliability of Microsoft's products.

Today, most firms are fully aware of the dangers of design undershoot. The U.S. auto industry has transformed itself over the past two decades through "zero-defect" supplier quality programs and lean manufacturing initiatives. Although they may not yet be the equals of Toyota, they have certainly closed the gap considerably. This begs a second question: Is it possible to *overshoot* the needs of the customer, in performance, features, and even (dare I say it) quality? Surprisingly, the answer is yes. If products were offered for free, this possibility would not exist. We must keep in mind, however, that value is actually the ratio of benefit to price. If added performance or features could be delivered at the same price, no customer would turn them down. However, if customers percieve no real benefit from an improvement, they won't pay a dollar more for it. As a result, any increase in performance, features, or quality that overshoots the needs of the market will typically result in an increase in development and manufacturing costs without an associated price increase. Hence, profits will decline despite the best efforts of design teams; *overshooting customer needs can be a significant source of waste*. This behavior is illustrated in Figure 4.2.

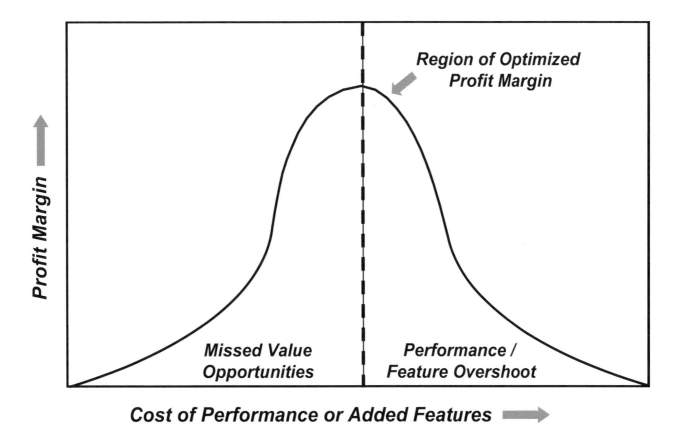

Figure 4.2: It is possible to either overshoot or undershoot the needs of customers. Undershooting will result in dissatisfied customers and a loss of price and market share, while overshooting can cause an increase in manufacturing cost and development time without an associated gain in market price. Optimal profitability and time-to-market is achieved by matching a product's performance, features, and quality to the needs of its targeted market segment.

Do I sense some skepticism on the part of my readers? I will attempt to prove my point. Let's begin with product performance. Not that long ago, buyers of personal computers anxiously awaited the release of the next generation of microprocessor, hungrily anticipating the added speed it would provide. Many of us willingly forked over thousands of dollars every year or so, casting aside our obsolete machines in favor of the latest speed demon. Shortly after the turn of the millennium, however, all of that changed. Most typical PC users became reluctant to relegate their still-new systems to the scrap heap, and many of us lost track of which generation of Pentium X was being released. As a result, the bottom dropped out of the personal computer market, and prices plummeted. Today, you can visit the Dell website and purchase an entire, highly capable system for under five-hundred dollars. If you're not satisfied with the speed of this low-end computer, you can upgrade your microprocessor to more than twice the power for about fifty dollars. What happened to cause this sea change? The answer is that once computers became fast enough for most users' needs, there was no reason to pay top dollar for increased processor speed. Fast enough was fast enough.

The same behavior can be observed in many other product categories. I had a friend who spent almost a thousand dollars for a cell phone ten years ago that was significantly smaller and lighter than others available at that time. Today, cell phones that make my friend's device seem downright clumsy are given away to new customers when they sign up for a year of long-distance service. Once cell phones reach the size and weight of a credit card, customers will no longer be willing to pay a premium for an even more miniscule model. This is true for essentially every performance attribute; eventually an attribute will become good enough, and will lose its ability to drive an increase in price. If you owned a cell-phone manufacturing company today, you would be ill-advised to spend valuable time and resources on further miniaturization. You would be better off shifting your attention to developing cell phones capable of taking digital video, receiving the latest TV programs, or serving as a heart defibrillator.

Speaking of added features, how does design overshoot manifest itself in this domain? Take a look at your DVD remote control. At least a hundred buttons, and probably a function key to create another hundred buttons. Do you use even a fraction of the functions that those buttons control? Feature overshoot is a common occurrence when a mature product category is in danger of becoming commoditized. Designers struggle mightily to avoid a loss of profit margin by adding any attribute that they believe will retain their product's differentiation. This can work for awhile, but ultimately the added features cease to provide real benefits to customers, and the strategy fails. Despite a rich spectrum of varying features, DVD players are a commodity; from the customer's perspective one is just as good as the next. The situation is no different for software. At this writing, the dominant concern in the software sector is security. Added features that fail to directly attack this critical problem are largely ignored by buyers. Most of us couldn't care less whether the next generation of Windows has a patronizing "paper-clip" help feature, or adds annoying squiggly green lines under our text that provide grammatical suggestions (especially since the recommended changes rarely make any sense). We want better blockers, firewalls, and parental controls; these features will determine a buyer's choice and willingness to pay.

We now come to the most controversial aspect of design overshoot. Is it possible to overshoot on product quality? I submit that for a given market segment, there is a "right" amount of quality; anything beyond that point will not impact either price or market share. Several years ago I heard an example given at a conference that is apropos. The gentleman who told this story was responsible for the paint and finish portion of one of Suzuki Motors vehicle assembly lines, and had spent enormous energy making that department the very best that it could be. Paint thickness was controlled to a microscopic level, appearance was obsessed over, and detailing was taken to new heights. After years of quality improvements, he was given a chance to present his department's status to the VP of Operations for Suzuki North America. He finished his presentation, fully expecting to be given a plaque or some other recognition for his group's success. Instead, the vice president made a surprising comment: "Your paint quality is too good." The VP went on to explain that buyers of low- to mid-priced cars do not expect their paint jobs to look like the finish on a Ferrari, and would not be willing to pay the considerable added price associated with such a finish. The paint and finish manager was asked to reduce the cost (and associated quality) of his department's finishes to a point that was appropriate for the market segment that was targeted by Suzuki's vehicles.

You might be thinking that this is all well and good for something as trivial as a car finish, but what about situations where less than obsessive quality might cause catastrophic financial or human loss? Certainly this overshoot stuff cannot apply to the quality of aircraft parts, medical products, and so on, right? A number of years ago, a major pharmaceutical manufacturer was the first to develop a synthetic form of human insulin. There was a tremendous potential market for this innovation: at the time, millions of diabetics were forced to use insulin derived from natural sources, which were of marginal consistency and purity. When the first batches of this new product were produced, however, there was a problem. The synthetic insulin was only .99 pure, and the impurities were causing serious negative side effects in roughly one in one-thousand users. Despite huge market interest, most doctors and patients were not willing to accept that level of risk. The firm immediately invested millions of dollars to build a new manufacturing facility that was capable of producing .999 pure synthetic insulin, resulting in a product that generated negative side effects in only one in ten-thousand users. The market for this product exploded. Buoyed by success, the firm decided that yet another round of improvements would surely garner even higher prices and greater market acceptance. They again invested millions in a new manufacturing facility, and were able to achieve .9999 purity, along with another significant reduction in negative side effects. They released the medication into the market at a substantially higher price point, and what do you think happened? They couldn't get a penny more for their improved product. Both patients and doctors were satisfied with the relatively low risk associated with the previous generation. The substantial investment required to go beyond that level of quality could not be recovered.

Let me be clear that it is generally a good idea to *slightly* overshoot the needs of your target customers. Market segments are not homogeneous, and some buyers may have higher standards than others. Moreover, it is not always clear where the quality line should be drawn. I'm not sure it would have been possible for the pharmaceutical firm mentioned above to know in advance that their market would behave in that way. What is important is to recognize that *every attribute of your new product has an overshoot threshold,* and that going beyond that threshold will result in wasted time and money.

The "Least Discernable Difference"

You can begin to identify the overshoot threshold of a product by using a clever concept derived from marketing theory. Imagine that there are two competitive products sitting on a table in front of you. You carefully examine both items, test them under use, and generally give them a good once over. After this evaluation, if you can identify something about one of the products that would cause you to choose it over the other, then that product is differentiated from its competitor. If there is no difference that is substantial enough to drive your choice, then the two products are identical from a desirability standpoint. In marketing theory, this is called the "test of the least discernable difference," as shown in Figure 4.3. In truth, this test is often stated in a more stringent way: "If a customer would not be willing to spend one dollar more for a product improvement, then that improvement falls below the least discernable difference threshold." Either way, it seems that if added performance, features, or quality are not significant enough to attract the market's attention, the time spent on that improvement was essentially wasted. As usual, an example should make this point clear.

A few years ago, I worked with an apparel manufacturer that was well-known for their trendy sportswear. In one of their conference rooms, they had on display along the back wall a dozen versions of one of their products. The first item looked quite nice; certainly something that appeared to be ready for market. The second version was remarkably similar to the first, with just some minor changes to stitching. The third used a different lining that was virtually indistinguishable from the first two. And so it went, with each version possessing some inscrutable change over the last, but none substantial enough to be noticed by an average buyer. At the end of the line was the final version, which had come full circle and most closely resembled the first iteration. These dozen products represented a full year's worth of prototyping, with the design team obsessing over relatively minor aesthetic changes. Unfortunately, by the time the product was deemed to be the best that it could be, the styling trends in that market had changed, and the product was considered to be out of fashion. It was never brought to market. The reason for the display was to remind future designers that changes which were not discernable by customers had caused a year's worth of waste.

So how can a firm avoid the trap of overdesigning a new product? The best approach is to gain iterative feedback from real customers throughout the design process, as shown in Figure 4.4. Once an initial concept has been proposed, consider generating a rough prototype and seeking early feedback from well-targeted potential customers. Focus your questions on attributes that have ambiguous benefits and try to gain insight into which performance levels or features are truly differentiating. With the proliferation of rapid-prototyping technology, it is possible to economically create a three-dimensional representation of most products (a scale model would be appropriate for larger items). These physical models are often referred to as "boundary-spanning objects" because they help span the intellectual boundaries between designers and customers. Once this early

Test for value using the "Least Discernable Difference":

"Will the customer recognize the VALUE of this improvement?"

Or in other words...

"Will the customer pay ONE DOLLAR MORE for this improvement?"

▶ *Minor styling or cosmetic changes*

▶ *Excessive number of versions or options*

▶ *"Hidden" benefits that customers never see*

▶ *Performance enhancement beyond customers' needs*

▶ *Unnecessarily detailed documentation*

Figure 4.3: If customers are not aware of a change or improvement to a product, it will not affect their buying decisions or the amount they will pay. The "least discernable difference" represents a threshold of customer perception, below which there is no market advantage.

feedback has been gathered, modify the design and take it to a more detailed level. Again create a model or prototype, perhaps with some built-in functionality. Gather additional customer feedback, and iterate once more. This cycle may seem time-consuming, but in reality it can be integrated noninvasively into a development timeline, provided that you have relatively easy access to willing customers. If this is not the case, identify surrogates within your firm that have the greatest insight into the minds of your target customers. These surrogates should probably come from your marketing group, but I've found that including field engineers, sales people, and any other employee who has regular customer contact, can provide a more balanced perspective. However you gather your inputs, the best way to avoid design overshoot is to respond to the pull of the market, rather than wasting time and energy gold-plating an already optimal design.

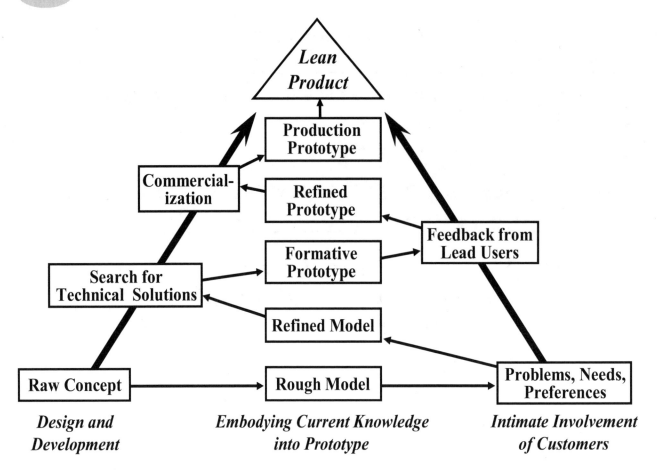

Figure 4.4: One of the best ways to avoid overshoot or undershoot of market needs is to gain iterative feedback from actual customers throughout the development process.

Must / Should / Could
Prioritization

Section

One of the most powerful ways to reduce waste and accelerate new product development is to consistently apply your team's efforts to the highest priority work at hand. Unfortunately, it is often difficult to determine which tasks should take precedence, which features are the most important, or which tests should be run first. Even if clear priorities are known, how can they be easily communicated to the design team? The lean method described in this section is one of the most widely adopted and successful tools covered in this guidebook. It provides a simple and effective way to both categorize project priorities and communicate them in a straightforward and unambiguous manner. Although the genesis of this technique is rooted in how customers prioritize product attributes, the method can be applied to essentially every aspect of the development environment, and even extended into your personal life.

The "Kano Model" of Customer Perception

A number of years ago, one of the gurus of the total quality management (TQM) movement, Noriaki Kano, created a model for customers' perception of product value. The Kano Model has become widely accepted as an insightful and accurate representation of how product attributes influence customer satisfaction. Before we go further, however, I must apologize to purists everywhere, including Kano himself. I have shamelessly co-opted this model to allow a far broader application of the underlying concept, as shown in Figure 4.5. In the original version, as in the one I've presented, customer satisfaction is plotted against product performance. However I've given Kano's curves somewhat different names. First allow me to make amends by telling the story of this model in the way its creator intended. I will then explain the liberties that I have taken.

Imagine that you are about to purchase a new automobile. Assuming that you have established your budget in advance, what factors would you consider when making your buying decision? With price held constant, you would likely compare mileage, horsepower, safety, legroom, styling – the usual differentiators that we are all familiar with. It is highly unlikely, however, that you would crawl under each of your candidate cars and check out their mufflers. The radiator would also be ignored, along with U-joints, fan belts, and so on. Why do we ignore these items? Because we assume that if the car is produced by a reputable manufacturer, these basic components will work acceptably well. In fact, there is little an automobile designer could do to enhance these elements that would influence our buying decision. The only time such basic components are noticed at all is if they fail. If

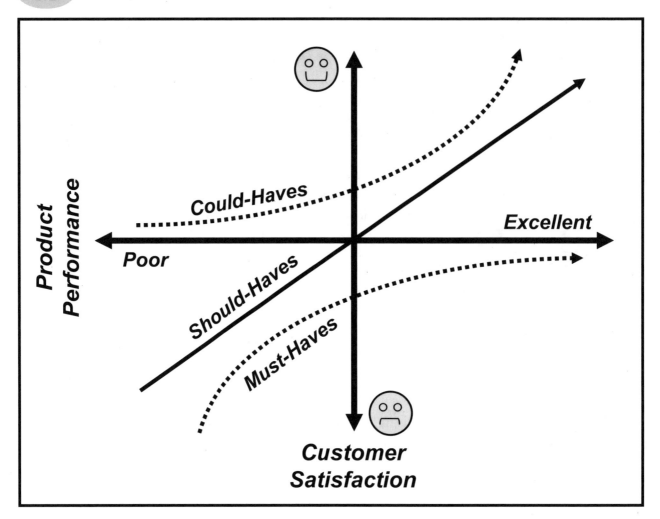

Figure 4.5: The "Kano Model" of customer perception identifies three categories of product attributes: "dissatisfiers" (which I've renamed "must-haves"), "satisfiers" (which I refer to as "should-haves"), and "delighters" (which I call "could-haves"). These categories can be used to effectively set priorities for development teams.

that should occur, we would be *dissatisfied*. The lowest curve in the figure was originally identified in just this way; attributes that follow this behavior were referred to by Kano as "*dissatisfiers*". They must be good enough to never become a negative, but there is little or no opportunity to delight the customer through enhancement of these design elements.

The center curve in the figure was originally titled "*satisfiers*," and was intended to represent those attributes that directly impact customer satisfaction. In our automobile example, characteristics such as mileage, horsepower, styling, and so on, would fall into this category. Finally, Kano made perhaps his most insightful observation. The top curve reflects how customers react when they are offered a new and highly beneficial innovation. Kano refers to these attributes as "*delighters*"; you could also think of them as providing a "wow factor". One of the key take-aways from Kano's model is that the greatest opportunities for product success lie in identifying delighters. Unfortunately, there is often significant risk involved. It would be far safer to have your development teams spend their time enhancing satisfier attributes, since they are a known quantity. Delighters require some level of breakthrough innovation, and may prove to be of little interest to the marketplace. Going back to our car-purchase example, a delighter (as of this writing) might be something like side-impact airbags, dashboard control through voice recognition, and most certainly, the hybrid engine. These features generate excitement, and can often make the difference in a purchase decision among roughly equivalent products. Yet many new improvements to automobiles have received poor marks from customers and have been relegated to the scrap heap. When was the last time you saw a new car with those automated seat belts that pull across your chest when you start the engine? After several million hot cups of coffee spilled onto an equal number of drivers' laps, the "wow factor" seems like a distant memory.

Although Kano's terminology works well in the context of customer satisfaction, I prefer to broaden the applicability of his insights to virtually every aspect of product development work, as shown in Figure 4.6. The result is a simple, three-category prioritization tool: must-haves (dissatisfiers), should-haves (satisfiers), and could-haves (delighters). The must / should / could approach to prioritizing customer needs is somewhat more coarse than quality function deployment. (See Section 2.1 of *The Lean Design Guidebook* for a complete description of this voice-of-the-customer methodology.) Yet what it lacks in specifics, it makes up for in ease of communication. In the following subsections, I will describe several opportunities to use must / should / could (M/S/C) within the context of product development work. Don't restrict yourself to this arena, however. A consultant friend recently mentioned that she is using M/S/C to help her son prioritize his homework. *All* of our time is valuable, not just time spent in the workplace.

Application #1 – Product Features and Requirements

The most obvious application of M/S/C is in the prioritization of product features based on their impact on customer satisfaction. Much as Kano observed, must-haves represent features or performance levels that are both basic and essential; falling short in this area will have a negative impact on the perceived value and market acceptance of a new product. It follows that should-haves are those attributes of a design that directly address known customer wants and needs, and will have a reasonably predictable impact on price and value. Finally, the could-haves represent new innovations or unique design elements that may capture the imagination of the marketplace, but may also prove to be of little or no benefit if the market fails to respond. Naturally, the best source of insight into which attribute falls into which category would be direct feedback from representative customers. The M/S/C methodology can be used as an informal voice-of-the-customer tool, either through surveys or through individual or group interviews. Again, ease of communication plays a powerful role; it is often difficult to get customers to sit through a Lean QFD (i.e., quality functon deployment) exercise, for example, but M/S/C feedback can be gathered in seconds.

From a project execution standpoint, a development team should ensure that all must-haves have been bedded down in the early stages of a project, and then spend most of

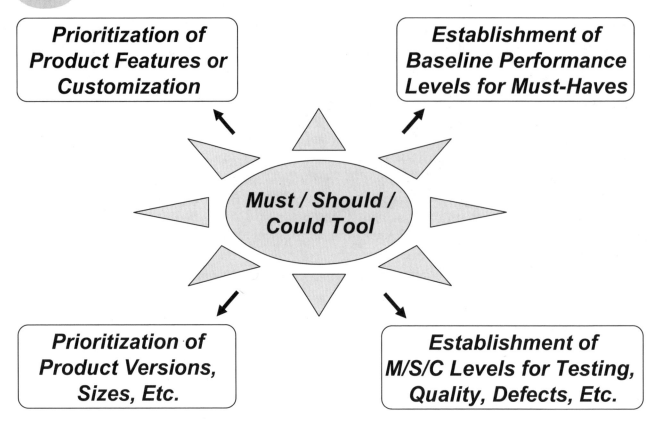

Figure 4.6: The must / should / could (M/S/C) prioritization tool can be applied to every aspect of new product development, from the features to be included in a product to the time spent on testing and qualification.

their efforts optimizing the should-haves. If time and money permit, the could-haves can be pursued, but only consistent with meeting the product's intended launch date – these aspects of the design might be trimmed to avoid excessive delays in product shipment. The only time this logic fails is if the new product is intended to be a breakthrough design, in which case the could-haves may represent the primary reason for investing in its development.

I recommend adding a column to your product specification document that explicitly captures the priority of each important requirement, as shown in Figure 4.7. Basic functionality and baseline performance would be assigned must-have status, with the shoulds and coulds falling into place as appropriate. The assignment of M/S/C priorities can trigger vital negotiations among marketing, engineering, and executive management. Conducting these negotiations at the beginning of development can save designers from wasting time on nonessential aspects of a new product, before core functionality has been addressed. Note that it is possible, and indeed beneficial, to identify must, should, and could levels of performance for a *single* product attribute. For example, the specification for an automobile might state that thirty miles-per-gallon is a must-have, thirty-five mpg is a should-have, and forty mpg is a could-have. In this context, the could-have becomes a "stretch goal" for the design team, while the should-have level represents the actual target for designers. The must-have baseline serves as a last resort; if the product is significantly delayed, the coulds and shoulds may be compromised somewhat, but the product cannot enter the market without meeting the must-haves.

Continuing with the last point, I have found it valuable in some cases to create a separate must-have specification at the inception of a development project, as shown in Figure 4.8. The idea is to provide the design team with a baseline for every critical specification, below which the team cannot go without invalidating the product's business case. The inputs to this must-have spec might be based on achieving parity with competing products in the marketplace, or may be derived from an understanding of market expectations and essential quality thresholds. However the requirements are selected, they must truly represent a "no-go" threshold of performance or features. Why is this beneficial to a design team? As the development process proceeds, it is often necessary to perform multidimensional tradeoffs to achieve the best possible mix of desirable attributes. When performing these trade studies, it is essential that designers understand the full space in which they may work. The must-have specification represents a firm lower boundary for any performance tradeoff, thereby enabling the team to avoid wasting time chasing possibilities that are simply not viable. In my experience, compromises to the initial product specification are generally made at the end of the development process, triggered by unacceptable slips in schedule or excessive cost. It is far better to proactively determine possible lower limits up front, so the team can use this information at those times in the process where it can provide the most benefit.

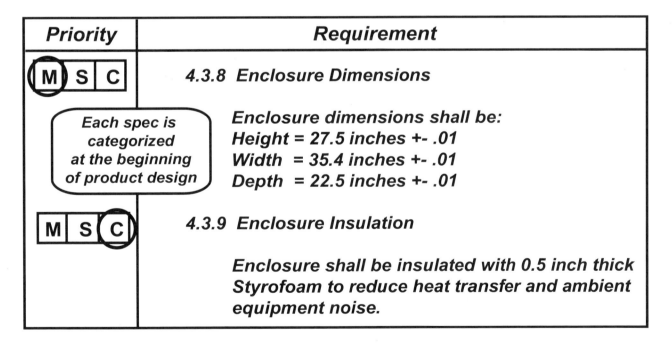

Priority	Requirement
Ⓜ S C	**4.3.8 Enclosure Dimensions**
Each spec is categorized at the beginning of product design	**Enclosure dimensions shall be:** **Height = 27.5 inches +- .01** **Width = 35.4 inches +- .01** **Depth = 22.5 inches +- .01**
M S Ⓒ	**4.3.9 Enclosure Insulation** **Enclosure shall be insulated with 0.5 inch thick Styrofoam to reduce heat transfer and ambient equipment noise.**

Figure 4.7: The must / should / could priority of each product requirement can be shown explicitly within an engineering specification document. In some cases, a single requirement might have a must-have level of performance, along with should- and could-have levels that represent challenges for the development team.

Priority	Requirement
(M) S C	**1.0 Maximum acceptable tolerances**
(M) S C	**2.0 Essential functionality**
(M) S C	**3.0 Minimum feature /option set**
(M) S C	**4.0 Mandatory cosmetics and ergonomics**
(M) S C	**5.0 Required testing and approvals**
(M) S C	**6.0 Market-driven performance levels**

Figure 4.8: It is often useful to create a "must-have specification" for a product at the inception of product development. This baseline can then be used throughout the process as a touchstone for the team when conducting performance tradeoffs.

Application #2 – Prioritizing Tasks Within a Development Project

Although the application described above comes the closest to Kano's original intent, it is the prioritization of tasks within a product development project that will provide design teams with the greatest schedule benefit. The M/S/C concept can be used in this context, both as an initial planning tool and as an ongoing means of communicating the priority of project tasks. Initially, those activities that are on or near the critical path should be given must-have importance. Should-have tasks would be those that involve significant technical or quality-related issues; clearly important but not necessarily on the critical path. · Finally, any task or activity that can be postponed until later in the project (or perhaps until after the first units are shipped) would be assigned could-have priority. As the project progresses, these priorities should be modified as needed to reflect the team's current situation. A task which was on the critical path at the beginning of development, for example, might move to a lower priority due to some unforeseen change in project direction.

Keeping all team members focused on either schedule-critical or technically challenging aspects of a project is a powerful way to ensure the highest levels of productivity and efficiency. Moreover, using M/S/C can enable far greater control of project schedule, as shown in Figure 4.9. The could-haves represent a "shock absorber" for time-to-market, allowing the team leader to pull the project schedule back into line if slips occur. Recall the three-legged-stool analogy used in Section 3.3 to illustrate the impact of change on a project: if one leg is too long, the stool (and by reference, the project) is unbalanced. If M/S/C is employed and the schedule leg of the stool becomes longer than desired, the scope leg of the stool can be adjusted by shaving could-haves until the project is back in good graces. In a sense, the trimming of could-have requirements or features gives the team leader an adjustable leg on the project stool. What tasks might this include, you ask? Virtually every aspect of a project is a candidate: design niceties, low-priority documentation, sizes of the new product that have low sales potential, and even selected qualification tests that can be performed either during or after product launch. If you've ever been on a product design team, it is likely that you have seen this approach in action...or perhaps I should say, in *reaction*. When a project gets into schedule trouble, it is amazing how many essential activities become optional. Rather than being unprepared for the inevitable push at the end of a project, why not use the M/S/C tool to provide both the team and its leader clear priorities up front. This way, the project might not get into schedule trouble in the first place.

Application #3 – Testing and Documentation

Of all the activities that constitute new product development, the ones that get the least respect are testing and documentation. Since the outputs of these tasks are not directly observable by customers, it is always tempting to cut a few corners, particularly

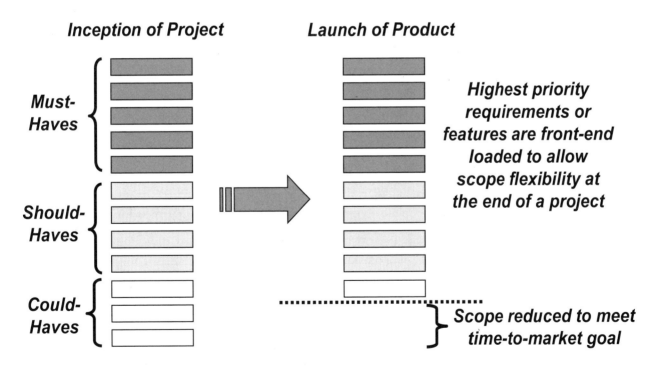

Figure 4.9: By applying must / should / could prioritization throughout product development, it may be possible to downscope a project without significantly affecting either quality or market price. The could-haves can be used as a "shock absorber" to protect a project's schedule.

when time (and your manager's temper) gets short. Having spent several years running a semiconductor testing laboratory, you might think that I would scold you for such heretical thoughts. Actually, just the opposite is the case; I recommend that you *plan* for cutting corners in testing and documentation. Perhaps I should explain myself.

What types of activities must be scheduled near the end of a development project? That's right, preproduction testing and product documentation. And when is time pressure the greatest? Very good, now you are starting to see my point. Although it is true that external customers are typically not aware of which tests you've run or how many levels of drawings you've released, the main reason why these activities get no respect is that they are in the wrong place at the wrong time. If the universe were to run backward, we would probably find ourselves happily performing test after test early in a project, but would be forced to shortchange innovation and conceptualization as the completion date approaches. In the absence of excellent planning and disciplined execution, whatever comes last will probably get short shrift.

So why should we *plan* for a crunch at the end of a project? Isn't this just admitting defeat? Rather, I believe that this is a matter of accepting reality. If you manage to pull off the "perfect storm" of ideal project scheduling and effective team leadership, than having spent a few hours putting together a contingency plan will be easily forgiven. On the other hand, if your project goes the way of most, knowing in advance which tests can be scaled back and which documents can be delayed or waived will avoid desperate flailing as your launch date approaches. How many preproduction units *must* be tested to have adequate confidence in a new product design prior to release? Which documents *must* be in place, because they impact vital areas such as production, quality, rework, and repair? If we are to fully protect our customers and our firm's reputation, what testing *should* we perform? For the benefit of future projects, which clever ideas or lessons learned *could* we capture? In my experience, applying M/S/C prioritization to activities that occur just prior to product commercialization is essential to launching a quality product. If appropriate priorities are followed, both your firm and its products will be protected from last-minute pressures to "get this thing out the door". Of course, our goal should be to execute a disciplined process that allows adequate time for the musts and shoulds, and even some of the coulds. When the going gets tough, however, and testing and documentation tasks end up on the chopping block, it will be a relief to know where and how deeply you can cut.

Application #4 – Daily Work Activities

Like many of you, the first thing I do each morning is make up a list of what I'd like to accomplish that day. Also like many of you, at the end of the day there are an intimidating number of items that I've failed to complete. The difference is that *I always complete my must-have activities*, and usually make significant inroads into the should-haves. The next morning, my list gets updated. With great joy, I scratch through those items that I've completed, and add new tasks that have come up since the day before. I then reevaluate my priorities, often elevating the shoulds and coulds from the prior day to musts and shoulds. This may sound a bit anal-retentive, but setting priorities in this way has allowed me to grow my business and still have time to enjoy life.

This concept can easily be adapted to the day-to-day execution of product development projects, as shown in Figure 4.10. The template presented in the figure is just a strawman; you can modify its format in anyway you wish. I've found that looking two weeks ahead is about right for most projects, and it is important that the action items be assigned to responsible individuals. Beyond that, any format will work just fine. As with my personal example above, the "rule" for a design team should be to complete all must-have actions as soon as possible and apply significant effort toward moving the should-haves forward. Could-have activities are kept on the back burner, awaiting available resources. As the project progresses, completed actions are removed from the list and the priority of remaining items is reevaluated on a regular basis. I could go on about how effective this tool has been for the teams that I've managed, but enough about me. Try this application of M/S/C for yourself and you will almost certainly be sold.

Application #5 – Filtering Design Concepts

This final application of M/S/C is really just an excuse to present one of my favorite innovation tools. In his excellent book, *Total Design*, Dr. Stuart Pugh describes a simple method for sorting through various design concepts and quickly identifying those

Two-Week Action Tracking Sheet				
Action Item	**Responsibility**	Priority		
		M	S	C
Finish critical-path tasks	S. Carton	X		
Order long-lead parts	C. Darney	X		
Submit regulatory documents	L. Mannette	X		
Review and approve final drawings	D. Copperfield		X	
Complete and release test plan	O. Twist		X	
Finalize bill-of-materials	T. Tim		X	
Begin creating product sales literature	E. Scroog			X
Update software documentation	B. Cratchet			X
Do other non-schedule-critical stuff	C. Dickens			X

Figure 4.10: Another example of how must / should / could prioritization can be applied to a wide range of project activities. Here it is used to help development team members prioritize their near-term actions.

candidates with the greatest potential for success. This so-called Pugh Method is shown in Figure 4.11. Pugh notes that one of the most difficult aspects of creative brainstorming is filtering out the good ideas from the not so good ones. He suggests that at the end of any brainstorming session, a two-dimensional matrix be created. Along the top of the matrix, various design concepts are listed. On the left side of the grid, he suggests identifying a number of must-have criteria for the future product. For each design concept, scores are chosen that reflect how well that alternative satisfies each of the must-have requirements. To illustrate this methodology, I'll describe a real-life application.

Several years ago, I facilitated a brainstorming event for a firm that produces vacuum cleaners. They were embarking on a major new project to design their next-generation portable canister vacuum. As with most mature products, profit margin was a significant issue, so each required function of the new vacuum was put under intense scrutiny. The goal was to identify opportunities to reduce production cost while maintaining high levels of customer satisfaction.

One of the attributes of the product that was addressed was the "allow-movement" function. We brainstormed on various ways to achieve portability, and came up with a wide range of ideas. These concepts were then organized as shown in Figure 4.11 (the drawings are optional, but they can help ensure that everyone visualizes the concepts correctly). The most familiar approach was selected as a "default" design; if no better idea came along, "four wheels" would be the logical choice. The group then generated a list of must-have filtering criteria. For example, the allow-movement solution would have to support the projected weight of the vacuum, move smoothly over various surfaces, and most important, cost less than the default design.

Once the matrix was constructed, the group went through each alternative concept and compared it to the default design. If an alternative was worse than the default with respect to a given must-have criterion, it received a minus (-) score. If it was better than the default, it received a plus (+) score. Finally, if there was no significant difference between an alternative and the default design, the alternative received an "S" for "same". Upon completion of this ranking exercise, the group totaled up the pluses and minuses for each design concept (ignoring the "S" scores, since they are neutral). Any concept that showed several pluses but no minuses represented a likely improvement over the default design. In this example, the three-wheel approach proved to be a winner. If an alternative concept earns a large number of pluses but also several minuses, there may still be a chance to salvage it. Perhaps there is a way to mitigate the minuses so that all must-have criteria can be met. Often this can be accomplished by combining the concept with elements from other design ideas. In this example, the "air-floatation" option looks promising, but it was projected to have stability problems. This drawback might be eliminated by adding skids (from one of the other concepts) to provide stability, while the air floatation would make the product glide like a hovercraft.

As you might have guessed, the firm chose the three-wheel design over the hovercraft option. The good news is that in a very short time (about a day of work), the design team in this example was able to interrogate a number of product functions and identify significant cost savings. Using must-have filtering criteria was the key to rapidly sorting ideas, and easily communicating why some clever concepts should be left on the drawing board.

Design Alternatives / Must-Have Criteria	4 Wheels (Default Design)	3 Wheels	Treads	Skids	Air Float	Casters	Handle	Backpack
Support 10 lbs.		S	S	S	-	S	-	-
Minimal Friction		S	-	-	+	S	-	-
Turning Radius		S	-	S	+	S	+	+
Smooth Movement		S	-	-	+	S	-	-
Light Weight		+	-	S	+	S	-	-
Nice Appearance		S	-	S	S	+	S	-
Handle Stairs Easily		S	-	-	-	S	+	+
Easy Assembly		+	-	S	+	S	+	+
Lower Cost		+	-	+	+	-	+	S
High Reliability		S	-	+	+	S	+	+
Number of Parts		+	-	+	+	S	+	+
Totals +	0	4	0	3	8	1	6	5
Totals -	0	0	10	3	2	1	4	5

Figure 4.11: The "Pugh Method" for filtering ideas generated by a brainstorming session. Here we use must-have criteria to effectively eliminate concepts that don't meet the product's baseline requirements, and highlight those design alternatives that should be given further attention. The "allow-movement" function for a portable vacuum cleaner is provided as an example.

Notes

An Overview of Set-Based Design

First, let me get the "lean trivia" out of the way. In the section that follows, we will discuss several of the powerful techniques that have made Toyota Motor Company's product development process one of the most productive in the world. However, when these methods were first published, they were given the unwieldy name of "Set-Based Concurrent Engineering". Doesn't exactly roll off the tongue, does it? So here's my thinking: In reality, the "concurrent engineering" part of the Toyota methodology is encompassed by their "3P" process (see Section 3.4). Hence, we can legitimately shorten the name to "Set-Based Design," when referring to the extremely powerful way that Toyota achieves their market-winning designs.

Several insightful articles have been published on the workings of set-based design, as well as an engaging fictional "business novel" by Michael Kennedy, entitled *Product Development for the Lean Enterprise* (see the Recommended Reading in Lean Product Development section). Therefore, I will ask my reader to refer to these references for in-depth coverage and allow me to offer a practical overview and some real-world examples. In particular, I will focus on two key elements of set-based design: the consideration of multiple, parallel design options, and the practice of delaying design decisions until as late as possible in the development process. Please keep in mind that these techniques are appropriate for firms that are already reasonably far down the improvement road. Each approach requires organizational discipline and an aggressive, team-based culture. If you are feeling a bit cocky about your well-honed development process, by all means give set-based design a try. However, if you are somewhat uncomfortable with your current process, it might be best to leave set-based design for Phase 2 of your lean implementation program...or even Phase 3.

Set-Based Design – The Concept

Imagine that you are shopping for a new car. Which of the following approaches would you choose? You could: a) do some research on available models, visit several dealerships, take test drives, and finally arrive at an optimal choice, or b) stop by the first car dealer you see and purchase whatever is displayed in the showroom. It seems foolish to make the rash "b" decision, given the substantial investment involved, doesn't it? Now consider how your firm develops new products (how's that for a segue). Do your teams: a) consider multiple alternative designs for each major new product and then merge the best attributes of each to arrive at an optimal solution, or b) quickly converge on a design concept and then convince themselves that they made the best possible choice? Hopefully you can see the parallel here. The primary reason to shop around for a new car is to evaluate as many alternatives as possible, so that you can select the car that best suits your needs. Why wouldn't the same logic apply to the design of new products?

Toyota Motor Company is well known for employing a set-based approach to new product development. The term "set-based" refers to their practice of considering a set of several design alternatives, and then merging the best features to arrive at a final concept. In fact, they typically form two or three *independent design teams* that compete with one another in parallel to create the best possible new car design. Once all teams have identified a preliminary design concept, they are brought together in front of upper management to present their ideas and defend their choices. The result of this competition is a "Frankencar" that combines the best attributes of all the alternatives. This set-based approach allows a far greater range of design possibilities to be considered than would be the case for a single team creating a single car design. There is a catch-phrase that describes this effect: "Conflict builds better cars".

In the 1990's, Ford Motor Company applied set-based design to the development of a new version of the Mustang. In this well-known example, Ford established three independent design teams, each of which was chartered to create a concept for the next-generation Pony Car. To ensure that the teams would not converge on similar solutions, they were each given a unique "name" that was selected to guarantee a diversity of designs. The first team was called "Rambo," and was asked to develop a muscle-car version of the Mustang. The second group was titled the "Schwarzenegger" team, and was chartered with creating an aggressive, middle-of-the-road version of the sports car. The final team was designated the "Bruce Jenner" team, after the Olympic decathlon gold medalist. This group was asked to develop a family-car concept with an "athletic" look and feel. The Mustang design that eventually went into production didn't look exactly like any of these alternatives, but instead drew from the best attributes of all.

The basic set-based design methodology is illustrated in Figure 4.12. Several parallel design options are pursued, either by independent teams (as described above) or by the same team, as an exercise in innovative thinking. It is often useful to define distinct "scenarios" for each of the alternative designs, that span the possible space of performance levels and product features. Once these diverse concepts have been fleshed out, they are compared with known customer preferences, and a compromise on performance and features is reached. After the overall design is clearly defined, the same set-based principle can then be reapplied to subsystems or components of the product to further optimize its value and appeal. Upon completion of each set-based iteration, critical design decisions are made, and the associated specifications are frozen before proceeding to the next phase of development (see Section 3.3 for a discussion of staged-freezing).

Clearly a set-based design approach is more resource intensive in the early stages of development. This may not be a roadblock when you have a deep bench like Toyota, but for smaller firms this can represent an insurmountable obstacle. Fortunately, even a relatively modest design organization can avail itself of the benefits of set-based design by using a slightly different tactic. Rather than considering discrete, parallel design alternatives, a development team can use "design bracketing" to define continuous ranges of possible performance levels and features. For example, rather than considering three distinct new car designs, a team could define the viable range for horsepower, handling, braking,

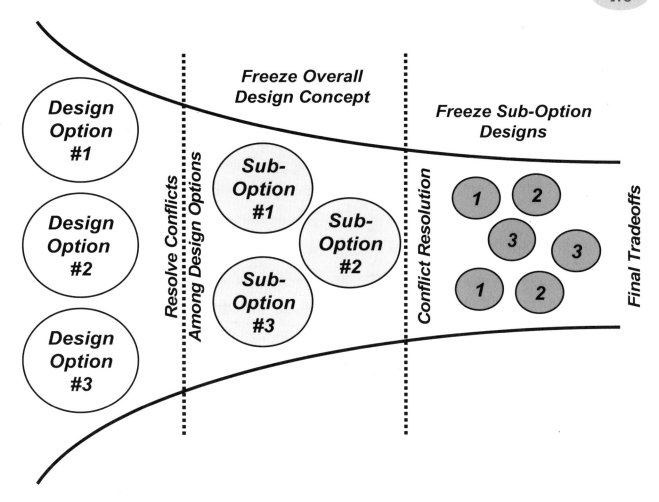

Figure 4.12: The concept of set-based design involves considering multiple versions of a product design and "competing" them against each other to arrive at an optimal product configuration. Hence, a "set" of designs are evaluated, rather than jumping directly to a single product solution.

interior noise, etc. At the beginning of development, these ranges would be kept intentionally broad. But as time passes, and both customer feedback and prototype test data becomes available, they would be systematically narrowed down until an optimal compromise is reached. A comparison of the two approaches to set-based design are illustrated in Figure 4.13.

Ultimately, the point of the set-based design methodology is to force development teams to consider a "trade-space" for a new product, rather than immediately jumping to a single, potentially suboptimal design. For a complex product, this trade-space could involve dozens of dimensions, but since only three dimensions can be illustrated graphically, that is how many are shown in Figure 4.14. Every point within the trade-space represents a possible product solution. As the design team moves through the development process, the volume of the allowable space shrinks, until only a point remains, representing the final compromise of all the parameters within the trade-space. This is as

Discrete Design Options –

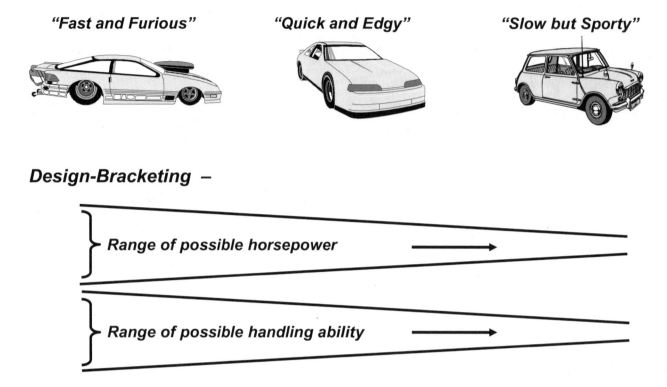

"Fast and Furious"   **"Quick and Edgy"**   **"Slow but Sporty"**

Design-Bracketing –

Range of possible horsepower

Range of possible handling ability

Figure 4.13: The benefits of set-based design can be gained either by considering several discrete design options, or by bracketing key performance attributes of a product and narrowing the range for each parameter until an optimal compromise is reached.

much a philosophical methodology as it is a technical one; without forcing design teams to embrace disparate concepts and divergent thinking, it is quite likely that your next new product will look an awful lot like all of your other products (emphasis on the "awful").

Set-Based Design – The Applications

Although the term "set-based design" was first used to describe the Toyota design process, they are certainly not the only company employing a set-based development strategy. In fact, this methodology is commonplace in a diverse range of industries. For example, one of the world's leading industrial design firms, IDEO, considers multiple alternatives in parallel, and then "competes" them to arrive at their groundbreaking product designs. Even the U.S. Department of Defense has been mandating set-based design for years, without even knowing it. It has been the DoD's routine policy since the 1960's to award parallel development contracts to several different defense contractors, and then down-select to the preferred design. If "conflict builds better cars," imagine what intense competition can do for the design of jet fighters. To demonstrate how ubiquitous a

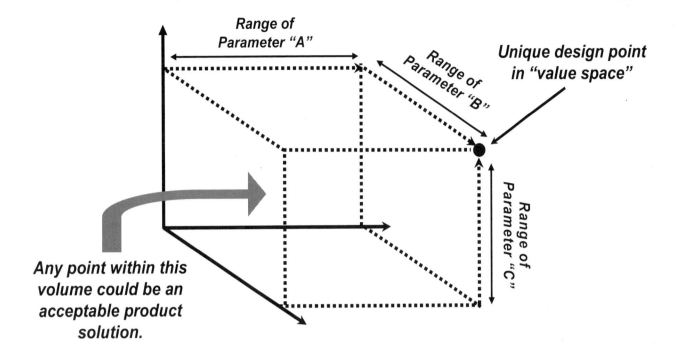

Range of Parameter "A"

Range of Parameter "B"

Unique design point in "value space"

Range of Parameter "C"

Any point within this volume could be an acceptable product solution.

Figure 4.14: The best way to understand set-based design is to imagine that your product's optimal design lies within a multidimensional "trade-space". As you analyze various design alternatives, the trade-space will systematically shrink until you arrive at the greatest possible value for your customers.

set-based design strategy really is, I'll offer two case examples that seem to have nothing in common: footwear and semiconductors.

Displayed on the wall of a leading footwear manufacturer are a dozen pairs of high-top athletic shoes, each one looking very much like the others. From a distance they appear to be identical, but upon closer inspection one can discern minor differences. These twelve shoe designs represent a reminder of the past; a time when this firm's design teams would create an endless stream of serial design iterations. The wall display illustrates how a year of development time could be wasted without arriving at an optimal product design. Today, the product development process within this firm has improved considerably. Although shoes and Toyota Camrys may seem very different, set-based design has proven to work equally well in both domains.

Instead of performing serial design iterations, this firm has adopted the methodology illustrated in Figure 4.15. At the inception of a design project, several discrete alternatives are generated for the new footwear product. One of the alternatives might exhibit "extreme styling"; bright colors and lots of cosmetic frills. The second design option would then fall at the other end of the spectrum; a conservative interpretation with a focus on comfort and performance. A third possibility might lie somewhere in the middle. All of these designs are intended to satisfy a well-defined market niche, and the choices of colors and styling for each alternative is made with these customers in mind. Prototypes of the three concepts are then created, and both internal marketing experts and external buyers are asked for feedback on the overall designs and on specific attributes such as color and detailing. This information helps the design team to narrow down the range of possibilities for their second round of prototypes. In the second phase, two concepts are created within the allowed range of design choices. Again physical prototypes are fabricated, and again they are used to harvest feedback from internal and external sources. The third design iteration is the last and the best (at least in principle). Unless unforeseen manufacturing issues arise, this is the design that is destined to become a commercial product.

From a time-to-market perspective, this footwear icon has reaped major benefits from using a set-based design approach. Whereas it used to take them up to eighteen months to launch a new shoe style, their development process can now be completed in eleven months. Moreover, the use of a set-based approach has allowed them to enfranchise their primary customers, fashion buyers for major retail outlets, into the design process. In a sense, the development of a new shoe design has become a collaboration between buyers and designers. After all, it is hard not to like (and buy) a product that you have had a hand in creating.

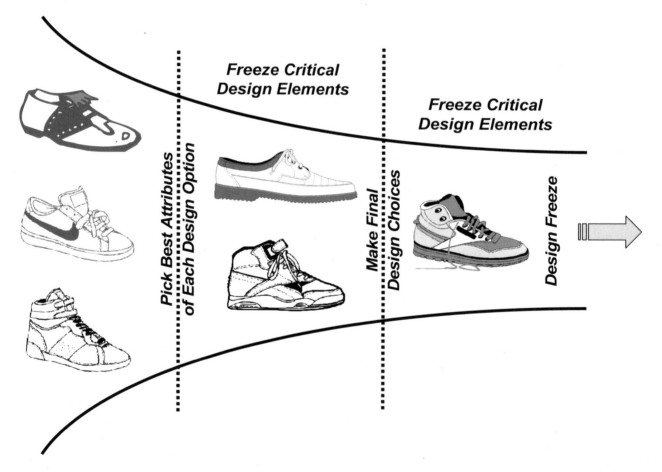

Figure 4.15: An example of how set-based design has been successfully applied to the development of a footwear product. Several discrete versions of a shoe are prototyped and the best features of each are incorporated into the next design iteration.

Now for a dramatic change of pace. We will leave the realm of high-fashion footwear and enter the pragmatic (not to mention microscopic) world of advanced semiconductor devices. The next example is drawn from my own experience, and illustrates both the "discrete design option" approach and the "design-bracketing" approach to set-based design. Although the anecdote is personal, it should be emphasized that the consideration of multiple, parallel design alternatives has been an integral part of the semiconductor industry since its inception. We didn't call it set-based design, of course. We just called it common sense.

Have you ever wondered how an IPod can store all of those thousands of songs? The answer is that it takes millions of transistors. (Note: The following example is intended for laypeople, so if you are a microelectronics expert, please cut me some slack.) In the early days of the industry, the two major factors that determined the market success of many new semiconductor products were the performance of each transistor, and the number of transistors that could be crammed onto a single chip. Amid fierce competition, firms would try to push the "bleeding-edge" limits of the technology in both of these critical areas. From a time-to-market standpoint, however, there was a seemingly insurmountable obstacle; it took from six to ten weeks to fabricate a prototype "lot" of silicon wafers. In other words, if you got a design wrong (either through errors, or by undershooting or overshooting the capabilities of the technology), it would be *two months* before you would find out. With our design team's ability to learn being paced by long lead-times for prototypes, we had no choice other than to use a set-based design approach.

A typical development cycle for a semiconductor product is shown in Figure 4.16. The first prototype lot would be used as an opportunity to test several different transistor geometries. Fortunately, since each lot consisted of twenty to forty wafers, it was a straightforward process to "split" it into smaller sets of wafers, each representing a unique design alternative. Rather than choosing two or three alternatives, however, we would often include six to ten different transistor configurations. Once the test data from this first wafer lot was available, we would analyze the performance of each version of the transistor, and use interpolation techniques to determine an optimal geometry. Since the final design parameters could fall anywhere within the spectrum of prototype config- urations, it can be said that we were using a design-bracketing approach.

Once an optimal transistor geometry had been identified, the second design iteration focused on the number of transistors that could be included on a single device. The limitation here was yield; as the number of transistors grew, the yield of fully functioning devices would decline. At a certain point, the cost per device would become unacceptably high (it turns out that the term "high" is surprisingly relative – in this case we were developing a *military* product). Hence, for our second round of prototype wafers, we would span the range of the possible number of transistors, from fairly conservative to irrationally exuberant. Again, we would wait the obligatory two months, and based on the resulting test data we would down-select to a final device design. One of the side benefits of our set-based approach was that our technical risks were significantly reduced. In a competitive market, it is common for design teams to feel obliged to push the limits of technology. If only one design alternative was being considered, and that alternative turned out to be overly aggressive, much time and money could be wasted. Since we *always* included a low-risk backup configuration as part of our design set, we were assured

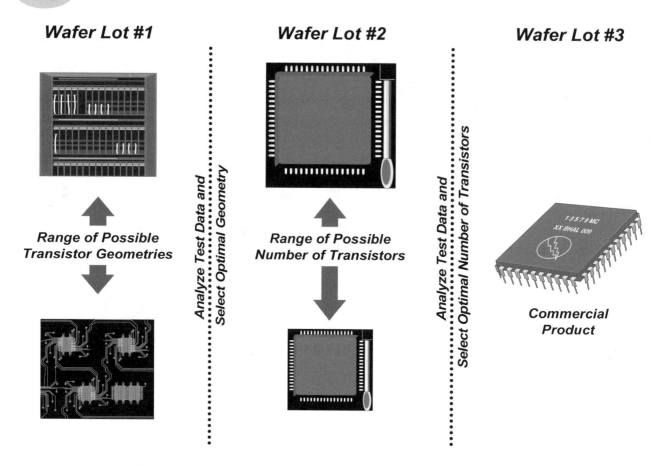

Wafer Lot #1   **Wafer Lot #2**   **Wafer Lot #3**

Range of Possible Transistor Geometries

Analyze Test Data and Select Optimal Geometry

Range of Possible Number of Transistors

Analyze Test Data and Select Optimal Number of Transistors

Commercial Product

Figure 4.16: An illustration of the design-bracketing approach to set-based design. In this example, a semiconductor chip is optimized by first evaluating a continuous range of transistor geometries, and then by considering a range of transistor densities.

of having a product to sell even if the blue-sky alternatives didn't pan out. Incidentally, just how often do you think that the low-risk backup design saved our ____?

How Delaying Decisions Makes You Faster

You might be thinking that the title of this subsection is an oxymoron. How is it possible that delaying design decisions can get your new products to market more quickly? To understand this effect, consider how a college student might select the classes she should take each quarter. In an ideal scenario, our apocryphal student might begin her education by taking courses in a variety of subjects to learn more about what each field of study has to offer. After surveying a broad range of subjects, she would then focus on a general area of interest (e.g., the sciences as opposed to the liberal arts). Only after a year or more of study would she declare a major, and begin pursuing a specific curriculum. As she approaches her senior year, she would further specialize by enrolling in advanced courses that delve into unique topics of interest. At every step, she would be careful to consider any prerequisites, so that she was adequately prepared for the next quarter's coursework. Following this logical progression, it is possible for our student to actually complete a four-year college degree in four years.

Now consider a more common scenario (perhaps one you are currently experiencing with your own college-age children). Our mythical student decides to take any first-year course that strikes her fancy, and as each course is completed, she announces that she has found her "life's work". She then declares a major and is assigned an appropriate curriculum. Unfortunately, another interesting course comes along on a completely different subject that causes her to change her mind. A new major is declared, and a new coursework plan is established. This cycle continues for several quarters, with each new major requiring a different set of classes than the last. In her second or third year she finally decides on a firm major, only to discover that there is a year of prerequisites that must be completed before she can begin taking junior and senior classes. The result is a four-year degree that takes five or six years to acquire, all because our student made decisions *too early*.

The key to making effective and timely decisions is to recognize two critical considerations: *precedence* and *dependency*. In the context of decision-making, precedence reflects the order in which decisions should be made from an intellectual standpoint. Before you can decide whether you will major in clinical psychology or abnormal psychology, you must first determine whether you will focus your education on the social sciences or the physical sciences. If this precedence is ignored, much time could be wasted delving deeply into the physical sciences, only to realize later that you are better suited to a career in psychology or sociology. Not surprisingly, the concept of precedence is clearly reflected in the set-based design methodology; a narrowing-funnel approach to decision-making is an excellent way of visualizing how precedence affects design choices.

Dependency, on the other hand, is a more pragmatic consideration. In college, dependency is a no-brainer; prerequisites for advanced topics are clearly listed in a university's course catalog. The dependency of decisions in new product development is not so obvious, however. Should high-risk design elements be given attention up front, or delayed until more is understood about the overall design of the product? Is it better to deal with the physical aspects of a product design first, and then consider ergonomics and cosmetics later, or visa versa? The answers to these questions are highly product dependant, but for a given product type there is a logical set of dependencies that can be learned over time and then institutionalized in your product development process.

The Toyota Motor Company has become so adept at organizational learning (see Section 3.5) that they have identified the precise order of precedence for decision-making in automobile design. They also have a clear understanding of the dependencies of their decisions, enabling them to prioritize their choices based on both of these critical considerations. In fact, they are so confident in their knowledge that they delay design decisions until as late as possible in the development process, consistent with lead times and other schedule-driving factors. This allows their design teams to apply the greatest amount of useful information to each decision, and avoids their wasting time fixing the problems that can result from premature choices. After all, we are always smarter tomorrow than we are today (assuming that we are amenable to learning). Using this decision philosophy, Toyota has achieved a more expeditious time-to-market, despite what might appear to be a strategy of procrastination, as illustrated in Figure 4.17.

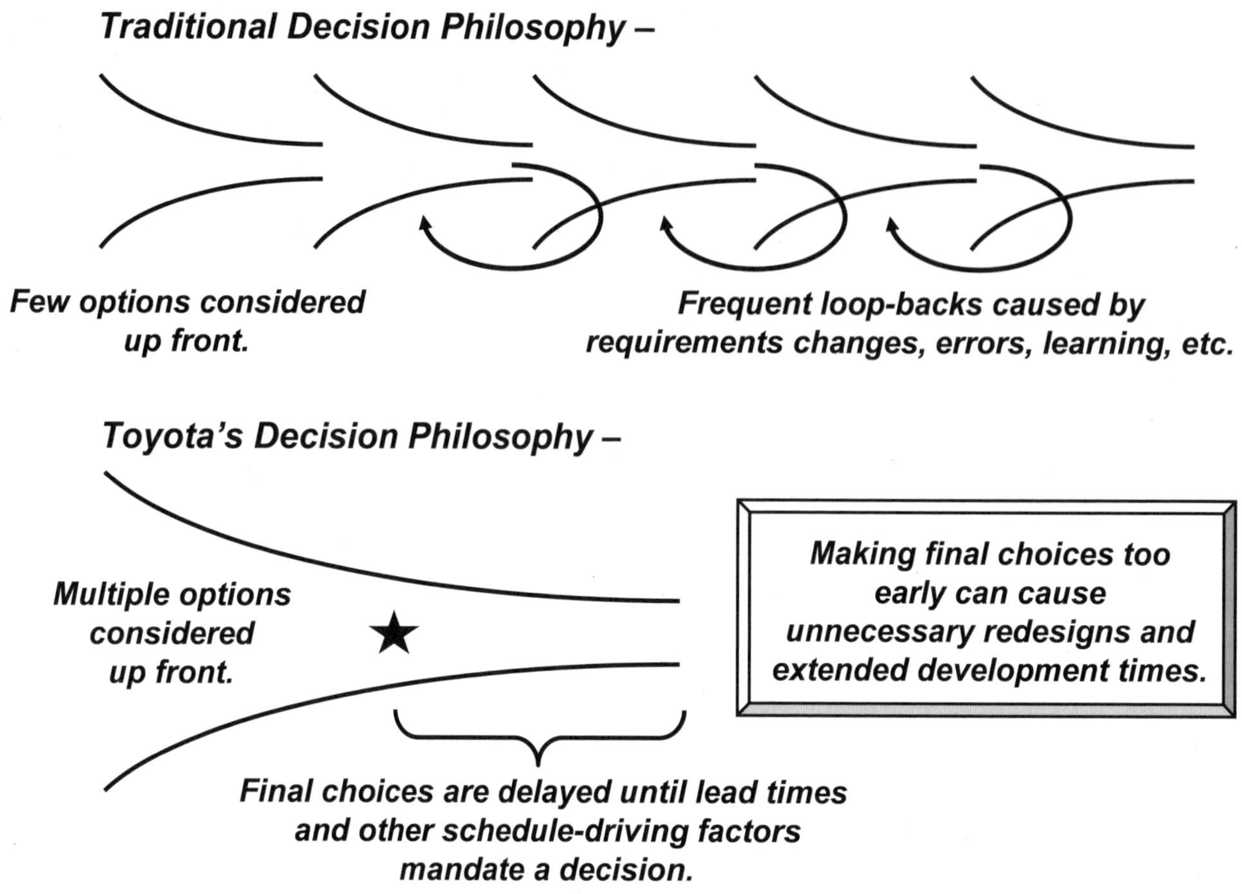

Traditional Decision Philosophy –

**Few options considered
up front.**

**Frequent loop-backs caused by
requirements changes, errors, learning, etc.**

Toyota's Decision Philosophy –

**Multiple options
considered
up front.**

★

**Making final choices too
early can cause
unnecessary redesigns and
extended development times.**

**Final choices are delayed until lead times
and other schedule-driving factors
mandate a decision.**

Figure 4.17: Toyota recognizes that design teams will always be smarter tomorrow than they are today. By delaying design decisions until the latest reasonable point in the development process, Toyota's teams have more and better information available to support their choices.

It is important to recognize that delaying design decisions is not for everybody. If your firm is not mature in its understanding of precedence and dependency, then delaying decisions will likely result in delaying your new product launches. I recommend that you begin your learning process by analyzing the critical path for a typical development project (see Section 5.4). This will provide you with a basic ordering of task dependencies. Furthermore, the use of a set-based design methodology can help you learn more about precedence, through the systematic consolidation of design alternatives. As confidence in your design teams' knowledge increases, you can begin scheduling key decisions at appropriately late points in the development process. Remember that making great decisions is not the same as making fast decisions. Avoid at all cost the "ready, fire, aim" mentality that serves as an all too common substitute for informed, high-quality choices.

Rapid Project Execution

*"Part of our time is snatched
from us, part is gently subtracted,
and part slides insensibly away"*

Seneca

Exception-Driven
Status Reporting

I've often said that the only way to improve a company is to change the way employees do their work every day. As obvious as it may seem, this simple mandate is often the most difficult part of a lean product development initiative. A firm can change its formal development process, slash waste from its policies and procedures, select more promising projects, set better priorities, and listen intently to the voice of the customer, yet still see little benefit in terms of time-to-market. Why? Because the designers themselves are still stuck in their old, wasteful habits; after all, the status quo is a very comfortable place to be. A telecommunications company will tell you that the hardest part of their infrastructure to improve is the "last mile" that connects their network to individual homes. Well, in lean product development, project execution represents that last mile.

As I've gained experience in traveling this final mile with design teams, I've learned that simplicity is king. For lean methods to really take hold they must: 1) make sense to pragmatic engineers and designers, 2) take virtually no time to implement, 3) be easy to communicate, and 4) require minimal effort to maintain. The lean project execution tools described in Part 5 are based on the same underlying principles as all lean enterprise initiatives: improved flow, reduced batch sizes, and an emphasis on pull. However, these tools have also survived a Darwinian selection process of real-world feedback to arrive at their current simplified state. This evolutionary process continues even as I speak, but for now these methods represent best-in-class ways to remove wasteful obstacles and allow value to flow from your design teams.

The status reporting method described in this first section is inspired by an improvement philosophy that predates lean thinking – statistical process control (SPC). Just after World War II, Dr. W. Edwards Deming and others from American academia were asked to assist Japan in its rebuilding efforts (this seems ironic when you consider the beating that U.S. firms received from Japanese companies just a few decades later). The statistical methods that Deming proposed for improving quality and production efficiency in devastated Japanese industries have revolutionized modern manufacturing. You will soon see that important gains can be achieved outside of the factory by applying the underlying concepts of SPC to the world of new product development.

Exception Management and Team Empowerment

The word *empowerment* has such an inherently positive connotation that you can't help wanting it to be applied to you. We all want to be empowered, and would like everyone we work with to be empowered as well. I'll bet the folks within your human resources department are huge advocates of this wonderful state of being, perhaps without fully understanding its ramifications. Beyond all of the platitudes, what does empowerment actually mean? The most common, and almost correct, definition is that a firm with empowered employees has embraced "distributed decision-making". Employees at all levels of an organization are encouraged to make local choices that directly impact their jobs, rather than following the traditional management hierarchy. This is not quite all there is to it, however. Based on this definition, workers would be allowed to make more decisions, but may still be subjected to constant scrutiny and second-guessing by upper management. As I will demonstrate below, true empowerment can only be achieved through the application of *exception management.*

Returning to Dr. Deming, sixty years ago, he and other improvement pioneers were challenged with bringing the manufacturing quality of Japanese industries up to world-class standards. While examining the traditional ways in which quality was assured, Deming was surprised to find that in most cases, every part that came off a production line was being individually inspected. Not only was this very inefficient, but it actually didn't work, since latent defects could slip through even the most diligent inspection. He proposed a more effective way to assure the quality of a manufactured product; by *controlling the process* rather than inspecting the *output* of the process. Using his statistical process control methodology, each manufacturing step is analyzed to determine the parameters that drive a product's quality. Control limits are then established, based on the range of each process parameter that will yield a part with acceptable tolerances. Finally, a control chart is generated that can be used to monitor the behavior of each process step over time, much like the one shown in Figure 5.1. As long as the process-control parameters remain within their limits, there is no need for external involvement. If a parameter gets close to a boundary (the grey zone in the figure), a warning is issued to the line foreman and appropriate maintenance personnel. If a limit is violated, an *exception* is recorded, and immediate action must be taken to remedy the situation and bring the process back to its acceptable baseline.

The identical logic that underlies statistical process control can be applied to the management of product development teams. What are the process parameters that determine the success of a design team? Adherence to schedule would be one, along with staying on budget, hitting critical performance specifications, and so on. These are reasonably quantitative metrics that can be used to establish an operating range for a team. Within this range, the team would be empowered to make decisions that impact their project. But here's the real kicker of an exception management approach: *The team should not require management oversight unless one of their parameters violates its allowed operating range.* Within their boundaries, the team should be left to function autonomously (within reason, of course). However, if an exception occurs (meaning that a boundary has been violated), the team should expect substantial management involvement until the situation is rectified.

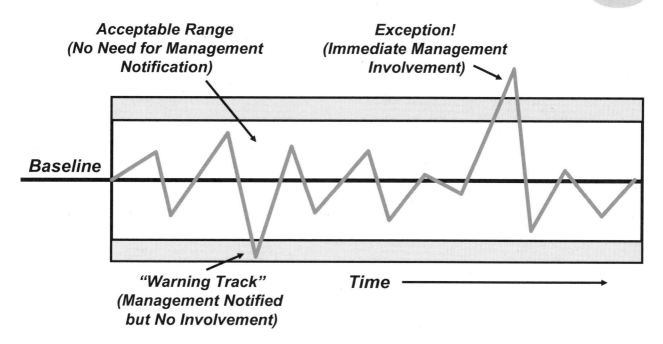

Acceptable Range
(No Need for Management
Notification)

Exception!
(Immediate Management
Involvement)

Baseline

"Warning Track"
(Management Notified
but No Involvement)

Time

Figure 5.1: The above diagram represents a simplified statistical process control (SPC) chart. If a machine on the factory floor is operating within its predetermined "acceptable" range, there is no need for management attention. If that machine's parameters wander into the "warning track," management is notified. Once a parameter violates either its upper or lower limits, immediate management action is taken. This same philosophy can be translated into an exception management approach to new product development.

The benefits to be gained from this approach to team management are significant. Not only do design teams have more control over their fate, but they are freed from the disruptions associated with reporting to executives that "the sky is still blue". Since upper management is already aware of the baseline project plan (e.g., delivery dates, budgets, performance specs), why waste the team's time reporting that the project is still following the plan? The only time a status report should be necessary is if the plan is violated in some significant way. When this occurs, the team should report on the nature of the exception, and describe how they intend to address the problem. In this way, management can focus their attention on assisting those teams that report exceptions to their project plans – the ones that actually need the help.

Lean Method: The "Stoplight" Status Chart

While the concept of exception management is quite attractive, does it actually work in practice? A brief personal story is in order. When I was just a young pup of an engineer, my first mentor was a brilliant scientist who also had tremendous insight into the management of design teams. After just a year of work experience, I was offered a chance to manage my first research project, so naturally I went to my mentor for suggestions. One of the tools he recommended was the red / yellow / green "stoplight" status chart. He said to me (in a heavy Catalan accent, as he was from Barcelona), "Ron, you don't want your team spending its time on formal status reporting. Just ask each team member to report to you by color each week; this way when a member's status is green, you can just move on to the next person." He went on to explain that a yellow status represented a warning that something might be awry, and a red status would demand my full and immediate attention. In short, a colorful application of exception management.

As my twelve-month project proceeded, I dutifully requested colors rather than status reports from my team members on programmatic issues such as schedule and cost, while focusing most of my attention on the technical details. All was well for the first six months or so, with mostly greens and a few yellows appearing on my status summary chart. As we approached month ten, however, things rapidly began to change, with significantly more yellows cropping into the picture. At month eleven, the entire status chart went red, and I spent a traumatic thirty days doing damage control to meet my project's deadline. Evidently, in the absence of clear, quantitative definitions for what red, yellow, and green actually meant, my team took some convenient liberties and delayed reporting exceptions until the last possible moment. When I brought this up to my mentor, he gave me a knowing smile and said, "The real challenge in leading a project is not managing status, it's managing human nature."

Indeed, exception management in general, and red / yellow / green (R/Y/G) status reporting in particular, suffers from a significant limitation; you have real people reporting on their personal efforts. Even under the best of circumstances, we all tend to paint a rosy picture of our endeavors. If things start to go south, most of us would rather pray for a miracle than report bad news. These natural, very human factors can wreak havoc on a project with a tight schedule and budget. After years of modifying my approach, however, I've found that R/Y/G status reports can work quite well, provided that you follow a few simple guidelines. I typically use a reporting format similar to the chart portrayed in Figure 5.2. The format itself is not important (as with most tools in this guidebook, you can improvise in any way you wish), but there are some key elements that should be incorporated into your approach. First, I keep the chart as clean as possible by only displaying the status of active tasks. Completed activities are deleted as they are finished, and upcoming efforts are included only when work actually begins. Second, there is always a single name associated with each active task, thereby assuring clear responsibility. Finally, my status chart includes several status metrics, such as schedule, cost, performance, quality, etc. These may vary depending on the type of development project involved and the level of attention that each metric requires.

Now here's the "human nature" part of my approach: I establish clear, and if possible quantitative, definitions for red, yellow, and green. For schedule status, you could define a "red" as indicating more than a week of slip in the completion date of a task. A cost exception might be defined as exceeding the budget for a given task by greater than ten percent. Performance status would receive a red designation if a critical product specification cannot be met. The actual exception thresholds that you use are up to you, but providing well-defined definitions is critical to finessing the subjective side of status reporting. For each red indicator, I require the responsible individual to provide additional details, along with a get-well plan. Greens require nothing more than a wave

Deliverable	Responsibility	Status to Plan		
		Cost	Schedule	Performance
Preliminary Circuit-Board Design	*Harry J.*	⇩	⇩	⬆
Circuit-Board Layout	*Tom H.*	⬌	⬆	⬌
Preliminary Enclosure Design	*Kathy M.*	⬆	⬆	⇩
Enclosure Supplier Selection	*Kathy M.*	⬆	⬌	⬆

- *Arrows indicate anticipated direction of change.*
- *If all tasks are GREEN, there is no need for a status review!*
- *A red arrow triggers management review and creation of a get-well plan.*

Figure 5.2: A simplified version of a "stoplight" project status report. This powerful visual tool allows clear communication of schedule, cost, and performance status for each active task within a project. Note that in this black-and-white diagram, black represents "red," gray represents "yellow," and white represents "green". Arrows indicate the predicted direction of status change in the short term.

and a smile. But what about the yellows? I have learned that a yellow status indicator, just like with a traffic light, should be a transient condition. It is just too tempting for team members to report a yellow status when their task is really a very deep shade of orange. To avoid the yellows being used as reds in disguise, I only allow this color to persist for one reporting period; by the next status report, a yellow task must either go to green or go to red. Lastly, I use arrows in addition to colors on my status chart. The direction of the arrow provides some useful information; a down arrow implies that things are projected to get worse over the short term, an up arrow suggests that the situation will improve, and a sideways arrow indicates that no change of status is anticipated over the next reporting period.

If you've spent much time working with product development teams, you have probably come across R/Y/G status reporting, so I won't belabor this basic tool. A few key suggestions to ensure successful application are summarized in Figure 5.3. Several of these points were discussed above, but one topic has not yet been addressed; for exception management to work, there must be trust and respect between design teams and their management. I recall a very tense executive meeting that I attended during my tenure as an R&D director. Our laboratory had experienced a shortfall of new contracts, and we were forced to lay off several staff members. As the discussion evolved, one individual was singled out as an "obvious" candidate for the unemployment line. The justification for this choice, it turned out, had nothing to do with the quality or quantity of this person's work. Several executives made comments such as "this guy seems to always be around when there's a problem," or "all I ever hear from him is bad news." I soon realized that this person was suffering from a near-fatal attack of the "shoot-the-messenger" syndrome. I patiently pointed out to my colleagues that this person was my top go-to guy for solving some of the most intractable problems in our laboratory. He was "always around when there's a problem" *because it was his job to fix problems.* It just goes to show how distorted our perspectives can become when superficial impressions and emotions take the place of facts and objectivity. If a team member reports that her status is red, your first reaction as a manager or team leader should be to *thank her for letting the team know in time to fix the problem.* You may have to grit your teeth, but keeping a smile on your face in these situations will generate the kind of trust that will enable you to manage human nature, not just project status.

You will find additional applications of exception management throughout the remainder of Part 5. One final note before we move on. I'm often asked to identify analogies between the methods of lean product development and the techniques of lean manufacturing that have proven to be so successful. In almost every case there is a clear connection, and exception management is, well, no exception. At a Toyota assembly plant, for example, a visitor can stand in an elevated mezzanine and view the miles of flow lines that can turn raw sheet metal into high-quality cars. From that vantage point, and with a neophyte's understanding of manufacturing, a visitor can quickly identify where the line is flowing properly and where there may be trouble. Colored lights on poles, referred to as *andon lights*, are positioned at each critical step in the assembly process. Green lights mean all is well, while yellow indicates a temporary parts outage or other minor delay. If a light turns red, it means that the line has stopped, and within seconds help will arrive to rectify the problem. Imagine the power of a method that allows instant visual identification and communication of problems; R/Y/G works as well in the conference room as it does on the factory floor.

Exception criteria must be explicitly defined, quantitative (if possible), and agreed upon.

People tend to be reluctant to report "bad news," resulting in inaccurate reporting.

Exception management requires trust and maturity – don't shoot the messenger!

You cannot have an empowered design team without exception management!

Figure 5.3: Some of the potential obstacles to the implementation of exception status reporting, and ways to minimize these issues. Note that for any lean method to be successful, it must be deployed with human nature in mind.

Notes

Stand-up Meetings
and Visual Project Boards

Not long ago, I facilitated a value-stream mapping workshop for a company that specialized in fulfilling custom orders. They received dozens of customer inquiries each month that required the creation of either a proposal or special-order quotation. Unfortunately, this quotation process had become unacceptably slow, often taking them weeks to respond to their customers. As a result, the firm was losing a large number of potential orders because customers grew impatient and went to a competitor instead.

After mapping out their current-state process (for more on value-stream mapping, see Section 6.1), it became evident that the primary cause of their glacially slow response time was the existence of several *time batches*. A time batch is analogous to a process batch in the factory; a number of items or actions are grouped together, ostensibly to improve efficiency. As we know from experience in lean manufacturing, large batches can result in significant waste, including slow production cycle times, excessive movement of materials, increased work-in-process inventory, and the potential for costly scrap. Batch-size reduction can yield significant efficiency improvements in the factory, but how does this concept translate into the product development environment? The above value-stream mapping example provides an excellent illustration. The workshop team discovered, among other things, that an office worker had been gathering up two-weeks' worth of quotation requests in an "in-box" before processing any of these time-sensitive documents. When asked what his motivation was for causing this delay, he indicated that it was "more efficient" for him to work on a number of the quotes in one sitting. Better for him, worse for the company. The simple solution was to mandate that this individual immediately process any quotation request that crossed his desk. The result was an average savings of one week in their response time to customers.

Yes, I know. This section was supposed to be about stand-up meetings and visual project boards; two of the most powerful and universally embraced tools in this guidebook. However, a brief tangent to more fully describe the idea of time batches will help my patient reader to better understand why stand-up meetings are so effective in improving workflow efficiency and time-to-market. So bear with me; the practical stuff will come soon enough.

First, A Word About Time Batches

The best way to explain how time batches manifest themselves in new product development is to discuss the examples presented in Figure 5.4. Any regularly scheduled meeting can represent a time batch, because information flows and decision-making decline to a trickle in the interim between these meetings. In one typical situation, a company's executive team met on the second Tuesday of every month to reallocate resources among their portfolio of development projects. Unfortunately, most of the resource issues that were causing delays to this firm's projects were occurring on a day-to-day basis. By the time the regularly scheduled resource meeting took place each month, these short-term problems had already done their damage, rendering the executive team's review of priorities next to useless. A similar wasteful situation might occur when capital approval meetings take place on an infrequent basis. A development team may be forced to wait until the next approval meeting for permission to purchase critically needed capital equipment. In general, the frequency of meetings should be driven by the urgency of the decisions they generate; strategic topics can survive long gaps, while daily issues should be addressed far more expeditiously.

Another manifestation of the time batch can occur when a large task is performed with no intermediate outputs, particularly if other project activities are dependent on it. For example, it might take several months to complete a comprehensive test plan document for a new product. Only after the information in this plan is made available can the test engineers begin fabricating their fixtures and creating detailed test procedures. This serially dependant situation can result in significant project delays, especially if the testing activity is on the critical path of the development project. How might this potential problem be rectified? By establishing intermediate outputs from the test-planning task that provide critically needed information to the test engineers. Although the formal release of the test document may be weeks or months away, an early feed of information may enable the test engineers to perform a substantial amount of preparatory work.

A final ubiquitous example of time-batching was mentioned in the introduction to this section. In that situation, a worker had grouped together two-weeks' worth of tasks before acting on them. As became evident during our value-stream mapping exercise, a time savings on his part had resulted in substantial waste for his company. If time sensitivity is not an issue, a small amount of batching may make sense. But for any schedule-critical activity, work should be performed *as soon as it can be addressed*, and in the smallest increments possible. What if a team member has more than one time-sensitive task on her plate? There is an even greater potential for time-batching to occur when multitasking reigns; typically a worker in this situation will push along all of her tasks in parallel, trying to keep the wolves at bay. The negative impact of this time-batch behavior will be described further in Section 5.6, but for now keep in mind that work should always be done in the smallest increments possible, and *in priority order*. Multitasking (i.e., the juggling of multiple tasks without clear prioritization) is not a skill to be cultivated; it is a wasteful practice that should be replaced by effective workflow management methods.

Time batches can cause significant delays in information flow, loss of team focus, and wasted effort. Examples include:

▶ **Regularly scheduled weekly / monthly / quarterly meetings**

▶ **Large work packages with no intermediate outputs**

▶ **Awaiting formal release of documents (serial dependency)**

▶ **Grouping of tasks to improve "efficiency"**

▶ **Multitasking without focus on task priorities**

Figure 5.4: A time batch occurs whenever project activities, decisions, or critical information are unnecessarily grouped together, resulting in uneven workflow and potential schedule delays. Batch sizes should be minimized by dividing large groupings of work into smaller increments, and by reducing wait times for critical information and decisions.

A Driving "Drumbeat" for Project Execution

Is a team coordination meeting a value-added activity? Recall that for an activity within product development to be value-creating, it must transform a new product's design, or the deliverables required to commercialize it, in some recognizable way. In the strictest sense, a team coordination meeting does not directly transform anything; its purpose is to monitor status and progress, ensure that risks are adequately addressed, and set work priorities for the subsequent period. Hence, a team coordination meeting is a classic example of an *enabler*; critically important to project success, but not a value-creating exercise. That being said, improving the way teams execute this enabling activity can have an enormous positive impact on resource efficiency and time-to-market.

The first step to enhancing team coordination is to abandon the pervasive concept of the "regular weekly meeting". As we discussed above, regularly scheduled meetings represent a time batch. Although some team communication occurs in the interim between meetings, it is very common for critical information to be withheld until "the entire group can hear and discuss it". Likewise, important workflow decisions are often delayed until the next coordination meeting: Which task should take priority? How should we handle this requested design change? When can we purchase needed parts? In each of these instances, several days may go by without activity while team members wait for a decision at the next weekly get-together. You may have heard the old (and not very funny) joke about a stopped clock: it's right twice per day. Well, the only time that a weekly team coordination meeting is "right" is when project activities just happen to be moving at a pace that is ideally suited to weekly updates. The majority of the time this weekly time batch will either be too frequent (e.g., during early discovery activities or when a project is in hiatus), or too infrequent (e.g., when critical project milestones are rapidly approaching). The pace of coordination should be matched to the pace of the project.

In fact, I suggest using the team coordination meeting to generate a driving drumbeat for project workflow. To illustrate why this is advantageous, consider the following question: When is most of the work that is presented in a weekly team coordination meeting actually completed? Answer: The day (or even the hour) before the meeting. This universal truth is shown graphically in Figure 5.5. The histogram in the upper-left corner represents the amount of focus that team members place on project work relative to the number of days before the next weekly coordination meeting. As the meeting day approaches, the sense of urgency among team members increases, until everything else must be set aside to get project work done. After the meeting, the urgency drops to zero, only to go through the same cycle the following week.

How would this behavior change if teams were to meet daily (please suspend skepticism for a moment)? The histogram in the upper-right corner suggests that with more frequent coordination comes increased focus; the development team experiences a consistent sense of urgency regarding their project tasks. This may sound like theory, but my experience with numerous design teams that have adopted this tool has shown that this effect is very real. Frequent coordination has translated into an increase in total work output in almost every situation. By now you are most likely mumbling under your breath that although this might be true, how can one justify spending an hour per day on coordination? The obvious answer is that you don't spend an hour per day; *you spend just ten minutes*. Before I drop the other shoe and describe how to implement brief stand-up coordination meetings, there is one more time-batch effect that is worth considering.

Project coordination is like driving a car; each time the team meets, the group has an opportunity to change the direction of workflow in response to new information that was gathered since the previous meeting. If you are cruising on the freeway, an occasional tweak of the steering wheel is all that's needed to stay on course. Once you reach your off-ramp, however, and begin winding through city streets, you will need to change direction more frequently, both to avoid obstacles and to make the turns that will take you to your final destination. Now imagine that the steering on your car has a time delay; it takes a full minute for the car to react to a turn of the steering wheel (must be a rental). While driving on the freeway this would prove to be a minor inconvenience, resulting in some weaving in traffic, but otherwise not a problem. Once in the city, however, you would find it impossible to avoid missing turns, and would probably collide with the first unexpected obstacle. This same behavior is true for project coordination, as shown in the bottom two graphs of Figure 5.5. If the frequency of coordination meetings is not properly matched with the pace and urgency of development work, there is a real possibility that team members will go off in wrong directions during the period between meetings. When project activity is hot,

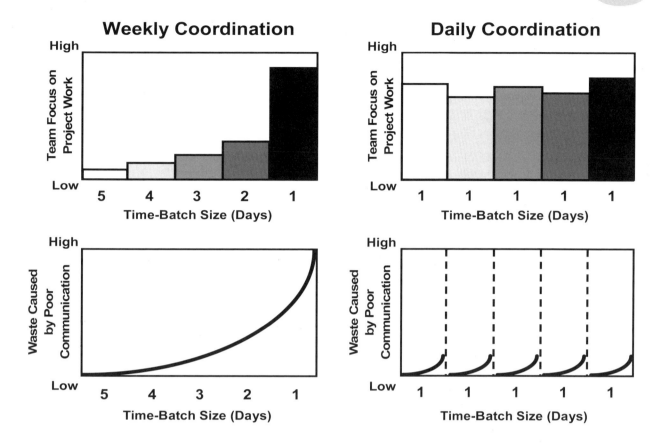

Figure 5.5: A weekly team coordination meeting represents a time batch that can distort the flow of work and may not adequately focus team efforts. The above graphs show the typical behavior of design team members when either a weekly or daily coordination meeting is employed. Although daily meetings are not essential, more frequent, short-duration stand-up meetings can increase team focus, drive product schedule, and avoid wasted effort due to relatively long delays between communication opportunities.

frequent coordination meetings allow the team to redirect resources, shuffle priorities, try new solutions, and so on, in response to rapidly changing events.

Lean Method: The Stand-Up Coordination Meeting

My first use of daily stand-up coordination meetings was a matter of "necessity is the mother of invention". One of the most challenging projects that I've worked on involved a team of scientists whose ability to make tangible progress was inversely proportional to their IQs. Upon taking over the leadership of this team, I dutifully set up weekly coordination meetings, and found myself aghast at the confusion, misdirection, and general lack of forward movement that occurred between meetings. After a particularly frustrating lack-of-progress review, I took a stress-reduction walk through the factory. As I strolled onto the shop floor, I noticed a production supervisor holding a daily shift-change meeting.

He and perhaps two-dozen workers were crowded around a white board, energetically discussing their plans for the day. Within ten minutes, all issues were settled, all assignments had been made, and the shift team was off to their work stations. The application of this approach to my troubled project was immediately apparent. The next day, I notified my team of eggheads that we would meet for ten minutes every morning. There would be no detailed discussions, no long-winded explanations, no tangents; there was plenty of time during the day to delve into these technical issues. At every meeting, I asked each team member to answer three simple questions: 1) What have you accomplished since the previous meeting? 2) What work are you planning to complete before the next meeting? And finally, 3) What do you need from your teammates or management to meet your objectives? I allowed roughly one minute per person, and was quite strict about holding people to this limit. If an important issue was raised, rather than discussing it on the spot, I captured the topic on a flip chart for disposition at the end of the meeting. Once all team members had answered the three questions, we collectively agreed to a plan of action for the day, and determined if any follow-up meetings were needed to dig deeper into issues that had been raised, or to make decisions that were needed to maintain the project schedule. Like clockwork, after ten minutes the meeting was adjourned.

The results were nothing short of spectacular. Once the moaning and groaning subsided (this took several days and required some cajoling on my part), everyone on the team began to recognize that something was different. Questions were being answered in a timely manner, connections among the team members were easily made, priorities were always clear, and a sense of team camaraderie was emerging. After only a few weeks of daily stand-up meetings, the project was back on schedule and progress was being made at a reasonable clip. Keeping these scientists on track was still like herding kittens, but frequent coordination enabled this team to achieve a level of productivity that would have been impossible otherwise.

Since that time, the companies that I have worked with have morphed the stand-up meeting concept in many ways. Despite its myriad variations, however, there are some fundamental ground rules that should be followed to ensure both the acceptance and success of this lean method, as shown in Figure 5.6. First, let me be clear that at a stand-up meeting, *people actually stand up*. No one gets comfortable, no doughnuts, no newspapers, just the team gathered around a visual project board (which will be covered later in this section). The starting time for the meeting is arbitrary, but first thing in the morning works best, in my opinion, since people are fresh and the workday is ahead of them. Just before lunch has also proven to be a popular timeslot, particularly if team members have flexible schedules. The only meeting time that I would not recommend is at the end of the day, since by the following morning all will be forgotten.

Although timing is important, it is the duration of your stand-up meeting that will determine whether it succeeds or fails. The most common reason why this type of meeting is poorly received by participants is that they become bloated with too much detail, or are co-opted by individuals who divert the meeting to their own agendas. If your experience with stand-up meetings has been less than stellar, it is almost certainly because they have lasted so long that your feet began to hurt. Here are my strong recommendations: When you first establish your stand-up coordination meetings, ask the team to agree upon some ground rules, the most important of which should be to stick to a fixed duration. I believe

---

1. Should be held either at starting time or just before lunch hour.

2. Should last for no more than one minute times the number of attendees (fifteen minutes MAXIMUM duration at first...the team can always agree to a longer duration later).

3. The entire core team should attend – off-site team members can call in on a speaker phone – overseas members can be connected through a designated "liaison".

4. The meeting facilitator should ask each attendee to respond to three basic questions:

- **What work did you complete since the last meeting?**
- **What work will you accomplish before the next meeting?**
- **What do you need from other attendees to achieve your goals?**

Figure 5.6: Some basic rules for holding stand-up coordination meetings. As obvious as this tool may seem, its success depends on proper facilitation and discipline. If your meetings are allowed to drag on, for example, they will quickly lose favor with team members.

that fifteen minutes should be the absolute limit, at least until the team has become comfortable with this format. The meeting should start precisely at the agreed-upon time (lateness cannot be tolerated, since it is useless to show up ten minutes late to a ten-minute meeting). Far more important, *it must end precisely at the agreed-upon time.* If all members of the team have not had a chance to speak, they can be the first to contribute at the next meeting. In fact, several firms that have implemented this tool have purchased kitchen timers for their team leaders. The timer is set at the start of the meeting, and when the bell goes off, the meeting ends without fail. Some people may not be comfortable at first with this aggressive pace, but eventually everyone will come to appreciate the highly focused, rapid-fire communication that results. I should mention that I've seen stand-up meetings that have, by agreement of the team, been stretched to twenty, and even thirty minutes per day. Ultimately, you and your team own the meeting, so you may do with it what you wish. I still strongly suggest that you begin with fifteen minutes or less until the discipline has become embedded in your team's thinking. You can then carefully add additional topics or agenda items as the team sees fit.

Attendance should be mandatory for core team members. Naturally, one of the benefits of frequent coordination is that if someone misses a day or two, they can rapidly catch up. However, missed meetings should be the exception, not the rule. In addition to the core team, any extended team members who are currently active on the project should also attend. In some cases, it may make sense to have these supporting individuals attend just one meeting per week (on an agreed-upon day), especially if they are being shared among several development projects. If a team member is located in a distant building or at another site, they can call in to a speaker phone at the designated time. Team members who are located in significantly different time zones can participate through an assigned "liaison"; a member of the local team is asked to contact each overseas participant several times per week and report on their progress and needs during the regular meeting.

The format of your meetings is extremely important. People like routines, so work with your team to reach a consensus as to how the stand-up meetings should flow, and then stick to it. The three questions that I've suggested are critical, but they can be adapted to suit your team's specific needs. At the end of the meeting, it is important to spend a moment dispositioning issues or problems that have been raised. If a technical problem has occurred, ask the involved parties to agree upon a separate time to meet on that subject. If team members require a decision to be made, either make it on the spot, or set up a time for that discussion as well. The point is not to resolve every issue in the stand-up meeting itself, but rather to ensure that all issues will be resolved promptly as the workday progresses.

While the duration of your stand-up meetings can have a dramatic impact on team members' acceptance, it is the frequency with which they are held that will raise the most eyebrows. Although I suggested above that a daily stand-up meeting can make sense in certain situations, a once-per-day frequency is no more "right" than a once-per-week frequency. The occurrences of these coordination meetings should be matched to the pace and urgency of the project, as shown in Figure 5.7. For example, I've seen several in-company improvement teams hold a monthly stand-up meeting to update the status of long-term initiatives and establish action lists for the following month. A development team might agree to meet once per week during periods of low schedule pressure, but increase the frequency to three times per week as important milestones approach. Finally, during crunch times on a project, daily meetings may be warranted. In fact there have been several times that I've held a stand-up meeting first thing in the morning and another right after lunch (e.g., during periods in which a number of prototype tests are being run prior to a customer demonstration or design review). It is important to remember, however, that once the schedule pressure subsides, the team can agree to reduce the frequency of the stand-up meetings back to three times per week or less. The best way to ensure the acceptance of this powerful coordination tool is to periodically ask your team whether the agenda, frequency, and duration are optimal, thereby enfranchising the entire team in the success of this lean method.

Beyond the reduction of time-batching mentioned above, holding frequent stand-up coordination meetings can yield additional benefits, as shown in Figure 5.8. Some of these gains may seem nebulous: "creating a shared language," for example, or "building team identity". Keep in mind that although it is hard to quantify these effects, they are as real as any schedule milestone. A team that comes together as an emotionally committed unit can achieve exponentially higher creativity and productivity than one that is a team in name only. Ultimately, your goal should be to evolve a product development culture within your firm that embraces urgency, encourages timely decision-making, and fosters true team empowerment.

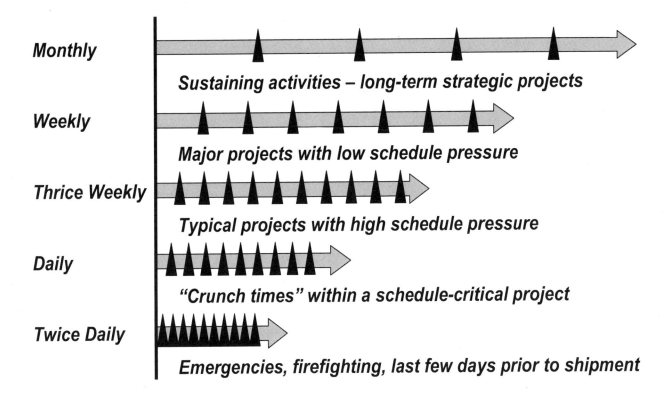

Figure 5.7: The frequency of stand-up coordination meetings should be driven by the urgency of information flows, the duration of the development effort, and the criticality of project schedule. For long-term, low-urgency projects or sustaining activities, a monthly get-together may be adequate, whereas for emergency situations (such as preparing for the launch of an important product), meetings might even take place twice per day for short periods.

Finally, it is interesting to consider just how far an organization can go in exploiting the benefits of the stand-up meeting. A major satellite communications firm has embraced daily get-togethers at all levels of management, from the bottom to the top. At 7:30 am every morning, the CEO meets with his executive team for ten minutes. At 8:00 am, each of these executives holds a stand-up meeting with their direct reports. By 9:00 am all functional departments and project teams are holding their working-level meetings. In principle at least, the CEO can make a decision at 7:30 in the morning and have it communicated throughout the entire organization before the coffee runs out in the break room.

Several companies that I've worked with have been quite creative in their extension of the stand-up meeting format into areas other than team coordination, as shown in Figure 5.9. One aerospace firm has set up several dedicated meeting rooms that are configured specifically for holding stand-ups. There are no chairs; only a waist-high table with a PC projector mounted underneath it. The projector is connected to the company's internal network, allowing groups to pull up whatever information they need for their meeting and

- ► **Creates a shared language among team members**

- ► **Allows for real-time reallocation of resources**

- ► **Encourages a focus on value-creating activities**

- ► **Establishes a clear, prioritized work plan for each day**

- ► **Provides a mechanism for cultural change**

- ► **Builds team identity and emotional commitment**

Figure 5.8: Some of the key benefits of using short-duration stand-up meetings for project coordination. A team is shown holding a stand-up meeting in an office hallway. A type of visual project board known as a "Wall Gantt" is displayed next to them.

display it for all to see. These dedicated rooms are scheduled in fifteen-minute increments, and are generally booked solid. In addition to coordination meetings, the stand-up format is used by this firm for a weekly "drawing signoff party," several data-sharing meetings, and to address surprises that seem to come up on a daily basis.

I encourage you to be creative with this tool. Many of the one hour and longer meetings that you are currently suffering through may be candidates for stand-up meetings instead. Although it may not seem like much when considered individually, a half-hour saved here and there can add up to a lot of productive time. On the other hand, you shouldn't assume that everything can be crowbarred into ten-minute quickies. There are many situations that demand longer meetings, not the least of which is an occasional team-building activity whose sole purpose is to share personal stories and learn about "big-picture" happenings in the company. I used to hold a weekly meeting at a local pizza parlor from noon to 2:00 pm each Friday. All team members were invited for free food and "open microphone" discussions of wide-ranging topics. It was just for fun, but it served an important purpose. When the project was cruising along and the team was experiencing minimal pressure, attendance at my pizza meetings was spotty. However, when things got hot and the team was stressed, virtually every member was there to blow off steam. Stand-up meetings get the job done in many situations, but there are times when bringing back the chairs and doughnuts makes the most sense.

Drawing Signoff

Conflict Resolution

Firefighting

Data Sharing

Figure 5.9: The concept of the brief stand-up meeting can be extended to many other facets of project work. A quick drawing (or engineering change notice) signoff meeting can be a great time-saver. Other schedule-critical situations can also benefit from more frequent, short-duration get-togethers.

Lean Method: The Visual Project Board

One of the hallmarks of lean thinking is the use of visual communication techniques. Presenting information in a simple graphical form can significantly reduce the risk of errors, and ensure that the right work is being done at the right time. In Section 5.1 we discussed the use of red / yellow / green "stoplight" charts to communicate the status of a project – clearly an application of visual communication in the product development environment. Starting from this humble beginning, we are going to build a customized and highly effective visual project board for your next development effort. A project board serves as a repository for all critical project information, and can become a dynamic focal point for stand-up coordination meetings (assuming, of course, that the meetings are held in view of the project board).

Let's begin building your customized visual communication tool by taking your red / yellow / green exception status chart and placing it up on a wall or white board in a convenient location. Looks kind of lonely up there all by itself, don't you think? Why not add the deliverables roadmap that we created in Section 3.2? Alternatively, you could display the "lean project schedule" that will be described in Section 5.4. Now that you have the high-level project status and a roadmap for future activities included on your project board, what other information might be useful to your team? Since the big picture has already been adequately addressed, perhaps some detailed workflow information might be beneficial. For example, an action tracking sheet would enable the team to better understand short-term priorities and upcoming milestones. This type of tracking sheet will also be discussed in Section 5.4, but for now just imagine a list of open actions, responsible individuals, and due dates. With the three key pieces of project information described above, you have all the essentials for holding an effective stand-up meeting... assuming that nothing new comes along. How will you handle issues, problems, and other unexpected situations? Rather than carting around a separate flip chart easel to capture these exceptions, you could simply add a fourth quadrant to your project board for this purpose (after all, that is why they are called *quadrants*). You have now arrived at the visual display shown in Figure 5.10.

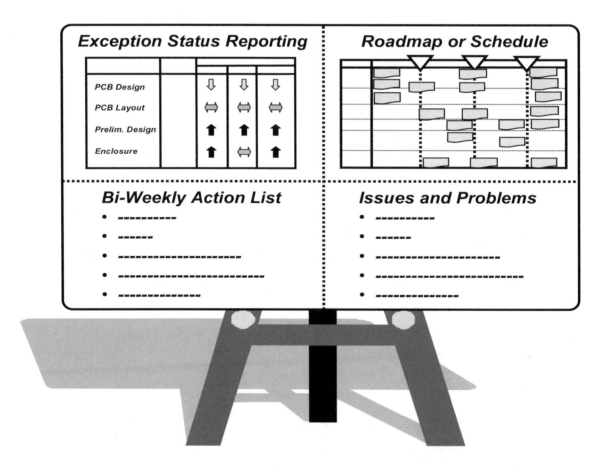

Figure 5.10: An example of a basic visual project board. This tool serves as a powerful enhancement to stand-up coordination meetings, or can be used on its own as a centralized repository for critical project information. Either a physical board or a virtual version can be used.

This basic format has been adapted and enhanced in many ways. Once you recognize the utility of the project-board concept, it is easy to envision other "quadrants" that could be beneficial. Displaying risk-mitigation activities, for example, could serve as a useful reminder to the team, and would help ensure that these important tasks are given proper attention. If your project involves a contract customer, perhaps space could be allocated for recent customer communications or change requests. One of my personal favorites is to include a lessons-learned list that can be updated in real time, rather than waiting until the end of a project to dig through rapidly fading memories. Anything and everything that is of interest to a project team is a candidate for inclusion. The comprehensive visual project board shown in Figure 5.11, for example, displays a broad range of information divided into nine nonants (okay, so I made that word up, but quadrants just doesn't make sense here). The choice of which elements to include is up to you, and you will learn over time which items are helpful and which are merely clutter. Once you have arrived at an effective format, consider creating a standard template for each item that can be adapted by future teams to their specific needs.

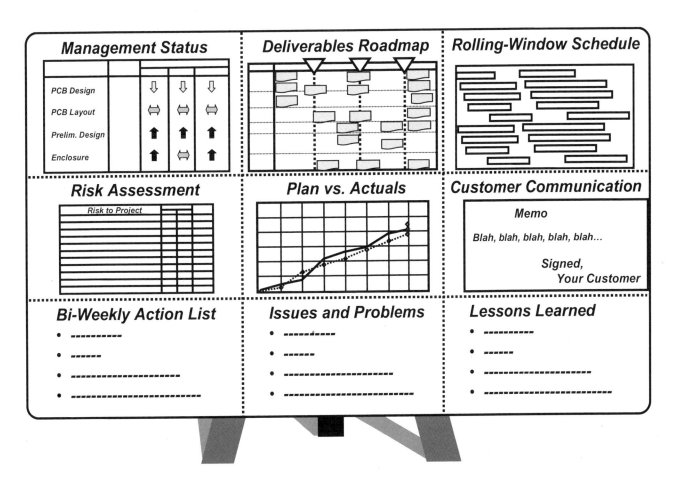

Figure 5.11: A fully realized visual project board used during the development of a complex aerospace system product. Any and all of these categories of information might be included in your version of a project board; select whichever makes the most sense for your firm's products.

You may have already guessed that a physical project board is not the only route you can take. Why not create a virtual version that can be accessed through your firm's network server or intranet site? This approach has been successfully implemented within a number of firms: Intel, for example, uses a "dashboard" of tailored information as the home page for each functional department and project team. A less sophisticated approach might be to provide a shortcut icon on the computer desktop of all team members (and possibly upper managers) that will link them directly to the visual information they need. You can still use this virtual version of a project board to support your stand-up meetings by projecting its image on a screen (as mentioned in the previous subsection), or by asking team members to pull it up on their laptops. The benefits of a virtual project board can be substantial, particularly if your team members and / or managers reside at different physical locations, or if wall space is at a premium.

Finally, it is important to note that a visual project board can display more than a single project's worth of information. It is common for a team of designers to be working on a number of projects at the same time. Why not create a multi-project board? Each project could be allocated a separate region of the board, or they might be merged together for the purposes of day-to-day team workflow management. This possibility suggests that you could also hold multi-project stand-up meetings in front of your multi-project visual display. In fact, this approach proves to be one of the best ways to optimize team productivity in a multi-project environment. Personally, I've used this technique to work through some intractable resource allocation problems. In one case, I was managing a team of twenty engineers who were responsible for a dozen small projects. It was impossible to hold separate stand-up meetings for each of these efforts, and it wouldn't have made sense to do so even if time permitted. Since the progress of each project depended on the resource demands of the other eleven projects, the best way to handle this situation was to hold a single stand-up meeting that covered all twelve co-dependant activities. Two or three of the projects were important enough to discuss daily, while the rest were assigned one day of the week for their turn in the spotlight. Yes, it was challenging, and yes, we had to run twenty-minute meetings instead of ten. However, all projects were completed successfully, and most (but not all) of the participants were able to keep their sanity.

Variations on a Theme...and Some Real-World Examples

There are two specialized forms of a visual project board that are worth discussing in some detail. The first is often referred to as a "Wall Gantt," because it serves the same purpose as a typical project schedule, except with more flexibility and, of course, more visibility. Actually, this clever tool resembles the deliverables roadmap discussed in Section 3.2, except that the timeframe is dramatically condensed, as shown in Figure 5.12. Imagine that you are the leader of a software design team that is approaching the release of a major new application product. The release date was announced by your sales force several months ago, and a number of key clients are expecting delivery in just two weeks. Unfortunately, at last count there were over one-hundred minor fixes, bugs, documentation holes, security concerns, etc., that must be disposed of before the product leaves your building.

▶ **Horizontal Axis Represents Time - Typically Days of the Week**

▶ **Vertical Axis Displays Core and Extended Team Members**

▶ **Activities Needed to Meet a Critical Milestone are Assigned a Responsible Person and Due Date Using Sticky Notes or Index Cards**

▶ **Colors Can Be Used to Indicate the Priority of an Activity or Other Useful Information**

Figure 5.12: A "Wall Gantt" is a variation of the visual project board that is designed to disposition a number of quick and very urgent tasks over a short timeframe. A classic application of this tool would be during the final two weeks before the release of a new software product.

How would you handle this challenge? Clearly a weekly coordination meeting would be a waste of time – two meetings and the show's over. Even a daily stand-up meeting might not be adequate to keep track of dozens of minor tasks, some of which may only require a few hours to complete. At this point, it's time to abandon your run-of-the-mill project board in favor of a Wall Gantt. Find an empty white board (or bare spot on the wall) and list the core and extended team members along a vertical column. Every available body should be listed: remember that you are in a high pressure situation. Along the top of your white board, list the days of the week for the next two weeks. Now gather your team around your emerging Wall Gantt and write down every task that must be completed before the new product can be released. I suggest using sticky notes or index cards, with a separate note for each task. Once you've completed your stack of stickies, it's time to assign responsibilities. Beginning with the "must-haves," read out each task and ask for a volunteer to handle it. Start populating the center of your matrix by placing each task's sticky note at the junction between the day of the week in which it should be completed and the person who volunteered (or was assigned) responsibility. Continue until all tasks are delegated and placed somewhere on the Wall Gantt. This represents a rough plan to get you started, and will be continuously adjusted as the two-week period progresses.

From this point forward, you will hold your daily stand-up meetings in front of the Wall Gantt. Your goal for each day's meeting should be to hand out every task note affixed to the column for that day to someone on the team, with the initial assignments serving as a starting point. At each subsequent meeting, team members will return the task notes for completed tasks, and take new ones that they believe they can handle. If a team member will not be available for several days, this should be indicated by "out-of-office" notes placed along that person's row on the chart. When the final task note from the Wall Gantt is handed back to the team leader, the project is completed.

The beauty of this tool is flexibility. Although an initial plan was established, within a few days those assignments will become completely distorted by unpredictable task durations and unexpected disruptions. As these unforeseen events occur, the allocation of tasks can be adjusted to ensure that every person is being utilized to the greatest extent possible. I've used a software team as an example, because this is where I first observed the Wall Gantt in action, but it can be applied to any intense, short-term effort. Other possibilities include preparations for a major design review, management of an aggressive testing regimen, handling of an unexpected quality problem, and so on. I've even heard of this tool being used by an engaged couple during the final weeks of preparation before their wedding. Incidentally, it shouldn't be hard to guess the professions of these lovebirds (hint: they used Microsoft Project to plan out their entire six-month engagement).

A final useful variation on the visual project board theme is not a project board at all. In fact, it closely resembles the "pull boards" that are often used in lean manufacturing. Again I'll illustrate this approach through a real-world example. A few years ago, I came across a company that had a terminal case of procrastination, at least with respect to keeping their product documentation up to date. As you probably know, every product has a set of drawings associated with it that captures the details of the design, and includes instructions for its fabrication. In addition, there are other supporting documents, including test plans and procedures, quality and assembly work instructions, and so forth, that are essential to commercialization. Every time a change is made to either the product design itself or to the process used to manufacture it, an engineering change notice (ECN, aka engineering change order) is submitted and approved. This portion of the change control process is usually executed quickly, since product changes are often motivated by a production issue or customer problem. What *should* happen next is that the product's documentation is formally updated to incorporate the approved change and then re-released. This can be a time-consuming process, however, so many firms allow their operations group to "red line" the current version of documentation until a new release can be completed. Knowing human nature, what do you think is the weakness in this situation? You got it; once the red lines are in place, there is little motivation to go back and complete the formal change incorporation process. In this particular firm's case, they had hidden away their incomplete ECNs in a large file cabinet, and then a second, and a third. Over *three-hundred* incomplete ECNs had accumulated, representing three years of backlog at the current pace of incorporation work.

The solution to this problem was plain to see (pardon the pun); a visual tracking tool was needed to put a spotlight on this horrendous backlog and to assist in eliminating it. The firm set up a "trigger board" in their drafting area that was arranged by the software tool needed to incorporate the change (not all employees of this group were versed in all of the legacy documentation tools). Within each category, a set of backlogged ECNs was selected on a priority basis and placed into slots, as shown in Figure 5.13. Motivated by an executive mandate to bring all production documentation up to date within six months, the drafting group divided their three-hundred ECN backlog into twenty-six roughly equal sets. Each week, a new set was added to the trigger board, and as the week progressed, employees would pull cards (very much like the *kanban* cards used in a lean factory) and perform the associated tasks. The goal was to complete each set of cards by the end of the week, so that the team would be ready for a new set the following Monday. If any tasks remained on the board from a previous week, they became the highest priority, and the new week's set was added below. Red / yellow / green status indicators were used to communicate how far behind the team was relative to their agreed-upon pace of work (their *takt* time, so to speak – more on this in Section 5.6).

The good news for this formerly undisciplined company is that the executive mandate was met; within six months (give or take a month or so) the entire backlog was eliminated. Their visual pull board is still in use, now serving to keep track of current tasks and set daily priorities. This idea of applying a visual pull board to product development work can be extended to any recurring or repetitive activity. A more generic version might resemble the flow diagram shown in Figure 5.14. Some form of a trigger card (i.e., *kanban* card) is used to signal that a task is in need of attention. These cards are arranged in priority order on a pull board, and assigned to workers as their time becomes available. Once completed, the trigger card is placed into a slot on a "finished board" until it is recorded by a team leader or manager. The use of red / yellow / green statusing can help the team monitor its rate of progress. This general methodology could be used for

ECN "Trigger Board"

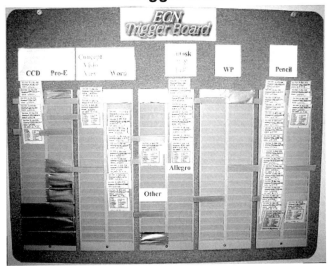

▶ *ECN trigger board sized for a two-week cycle-time and 150 drawings*

▶ *Arranged by the software tool used for change incorporation*

▶ *Red / Yellow / Green used to show completion status relative to the agreed-upon pace of work.*

▶ *Pull cards are used to assign change incorporation tasks in priority order.*

Figure 5.13: Another application of the visual project board concept, in this case to ensure the prompt incorporation of changes to engineering documentation. This board allows easy visual tracking and prioritization of all change incorporation tasks.

dispositioning corrective-action requests, the processing of purchase orders, responding to customer inquiries; essentially any recurring activity within new product development (or within the entire enterprise for that matter...but that must wait for another guidebook).

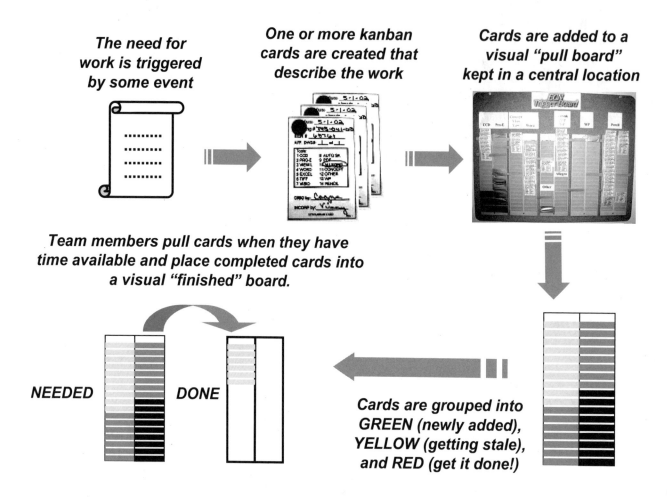

The need for work is triggered by some event

One or more kanban cards are created that describe the work

Cards are added to a visual "pull board" kept in a central location

Team members pull cards when they have time available and place completed cards into a visual "finished" board.

NEEDED   DONE

Cards are grouped into GREEN (newly added), YELLOW (getting stale), and RED (get it done!)

Figure 5.14: A generic flow diagram for an administrative "pull system" using a visual project board (referred to here as a "pull board") as its key element. Applications include request for quotations, customer inquiries, corrective-action requests, engineering change orders, drawings that need to be created or modified, and so on.

Time-Slicing and "Project Time"

Most of you are aware that the personal computer sitting on your desk is a multitasking machine. What might surprise you is that despite its ability to maintain multiple open windows and perform several tasks at once, your computer almost certainly has only a single microprocessor juggling all of these activities. How is it possible that a solitary chip, performing a serial stream of binary calculations, can do several things at once? The answer is that it doesn't. It does one job at a time, based on a priority list that has been generated by the operating system. By moving quickly from one task to another, however, it gives the *appearance* of performing many jobs simultaneously (this is often referred to as multiplexing). The amount of time that a microprocessor spends on each task is "sliced" based on priority, so that more important activities are allocated a greater percentage of any given time period. All jobs are active, but some may progress more slowly than others.

The application of *time-slicing* is not restricted to the realm of digital ones and zeros. The members of your product development team, for example, have something in common with microprocessors; they too are limited to performing one job at a time. Even someone with well-honed multitasking skills must focus on each individual task sequentially. When faced with many tasks, they simply multiplex amongst them, while doing their best to allocate the appropriate amount of time to each activity. Unfortunately, not everyone is adept at this time allocation process, resulting in a significant potential for waste, particularly if the relative priorities of various activities are not well-understood.

In this section, we will discuss several ways in which time-slicing can be used to reduce multitasking inefficiencies and to increase the flow of high-value work within a project team. All of these applications have been successfully implemented in real-world companies, and have survived the test of resistive cultures and deeply embedded inertia. They are not, however, as straightforward to implement as a stand-up meeting or a project board. In general, a relatively high degree of discipline is required to make time-slicing work effectively. If discipline is not your organization's strong suit, you may have to settle for some of the more basic improvement suggestions that I will provide. Those of you who are mates on a tight ship should consider the implementation of time-slicing a worthy challenge, with a substantial reward at the end.

A Time-Slicing Strategy for Capacity Allocation

Suppose that your family can only afford to own a single car. You and your spouse both work, and your teenage daughter has just received her driver's license. Moreover, your two younger children have signed up for every extracurricular activity imaginable, each of which requires roundtrip transportation across town. How would you make the best possible use of your poor, overworked automobile? If you were an expert in lean manufacturing, you might pull out your copy of *Quick Response Manufacturing*, by Rajan Suri, to see how he would apply time-slicing to handle this dilemma. Well, not *exactly* this dilemma, but a very similar one: the allocation of machine time in a mix-model manufacturing environment. Suri's first response to your car conundrum would likely be to recommend that you buy several small, inexpensive cars and share them among your various users. However, in factories, just like in families, this may not be practical. There are some types of capital equipment that are so costly, massive, or difficult to operate that owning a single machine may be the only realistic possibility. In this situation, the best alternative would be to carve up the available time on this equipment, based on the needs and priorities of the various product lines. For a family car, this would mean giving grandma's medical appointment a larger time slice than your daughter's burning desire for a mocha latte at Starbuck's.

Within the product development environment, people rather than machines represent the unique resource that must be efficiently allocated. If team members are active on multiple tasks, a time-slicing strategy would involve allocating varying percentages of their time, or even specific time blocks within their workday, to each activity. The relative percentage of time would be determined by the priority of the task; non-schedule-critical jobs would receive a much smaller time slice than critical-path activities. The general application and benefits of time-slicing in the context of new product development are shown in Figure 5.15. A specific timeslot within a team member's day might be allocated to project work that requires high concentration and intensive collaboration, while another might be dedicated to the handling of sustaining engineering tasks. Lower-priority work, such as the dispositioning of e-mails, might be given a small slice of time at the beginning and end of the workday. In some situations, the timeslots of several team members might be synchronized to improve communication efficiency (e.g., a fixed time during the day or week for meeting with the team's purchasing representative). The goal is not to treat professionals like machines, but rather to organize and synchronize their workflow so that the maximum output can be achieved in the shortest possible time.

Although the idea of regimented timeslots and militaristic workflow management may seem like the negative utopia of new product development, a small-scale application of time-slicing can be effective in even the most libertarian work environments. Time-slicing should be applied sparingly, and should be used as a solution to a problem, not as a broad and disempowering program. The applications described in the following subsections have been selected based on an eminently practical consideration: their worth has been proven multiple times in real-world situations. Consider these suggested applications as a starting point for your own innovative use of time-slicing during the execution of development projects.

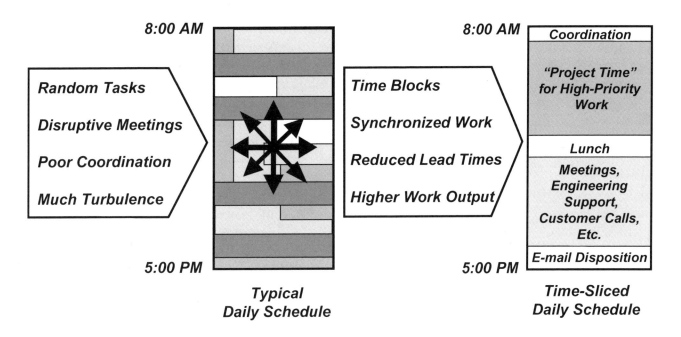

Figure 5.15: Time-slicing provides a straightforward way to allocate project resources to specific tasks in a multitasking environment, based on priority, urgency of completion, and long-term importance to the development effort. The primary benefit is reduced chaos and turbulence, resulting in an improved flow of value.

Application #1 – Multiply Productivity Through "Project Time"

I mentioned in Part 1 of this guidebook that a chaotic work environment is the greatest cause of wasted time within many firms. This is particularly true for product development teams, since their work often demands high levels of concentration for extended periods. The first application of time-slicing addresses this problem in a creative and pragmatic way. Rather than completely eliminating intrusive meetings, walk-in interruptions, e-mail alarms, and the endless choir of ringing cell phones, why not part the waters of chaos for just a few hours each day? Before I describe how establishing a dedicated "project time" can literally double your development team's work output, let me provide you with some insight into how the human mind reacts to constant interruptions.

A team of researchers recently performed a study of how the brain reacts to frequent interruptions while engaged in high-concentration work. A sample group of one-hundred typical office workers was given a series of challenging thought problems to solve (essentially an IQ test). In the first round of this experiment, the subjects were provided with a quiet work environment. Once the first round was completed, the same sample group was asked to return the following week and take a similar test, except that for this second session, the participants were constantly interrupted. They were expected to respond to e-mails and instant messages while taking the test, and were exposed to

205

unexpected walk-in interruptions by the researchers. After the second round of testing was completed, the researchers compared the test scores from both sessions. What they found sheds light on something that most of us have experienced many times: you are capable of far greater creativity and problem-solving acumen when you are not being continuously interrupted. In fact, the average test subject (temporarily) lost *ten IQ points* as a result of the chaotic testing environment. (For an overview of this experiment, see "Emerging technology: Is e-mail making you crazy," *Discover Magazine*, November Issue, 2005.) In a separate study, analysis of MRI scans from people engaged in high-concentration activities has shown that the human brain actually changes its mode of operation when exposed to invasive stimuli. A quiet environment encourages brain activity centered in the frontal lobes, where the highest levels of cognition take place. As soon as the brain senses turbulence and interruptions, a different, more primitive portion of the brain takes over. One could refer to these two distinct modes of thought as the "deep-think" mode and the "survival" mode.

So are your engineers and designers deep-thinking or just surviving? The problem of continuous interruptions is particularly acute in larger firms, where multitasking and interpersonal communication demands are the greatest. How can time-slicing alleviate this drain on creativity and productivity? Consider the following possibility: What if your organization were to adopt a policy that during the first two hours of each workday, no administrative meetings would be held, walk-in interruptions would be kept to a minimum (except in emergencies), and employees would be allowed to forward their phones to voice mail. Essentially, "library rules" would apply. Although this policy would be most beneficial to designers and engineers, there are few disciplines within a firm that would not embrace the chance to get some real work done. I call this focused work period "project time," and have seen this approach, or a variation thereof, successfully implemented in firms from virtually every industrial sector. Before discussing some possible variations (including several that don't require a dramatic shift in culture), I'll share an example.

A division of a large industrial conglomerate had developed a policy of "internal customer service," meaning that all employees were encouraged to make themselves available to anyone who needed assistance at any time. The goal was to break down barriers to communication, and to accelerate their business processes by ensuring that needed information would always be easily attainable. Over time, however, it became evident that this policy had backfired; employees who required periods of high-concentration were being bombarded by continuous interruptions, many of which were trivial or unnecessary. For example, design engineers were frequently being disturbed to provide product information that was readily available on-line, in the company's searchable literature. When combined with this organization's excessive meeting roster and a highly bureaucratic administration, new product development work had ground to a halt. Driven by desperation, this division adopted a strict policy of project time, as described in Figure 5.16. The first two hours of the workday were to be dedicated to project work, done either by individuals or small collaborative groups. The internal customer service policy was suspended during this period, except for a well-defined list of emergency situations (e.g., urgent support for the factory, a customer-related crisis, etc.). Functions not directly involved in product development were extended the same opportunity, except for those situations where it didn't make sense, such as for the sales and customer service teams.

In fact, to help remind people of project time, the organization purchased orange road cones that were handed out to all engineers and designers. Employees would place a road cone in the doorway of their cubicle to indicate that they were performing high-concentration work and should not be disturbed.

Without delving into the difficulties associated with the implementation of this policy (which will be discussed below), the results for this example firm were astonishing. Within weeks, project work was moving forward at an acceptable pace, and almost every participant acknowledged that the cause of this breakthrough was their ability to perform predictable, high-value work for at least a few hours each day. In fact, several months after adopting the two-hour time slice for project work, the organization decided to extend the project-time period to the entire morning for several key disciplines. Of course during the rest of the workday, the chaos returned and the interruptions were rampant. Yet the working environment within this division had fundamentally changed; employees were now able to get their assignments done during the normal workday, rather than consuming their nights and weekends.

If this aggressive implementation of project time seems beyond your organization's reach, several viable alternatives are listed in Figure 5.17. It is not essential, for example,

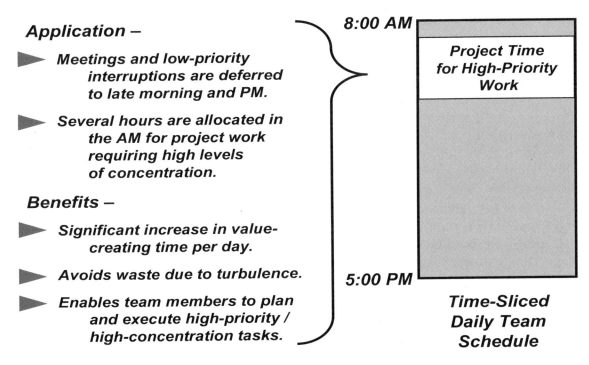

How to make time available for high-priority work:

Application –
- Meetings and low-priority interruptions are deferred to late morning and PM.
- Several hours are allocated in the AM for project work requiring high levels of concentration.

Benefits –
- Significant increase in value-creating time per day.
- Avoids waste due to turbulence.
- Enables team members to plan and execute high-priority / high-concentration tasks.

8:00 AM — Project Time for High-Priority Work — 5:00 PM

Time-Sliced Daily Team Schedule

Figure 5.16: One of the most powerful applications of time-slicing is the establishment of a dedicated period within each workday for development team members (and other employees) to perform high-concentration work. Both individual efforts and small-group collaborative activities are encouraged, but regularly scheduled meetings and low-priority interruptions would be delayed until after "project time" is over.

that everyone in your organization adheres to a synchronized project time. You could consider allowing each functional area to select their own project-time schedule, while maintaining several "core hours" during the middle of the day to allow for cross-functional meetings. One firm that I've worked with set up a "study area" within a block of unused office cubicles. These hideaways (which incidentally, did not have phones) were made available to any employee with a legitimate need. Time could be reserved in the study area in much the same way as one would reserve a conference room, with the caveat that the reservation be communicated to the requestor's managers. A similar idea has been used successfully in the software industry; programmers are allowed to work at home for a set of predetermined hours during the week. This approach has demonstrated dramatic productivity benefits. In one case, a software engineering firm reported that employees who worked at home were roughly three times as productive during these off-site periods. This work-at-home concept could be highly effective in alleviating schedule crunches on any type of project; individuals who are working on critical-path tasks could be allowed to work at home for well-defined periods until their tasks are complete. As a last resort, and assuming that your firm is just not up to the challenge of implementing any of the above variations, you could simply encourage your project team members to "call meetings with themselves" several times per week. For example, you might suggest that key designers block out two hours every other day for their own high-concentration work. These blocks would show up in Microsoft Outlook (or whatever scheduling tool you use) as a meeting, the priority of which would depend on the criticality of the task involved. Sure, it is likely that these self-meetings will be violated occasionally, but even a few blocks of dedicated project time can yield significant benefits.

Although most employees immediately recognize the benefits of project time, experience has shown that there are several obstacles that must be addressed to grease the skids for this lean method, as shown in Figure 5.18. The underlying motivation for project time is to free up quality time for engineers and designers, but from a political (and arguably, a fairness) standpoint, other disciplines should be included as well. It is easy for resentment to ferment when one set of employees is treated as though they are special. Offer project time to any discipline that can legitimately benefit from its implementation. Next, I suggest not jumping immediately to a policy statement and broad deployment, but rather to take a measured approach. Hold a group meeting that includes representatives from all affected disciplines and ask for collective feedback on how implementation should proceed. Then select a "showcase" group or project team to serve as pathfinders for the rest of the organization. Give this pilot effort a few months and then reconvene the initial steering group for a status update. Modify your approach as necessary and then move to a larger-scale deployment. Finally, it is essential that there be agreed-upon rules for project time. In particular, a list of acceptable "emergencies" should be created collaboratively by a multidisciplinary group within your firm. Everyone thinks that their needs are emergencies, but only a small fraction of these potential interruptions are so urgent that they cannot wait a couple of hours until project time is over.

If your design teams find themselves with precious few hours of "quiet time" within the workday, some variation on the project-time theme may be the most direct way for your firm to increase project capacity and accelerate time-to-market. Implementation can be

Some Project-Time implementation ideas:

 Establish a block of time each day that your team sets aside for focused project work, say 8:00 – 10:00 AM.

 Create a "study area" at your facility that can be reserved by workers who require short periods of high concentration.

 Consider a structured program that allows team members to work at home during periods in which they are on the critical path.

 Issue a "project-time guideline" to all employees that defines the timing and duration of project time, and rules for what constitutes an emergency.

 Use a "red flag" or other creative method for communicating when team members are engaged in high-concentration work.

 If a formalized project time is not practical, consider recommending to team members that they "call a meeting with themselves" for a few hours each day.

Figure 5.17: A number of ways to implement the concept of project time are shown above, each of which has been deployed successfully within one or more companies. The key consideration should be to match your project-time approach to the culture, discipline level, and management philosophy of your firm.

challenging, to be sure, but the discipline that you will develop will aid your organization in the integration of other, more-advanced lean methods in the future.

Application #2 – Managing Resources in a Multitasking Environment

Although project time is perhaps the most dramatic application of time-slicing, it is the managing of shared resources that brings out the best in this lean method. Possibilities include the sharing of extended team members among multiple projects, the sharing of capital equipment, and even the sharing of an individual team member's time among several project tasks. Whenever multitasking is required, time-slicing provides a means to ensure that all work gets done, and that the most important tasks get done first. Let's go through (in reverse order) an example for each of these three modes of use.

You are a core team member with a problem: too many critical activities on your plate. In addition to your primary responsibility, the designing of an innovative new widget, you have also been asked to generate a prototype test plan, and coordinate the certification of the new product by the regulatory powers-that-be. If this were not enough, your functional manager insists that you make progress on his pet R&D project. What would be the best way to allocate your time? Your first step should be to determine the relative priorities of your tasks, using either the must / should / could approach (see

Overcoming Obstacles to Project Time

Figure 5.18: One of the greatest obstacles to the implementation of project time is a failure to engage employees in the planning and deployment process. A combination of good communication and continuous feedback from impacted employees will give you the highest probability of success.

Section 4.2) or any other means that gives you a rank-ordering. In principle, all you need to do now is work on each task in sequence until your list of assignments is complete. Unfortunately, this just isn't practical in your situation, since all of these jobs require some level of attention on a daily basis.

Well, it's time-slicing to the rescue. Based on the priorities generated above, you could carve up your workday into segments. For example, you could allocate mornings to widget design, a few hours after lunch to working on the test plan, and the last portion of your day to handling regulatory issues. These timeslots would flex somewhat from day to day, but in general you would try to keep the ratio of allocated time roughly constant. If priorities change (e.g., you hit a regulatory stumbling block) you might temporarily shift your time allocations to focus on the more urgent situation. If you've allocated your time slices properly, you will have arrived at the best compromise from a project-schedule standpoint. Ah, but what about that pesky R&D project that never seems to have enough priority to warrant your attention? You could carve out a small time slice, say a few hours each week, to move this effort forward. Although only incremental progress will be made in the short term, in the fullness of time even this low-urgency effort will reach completion.

It is easy to see how this same approach could be extended to the sharing of laboratory equipment, rapid-prototyping systems, environmental chambers; really any resource that is in short supply. A "reservation system" can be established for any scarce asset so that all potential users can be serviced in an organized way. The amount of time allocated to each user would depend on the priority of their project, but all would be given at least a small amount of available capacity. A good example of a reservation system is the way in which time is allocated on the Hubble Space Telescope. Scientists from around the world covet time on this incredible machine, and yet only a single user can be served at a time. To address this problem, the Space Telescope Science Institute has set up a time-sliced schedule that extends far into the foreseeable future. A committee reviews requests for time on the telescope, and based on their scientific priority, time blocks are allocated. In some cases, a month of continuous observation might be granted, while minor projects may only be allocated a single night per year. In this way, a broad scientific agenda can be serviced by this unique instrument, rather than just a few high-visibility studies.

A final resource allocation issue that can be resolved through time-slicing is the sharing of extended team members among multiple projects. Not surprisingly, the solution to overworked and overloaded support functions is a form of reservation system, as shown in Figure 5.19. A real-world example will demonstrate how successful this approach can be. There is a small company in the Midwest that produces farm implements. Over a period of several years they had committed most of their product development resources to designing an entirely new suite of products, with a massive launch campaign scheduled for the next six months. Just as these designs were approaching commercialization, however, disaster struck. At the beginning of this major development effort, the firm had six full-time purchasing specialists supporting the various design teams. As the launch date approached, four out of the six buyers announced that they were leaving the company. Two of these employees were quitting due to burnout; the demands on their time had been so chaotic and stressful that they had found employment elsewhere. A third buyer left to go back to college, and a fourth exited due to the pending birth of a child. With only two purchasing people remaining, the massive new product launch seemed to be a virtual impossibility, and the company found itself in severe financial jeopardy.

The solution was, of course, to time slice the workdays of the remaining two buyers (something which, had it been done earlier, would likely have averted the loss of the two disgruntled employees). Each buyer was assigned several projects, along with the relative priorities that they should follow. The buyers then established set timeslots within the workweek for each project. During these dedicated periods, they were available to support the designated team, and only that team. Other projects were asked to wait for their timeslots unless an emergency situation occurred. In this way, the buyers avoided constant turbulence, were able to focus on one bill-of-materials at a time, and could complete significant blocks of work without interruption. The result was that all new products were launched on schedule. Moreover, after the dust had settled, the firm decided not to re-staff the purchasing group; with the aid of time-slicing, *two buyers were now capable of doing the work of six.*

How to efficiently manage shared resources:

Application –

▶ **Applies to resources that must be shared among multiple projects or teams.**

▶ **Make reservations for slices of time allocated to each project (e.g. "A" and "B" at right) on a priority basis.**

Benefits –

▶ **Ensures that highest priority projects receive prompt service.**

▶ **Avoids waste due to turbulence.**

▶ **Allows optimal utilization of a potential resource "bottleneck".**

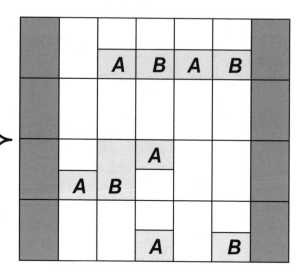

**Time-Sliced
Monthly Schedule**

Figure 5.19: Time-slicing can be effective as a means to reserve and allocate resources that are shared among several project teams (e.g., purchasing, drafting, quality assurance, and so on). By establishing prioritized timeslots for each shared resource, lead times can be reduced and chaotic multitasking can be avoided.

Application #3 – Balancing Sustaining Support and Project Work

Here is an interesting wrinkle on the shared-resource problem. It is one thing to set priorities within a project team, or even among multiple projects. But how can we protect team members' time from the undeniable demands of factory sustaining support? There can be no denying that if the production line is stopped, there is nothing more important than getting it moving again. Yet sustaining support can be the cause of considerable turbulence within a design group, with engineers being torn between their "deep-think" design work and fighting fires on the factory floor. There is at least one solution that I've seen work effectively: I call it a "filtering system," but it is really just another application of time-slicing.

Shortly before I left the corporate world to start my own business, I was offered an "opportunity" to manage an impossible project (the kind of project that's assigned to someone who has nothing to lose). The U.S. government had discovered a large sum of uncommitted funds that could be applied to developing a new infrared sensor prototype. The funds were more than adequate to accomplish this goal, but the money would disappear at the end of the fiscal year...only two months away. It normally would take at least twelve months to design such an advanced prototype, so the timeframe allowed for this project was comical. Yet both my management and the government were adamant that a best effort be made.

I agreed to manage the project under one condition: that I be allowed to direct the project team in any way that I wished – literally full and complete control. With this condition granted, I proceeded to move the entire team into a suite of offices that were designed for highly classified projects. This type of office arrangement is fairly common within the military contractor world, and all share a distinguishing feature; there is a combination lock on the only entry door to the office suite. Once the move was complete, I informed my management that any request for a team member's time would have to go through me first. Likewise, I admonished my team members to notify me if they were asked to do anything other than the project tasks they were assigned. In a sense, I volunteered to serve as a filter for my team. Occasionally, a request would be made that was so compelling that I was forced to release a team member for a brief period. Often, however, I would handle requests myself to protect my team from interruptions. By the way, only team members were given the combination to the lock on the office door.

I wouldn't have shared this example with you if the outcome had been a professional embarrassment, and in fact the results were a shock even to the team. A combination of enthusiasm, dedication, and protection from interruptions allowed this team to produce one of the best infrared-imager prototypes ever created by Hughes Aircraft Company, in literally one-sixth of the typical time. Although your projects may not warrant such draconian measures, the idea of assigning a filter to protect team members from interruptions can be highly beneficial. Suppose you were to assign an engineer to be the "on-call" person for factory support (or customer / sales support for that matter), as shown in Figure 5.20. During agreed-upon periods throughout the week, that engineer would be asked to handle as many requests for sustaining support as they could, before asking for help from other members of the engineering staff. Clearly not all problems could be solved by this individual alone, but many of the nuisance interruptions and minor issues could be readily dealt with. At the end of the week, a new engineer would be given the on-call role, with all members of the engineering staff being assigned this job on a rotating basis. Not only would this approach provide some level of protection from disruption, but it would also serve as an excellent training ground for the engineering staff. It is amazing how much engineers will learn about the products they design if they spend even a few days living with the problems their designs precipitate in the factory.

Application #4 – Making Time for "Important but Not Urgent"

In the discussion of Application #2, I mentioned an R&D task that never seemed to get the attention it deserved. There are typically a number of "strategic initiatives" within a company that have high importance, but essentially zero urgency. Training your employees in new tools and methods, for example, could generate significant gains for your firm, but tearing them away from their ponderous workloads would be highly inconvenient

How to handle sustaining factory / customer support:

Application –

▶ *Establish time-sliced schedule for engineering resources to be available "on-call" for factory or customer support.*

▶ *All other "emergency" needs are handled by a rotating "on-call" individual.*

Benefits –

▶ *Provides prompt support without disruptive turbulence.*

▶ *Enables team members to plan their work around "on-call" time slices.*

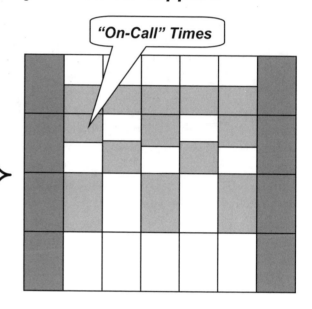

"On-Call" Times

Time-Sliced Monthly Schedule

Figure 5.20: Yet another example of how time-slicing can reduce or eliminate waste within the development process. Often core team resources are torn between their project work and critical sustaining activities. By designating a rotating "on-call" individual to handle most sustaining-support interruptions, the remainder of the team is freed to focus on their project tasks.

in the short term. Likewise, multi-year research projects tend to be shoved aside by even the most petty (but urgent) activities. Paramount on the list of things that get back-burnered are improvement initiatives, since most people seem to prefer hunkering down and doing it the old way rather than taking the time to apply something new. Steven Covey tells the well-worn tale of a man in the woods sawing firewood. It's been awhile since he last used his saw, and it has become rusty and dull. Yet even upon realizing that the tool was none too sharp, he still hacks away, making up for dullness with brute force. The irony of this fable, and of human nature in general, is that by taking just a few minutes to sharpen his saw, the job could have been completed in a fraction of the time.

Time-slicing provides an answer to this common problem. Although improvement initiatives and other strategic projects may never rise to the priority of short-term project work, they can still be allocated a small-but-finite slice of time each week or month to enable some degree of forward progress. You might consider, for example, setting aside the afternoon on Fridays as a time slice dedicated to process improvement or R&D project work, as shown in Figure 5.21. Hold a stand-up meeting at the start of these timeslots to quickly reset your team (assuming a team is involved) and set up an action plan for the remaining time within the slot. In this way, improvement initiatives and other important strategic activities can keep moving forward "in the background" while causing only a minor disruption to critical project work.

I once read an interview with a man who had become world famous as an art dealer and antiquarian. His personal fortune had risen above the billion-dollar mark, and his influence was felt in every corner of the art world. The interviewer suggested that this gentleman must possess some innate genius for picking great new artists and identifying incredibly rare antiques. The art dealer responded, "That is completely untrue. I was a *terrible* art critic in my youth, and picked more fakes than treasures when it came to antiques. *I've just gotten a little better at it every day.*" By setting aside small but consistent time slices for process improvements, research projects, and employee training, your firm will get a little better every day as well.

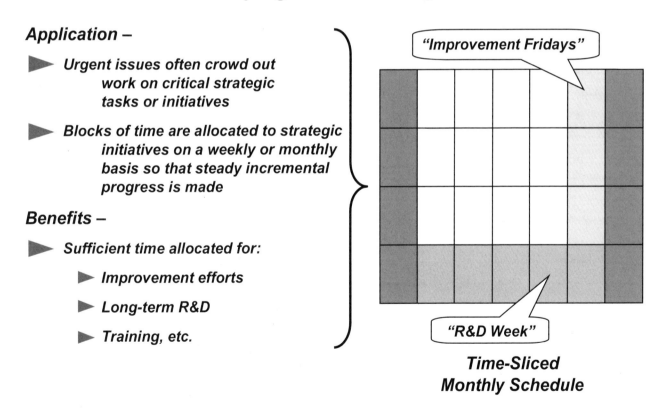

How to ensure progress on "Strategic Initiatives":

Application –

▶ **Urgent issues often crowd out work on critical strategic tasks or initiatives**

▶ **Blocks of time are allocated to strategic initiatives on a weekly or monthly basis so that steady incremental progress is made**

Benefits –

▶ **Sufficient time allocated for:**

　▶ **Improvement efforts**

　▶ **Long-term R&D**

　▶ **Training, etc.**

"Improvement Fridays"

"R&D Week"

Time-Sliced Monthly Schedule

Figure 5.21: A final application of time-slicing addresses a common problem in any business; having difficulty making progress on long-term strategic initiatives due to the pressures of short-term, urgent tasks. By slicing a time period each week or month for strategic work (e.g., improvement projects, long-term R&D studies, etc.), your organization will make assured (albeit slow) progress.

Notes

Lean Scheduling
and Value Milestones

From a project execution standpoint, scheduling is the eight-hundred pound gorilla. No product development effort can approach optimal time-to-market without first building and maintaining a valid schedule, yet the level of competency that I've observed in this critical discipline is spotty at best. At one end of the spectrum are firms that essentially ignore scheduling; management establishes an arbitrary launch date for a new product and expects their organization to dutifully respond. Not surprisingly, these managers are almost always disappointed. In stark contrast are those companies that have embraced full-blown project management, to the point of demanding obsessively detailed schedules and the calculation of complex "performance indices". The managers of these firms are also frequently disappointed, but for different reasons. Scheduling, as with any other aspect of product development, is susceptible to both overshoot and undershoot, resulting in waste at either extreme.

In this section, I'll describe a lean scheduling methodology that will provide your teams with all of the visibility and control they require, without the excessive formality and overhead that often accompanies it. A project schedule should serve as a useful roadmap for a development team, not a sinkhole for their time. The key is to incorporate the right amount of detail, the appropriate level of flexibility, and most important, a heaping helping of reality. The lean method that I propose is well-aligned with the *Project Management Body of Knowledge* (PMBOK – visit www.pmi.org for more information), but with a pragmatic and time-sensitive twist. If your firm performs major contract work, such as building dams or designing jet fighters, then set up your project management office, fire up Primavera, and go to town. For the vast majority of development projects, however, an informal schedule, some objective value milestones, and an efficient means of updating status is all that is needed to ensure a timely product launch.

Focus Attention and Resources on the "Critical Core"

One of the most fundamental concepts in project scheduling is the notion that tasks within a project can, and almost always do, depend upon each other. Let's build a house together to illustrate this point. We'll skip the design phase, and go directly to pouring our foundation. The footings have been trenched, and the concrete trucks are lining up to begin dumping their loads. If we were to start filling the trenches at this point, however, we would be in deep trouble (pardon the pun). Have the plumbers been on site yet to install the sewer and water mains? Has the underground electrical been routed? What about gas lines, cable TV, and phone connections? Each of these tasks must be completed before the foundation can be poured, so we could say that the concrete work *depends* on these other activities.

If we wanted to build our house in the shortest possible time, we would analyze all these dependencies and determine how we could best accommodate them. Any task that could be performed in parallel would be so scheduled, while some activities would have to wait until other work was finished. Once we've arrived at the shortest possible timeframe for project completion, we would find that there is a series of tasks that line up like little soldiers, each depending on the one before it, with no "slack time" in between. This is the critical path of our homebuilding project. If any of these critical-path tasks are delayed, even for a day, it will adversely affect our move-in date (as well as our sanity). Hence, it seems logical that we should focus most of our attention on ensuring that nothing delays the critical path.

Indeed, there is a whole school of project management thinking, referred to as critical-path management (CPM), that recommends exactly this strategy. As I've previously mentioned, I agree with the concept of prioritizing critical-path tasks. There is, however, a hidden trap in this naïve way of thinking. For a simple project, such as cooking a meal for example, the critical path is usually fairly obvious. However, as the complexity of an endeavor increases, the dependencies become intertwined, to the point of requiring sophisticated software tools to devine the precise critical path. In our homebuilding example, we noted that quite a bit of "groundwork" had to be completed before the foundation could be poured. What I didn't mention was that even these initial activities have their own dependencies: sewer lines must generally go in first, followed by plumbing, then electrical, phone, cable, etc. To demonstrate how much skill can be involved in critical-path management, consider that a typical home-construction project takes between six and twelve months. Recently, an association of builders in the San Diego area was able to construct a complete house, including landscaping and finish work, *in two hours*. I won't go into the details (fascinating as they are), but suffice to say that it took months of incredibly detailed planning, and a team of hundreds of tradespeople, to accomplish this feat.

Should your development teams spend months planning their efforts, hoping that once this magical schedule was created, the product could be launched in a couple of days? Of course not. Even in the well-defined world of construction, the costs associated with this kind of obsessive critical-path scheduling would be prohibitive, not to mention logistically impractical. Moreover, every product development project has risks and uncertainties. It would be impossible to predict every nuance of task dependency and duration in advance. In fact, this leads us to the trap that many critical-path managers fall into, as shown in Figure 5.22. In an ideal world, there would be an orderly string of tasks that constitute the critical path. As the complexity and uncertainty of a project increases, however, dependencies blur and the durations of activities begin to vary. If you were to spend an inordinate amount of time obsessing over critical-path scheduling, you would find that much of that time (not to mention your team's time) would be wasted, since the critical path will be constantly changing. I've found that it is far more effective to blur your schedule-thinking somewhat on projects involving substantial risk and uncertainty.

The Traditional Critical Path (a Nice Ideal) –

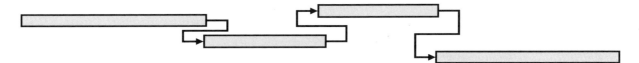

▶ **Single serial pathway that determines duration of project.**

▶ **A slip along the critical path causes a slip to the project's end date.**

The "Critical Core" (a Reality on Most Projects) –

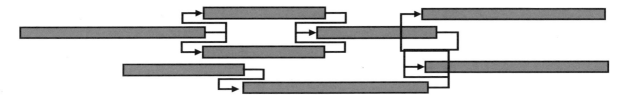

▶ **Multiple pathways, each of which MIGHT determine the duration of the project.**

▶ **Which pathway drives schedule is determined by resource constraints and other risk factors.**

Figure 5.22: The critical path of a project represents the theoretical shortest duration, based on the current plan. This is a nice ideal, but the reality is that there are typically a number of additional activities within a project that, although not on the critical path, are still schedule-critical. This broader group of tasks is referred to as the "critical core".

Rather than looking for a single critical path, it is more practical from a team management perspective to focus on what I call the "critical core".

The critical core is the set of tasks on a project that has a high potential to drive schedule. It includes the traditional critical path, along with other tasks that have high levels of dependency (i.e., many activities depend on it), or that have significant potential to drive schedule. A subtractive approach works nicely here: Any task that can move about within the project schedule without significant impact on the product's launch date is not included within the critical core. If a task must be accomplished at a set time, or in a set order, then it should be central to your scheduling efforts. I am not suggesting that non-critical-core tasks should be neglected, but the focus of the team leader and the priority of the development team must be directed toward critical-core tasks at all times, as shown in Figure 5.23.

Fortunately, the scheduling skills required to identify and manage the critical core is within the reach of any competent team leader. Even a cursory understanding of this

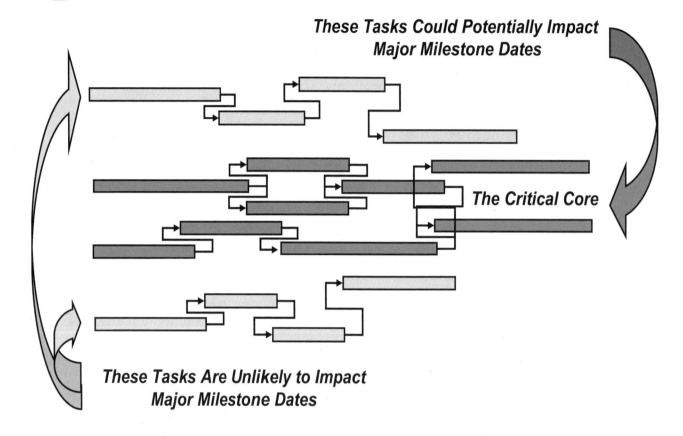

These Tasks Could Potentially Impact Major Milestone Dates

The Critical Core

These Tasks Are Unlikely to Impact Major Milestone Dates

Figure 5.23: From a schedule standpoint, the focus of a project team leader should be on ensuring that critical-core tasks are given the resources and attention they need to be completed on time.

concept will allow your team to achieve reasonable development cycle-times. As your experience grows, more sophisticated planning will become possible, and your ability to reduce a project's duration will increase. It still wouldn't make sense to spend excessive time and energy on detailed scheduling, since risks and uncertainties render this level of attention all but useless. Abandon all hope of a "two-hour project," but through careful attention to the critical core, your teams will have the potential to achieve dramatic reductions in time-to-market.

A Three-Tier Approach to Lean Scheduling

How much detail should a project schedule include? On the one hand, a highly detailed schedule provides team members with clear direction and allows them to better understand the complex interactions among tasks. Alternatively, one could argue that most of the time spent generating such a schedule would be wasted, since after the first month or two of a typical development project, the original schedule isn't worth the paper it is written on. Is this a justification for neglecting detail in favor of a 40,000 foot view? The three-tier approach to project scheduling that I propose solves this dilemma in a highly efficient way.

At the beginning of a project, the team leader would collaborate with her team to generate a high-level master schedule. A master schedule covers the entire projected duration of a development effort, but only includes the critical-core tasks and major milestones. Often several related tasks are lumped together into "work packages" that are represented by a single bar on a Gantt chart, with a single completion milestone at the end. The master schedule provides enough information to track progress at the executive level, and gives the team a picture of the overall project from start to finish. This is what I refer to as "Tier 1" of the three-tier approach illustrated in Figure 5.24.

At this point, traditional project management dogma would recommend that a more detailed schedule be generated that captures all of the intricacies and dependencies. Indeed, this is the next step in my process as well...but with an important difference. Once the master schedule has been agreed upon, the development team would be asked to provide the next level of planning detail for any work package that is scheduled to begin during the first three months of the project. The remainder of the schedule is left at the high-level planning stage. At the beginning of each month during the project's execution, the team will again be asked to look ahead three months and provide details on any work package that is scheduled to start within that period. This "rolling-window" schedule represents "Tier 2" of the three-tier methodology. The advantages of rolling-window

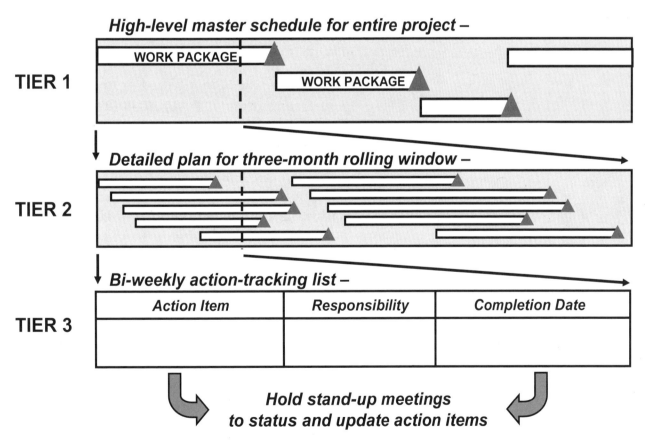

Figure 5.24: The "three-tier" approach to project scheduling minimizes wasted time on excessive planning detail, and provides a straightforward way to track and update the project plan.

planning are significant. The team gains all of the benefits of a detailed roadmap in the short term, while not wasting time and effort trying to see many months ahead into an uncertain future. Certainly there are some types of activities that may require many months of advanced planning (e.g., setting up complex test equipment for prototype evaluation), but in most cases, a three-month rolling window provides all the detail a team will need.

Even within this relatively short time-window there are limits as to how deep the Tier 2 schedule should go. I recommend using an "eighty-hour" rule, meaning that team members who are responsible for near-term tasks provide a measurable progress milestone on roughly two-week intervals. For example, a team member who is responsible for a work package with an eight-week total duration might identify four or five intermediate milestones that would be included in the Tier 2 plan. Obviously, these milestones don't have to occur at exactly two-week intervals, but this general rule ensures enough granularity to accurately track progress, without wasting time on excessive planning. Whenever possible, this informal milestone-setting exercise should be kept within the team, without the involvement of upper management.

This leads us to "Tier 3," which you are already acquainted with from our discussion of visual project boards in Section 5.3. The simplest way to track progress on a development project is to use stand-up coordination meetings as a forum for status updates, rather than expecting the team to mark up Gantt charts on a weekly basis. To accomplish this, a project team leader would create a two-week action tracking list, based on the milestones that appear on the Tier 2 schedule. Each Monday, the leader would look ahead two weeks on the schedule and capture any milestones occurring within that period on the action tracking list. As the week progresses, the responsible team members would be asked to provide the status of their milestones during their ten-minute stand-up meetings. At the beginning of the following week, any completed milestones would be so noted on the tracking list, and the two-week window would be rolled forward one week to capture new milestones. I like to use an Excel spreadsheet to create this two-week tracking list, so that as the project progresses, I can maintain a continuous record of milestones achieved and their completion dates. Although the spreadsheet retains the entire history of the project, I print out only the portion that displays the forthcoming two weeks.

A few comments regarding the implementation of three-tier scheduling are worth mentioning before we move on. First, the work packages represented on the Tier 1 master schedule can be gleaned directly from the deliverables roadmap that we discussed in Section 3.2. Each deliverable represents a neatly defined work package; all that must be added is a duration and it becomes a line on the master schedule. Again, it makes sense in some cases to group together a set of related minor deliverables into one work package for the high-level plan, and then decompose this package into its constituent parts for the more detailed Tier 2 plan. Second, I suggest using the Tier 1 plan as your "advertised" schedule for the development project. This high-level view is all that should be needed to inform upper management. In fact, showing too much detail can be confusing to executives and may encourage unnecessary micromanagement. If the project gets into trouble, the executives would be justified in asking for a Tier 2 perspective, but while the project is on track, major milestones should be adequate. Finally, you may be skeptical as to the effectiveness of rolling-window planning. Can this really work on complex, large-scale development projects? Let me assure you that this method actually works. In fact, my first exposure to this approach came from training that I received through the U.S. Department of Defense. The rolling-window planning concept is standard procedure on many defense projects. Why would the military ask for *less* detail in their long-term schedules? Because they (rightly) recognized that they were paying for unnecessary planning exercises that became obsolete almost overnight. If the Pentagon is not willing to pay for excessive planning detail, why should your firm?

Track Real Progress Using Value Milestones

At the core of any effective scheduling approach are the milestones that are used to track progress. A milestone represents both a point in time and a measure of value achieved. Measuring time is the easy part; determining the amount of value achieved can be considerably more difficult. Some major milestones such as design reviews are unambiguous, but how can we objectively measure progress for the other activities that constitute new product development? The most common approach is to estimate the "percent complete" of a project task. For example, a team member might be responsible for a task with a total planned duration of eight weeks. We could attempt to track this individual's progress by periodically asking him what percent of the work within his task has been completed. Actually, we don't even need to ask the question; after four weeks, it's likely that this worker would report that his task is fifty percent complete, after six weeks, seventy-five percent complete, and so on. These responses are not based on the amount of value that was created, but rather on the amount of time that has passed. The trouble with tracking progress using percent complete is what happens as the eighth week approaches. Suddenly the team member finds himself out of time, but in many cases, not out of work. There is a famous quip in project management circles that goes, "It's not the first ninety percent of a task that will kill you, it's the second ninety percent."

The challenge of effectively tracking progress on a project can be solved through the use of *objective and measurable* value milestones. In fact, an entire system for progress measurement has been developed around what is referred to as Earned-Value Management. To measure earned value, we must first identify milestones that are unambiguous measures of progress; actual accomplishments that represent substantial work. Some examples of such milestones are provided in Figure 5.25. The creation of a document, for example, could be divided into incremental milestones such as the completion of an outline, the distribution of a draft document for review, the incorporation of recommended changes, and the final release of the document. Each of these milestones can be objectively verified, and each represents a tangible amount of actual work that has been performed. If the team member who is creating this document is behind schedule in completing the initial outline milestone, both the worker and the team leader will know that the overall schedule for that task is in jeopardy. This early warning can be extremely important, since there would still be time remaining to take corrective action. Perhaps the team member is being distracted by other, lower-priority assignments. Alternatively, the slipped milestone might indicate that more resources will be needed to accomplish the task on schedule. In any case, knowing the objective status of completed work at intermediate points within a task can save a project from unrecoverable delays.

Examples of Measurable Value Milestones

▲ **Document outline complete**
▲ **Document out for review**
▲ **Document released**

▲ **Design simulation complete**
▲ **Prototype fabrication complete**
▲ **Prototype testing complete**
▲ **Prototype test results accepted**

▲ **Software modules defined**
▲ **Software flow diagrams complete**
▲ **Software coding complete**
▲ **Software code-check complete**
▲ **Software testing complete**
▲ **Software released**

Figure 5.25: Value milestones should never be based on a percent-complete estimate. They must always be objective, measurable (i.e., verifiable), and of sufficient granularity to provide both the team members and the team leader with adequate visibility into schedule status.

To illustrate how powerful the earned-value system can be in managing project schedules, consider the following real-world example. A public utility in a major metropolitan area was given the opportunity to build a large power substation for a local oil refinery. This type of privately funded construction job represented a significant source of revenue for the utility, and this contract was a major opportunity. The only drawback was that there was only one day in the year during which the new substation could be brought on-line without disrupting the oil refinery's operations. Hence, the contract mandated that the substation be ready to go live on that very specific day; any delay beyond that point would result in a substantial financial penalty. This penalty clause caused a great deal of trepidation on the part of the utility's management, since their history had shown that the timely completion of projects was not their forte. After a great deal of discussion, they decided to sign the contract, with the understanding that the team leader for this project would use some new management tools to ensure success.

The first "new tool" was the use of earned-value milestones, as shown in Figure 5.26. The team leader worked with the construction crew to identify objective value milestones, and to determine the estimated time required to achieve them. (Note that I have greatly simplified this example for clarity.) Once this list of milestones was identified, a Tier 1 master schedule was created, and due to the short duration of the project, a more detailed Tier 2 plan was simultaneously generated for the entire effort. As the construction work progressed, the actual completion dates of the intermediate milestones were carefully tracked and compared to the planned completion dates, as shown in Figure 5.27. This tracking system allowed the team leader to determine the "schedule variance" at any point during the project. If the schedule variance was positive, it meant that the project was ahead of schedule, as was the case for the second milestone shown in the figure. A negative schedule variance indicated that the project had slipped schedule, and the final completion date was at risk.

As you can see in the figure, after a good start, the project began to lag behind schedule by a few weeks, and despite the team's best efforts, this slip could never be completely recovered. Fortunately, the team leader had employed a second new project management tool that ensured a successful outcome, and avoided a painful penalty. During the initial planning of the project, the team agreed to insert a "risk buffer" at the end of the effort to serve as a shock absorber for any unexpected delays. This two-week buffer literally saved the project. As it turned out, the team completed construction with a few days to spare, and what would have been a disaster became a shining success.

The concept of a risk buffer is derived from another school of project management thinking that is referred to as Critical-Chain Project Management. I will grant you that the use of this type of buffer is not always successful. If the team knows that it exists, they may simply ignore their intermediate milestones, assuming that the buffer is theirs for the

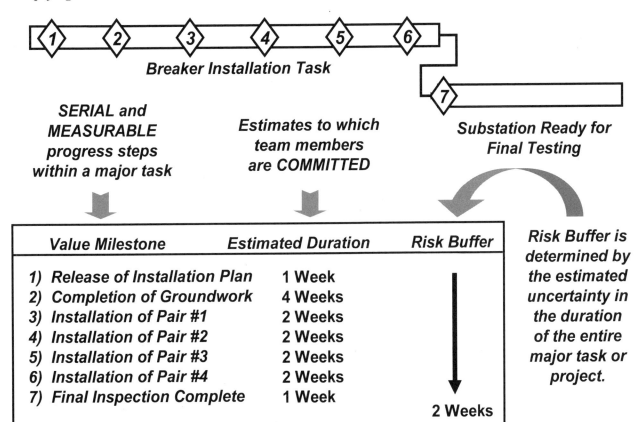

Figure 5.26: A real-world application of earned-value milestones and project risk-buffering. In this example, a public utility is under contract to install a new power substation for an oil refinery.

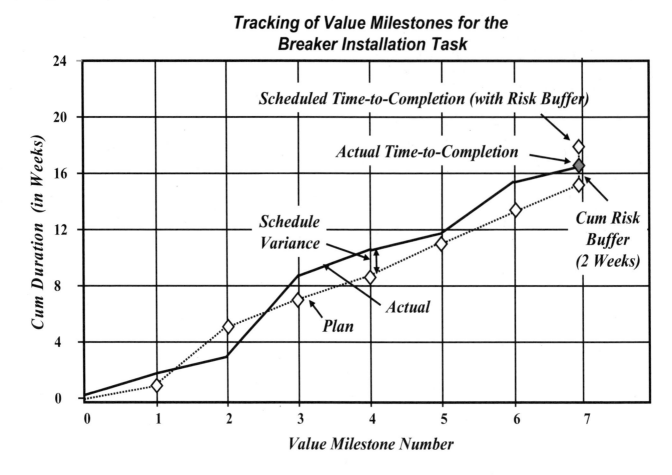

Figure 5.27: A continuation of the power substation example. The diagram above provides clear visibility into the current schedule status of a project, the variance between planned and actual progress, and the estimated time-to-completion. Note that a two-week risk buffer was added during the final stages of the effort to protect the project from unexpected delays.

taking. Likewise, it is possible that management will view the buffer as "slack time" that can be eliminated to permit an earlier completion date. That being said, if both the team and management understand the negative consequences of ignoring the buffer, this type of shock absorber can help guarantee the timely completion of a project.

One final note regarding both Earned-Value Management and Critical-Chain Project Management. Both of these methodologies are far more complex and sophisticated than I have implied in this example. If the reader is interested in learning more about these topics, there are a number of excellent books available. For the average product development project, however, a very basic application can yield significant benefits. I've observed varying degrees of success with the use of risk buffers on product development projects, but the tracking of objective earned-value milestones has been an unambiguous positive for every project that has implemented them. So stop fooling yourself with percent complete and start tracking the *real* creation of value.

Putting it All Together – Lean Scheduling in Ten Minutes Per Day

We now have all of the pieces necessary to manage a product development project in ten minutes per day. The earned-value milestones discussed above are, of course, the same detailed milestones used in the Tier 2 schedule previously described. These milestones become the items captured on the Tier 3 action tracking list, which can then be easily displayed on a visual project board. Updating these value milestones can be accomplished during a project team's stand-up coordination meetings. In this way, the loop is closed: lean scheduling, brief stand-up coordination meetings, and a visual project board represent an integrated system for highly efficient management of a development project, as shown in Figure 5.28. There is certainly more that a team leader can do to analyze the progress of a project, but in most cases, this basic system is all that is needed to ensure timely project completion and provide ample visibility. Remember that project management is an enabler; a tax on the time and resources of a project. As essential as this function may be, there is certainly no reason to spend more time on it than is necessary. If your projects warrant additional management overhead, there is much more that can be done. In most situations, however, the approaches described above will yield successful outcomes in a fraction of the time.

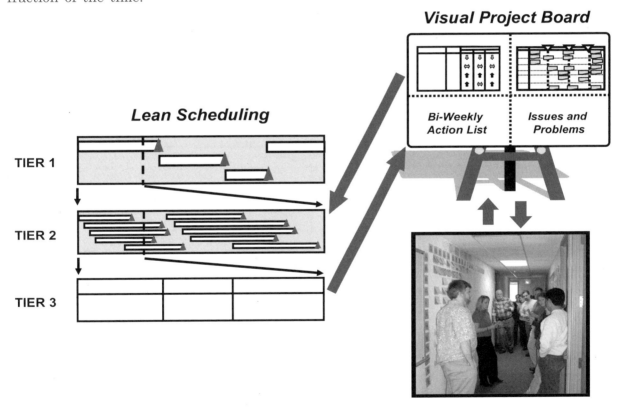

Figure 5.28: By combining lean scheduling, earned-value milestones, a visual project board, and stand-up coordination meetings, a project team can achieve high levels of schedule control and visibility with a minimal commitment of time.

Notes

E-mail Rules, Lean Meetings, and Other Time-Savers

When it comes to freeing up valuable resources and accelerating development projects, time saved is time saved. I say this because some of my readers may feel that improving the use of e-mail, for example, or the way that meetings are run, is not sophisticated enough to warrant serious attention. The time studies that I have performed in a wide range of firms have shown that, on average, *over half of a project team member's workday* is spent dispositioning e-mails, attending meetings, or engaging in other forms of communication or correspondence. The fact is that although it might seem mundane from a theoretical standpoint, implementing a few simple time-saving techniques can eliminate as much waste as any of the other lean methods described in this guidebook. Consider them a guilty pleasure; quick ways to see measurable improvement in a matter of days rather than months.

The Art of the Lean Deliverable

As I mentioned in Section 3.2, when it comes to development work, all value is embodied in the essential deliverables required to commercialize a new product. Hence, it is logical to begin our quest for quick-hit time savings by scrutinizing the way in which deliverables are created. The potential for waste in this regard became crystal clear to me while working with a high-technology electronics firm in Silicon Valley. Unlike many progressive firms in the region, this company was still in the dark ages when it came to cross-functional collaboration. Each engineering function was an island unto itself, with documents and other formal deliverables serving as the *de facto* lines of communication. After reviewing a rather tall stack of such documents, I came across a test plan that gave me pause. It was a beautiful thing to behold; laminated cover with full-color graphics, spiral bound, and over one-hundred pages of arcane descriptions and detailed discussions. Simulation results were presented, operating modes were described, and virtually every aspect of the product was thoroughly documented. A few days later, I had the opportunity to see this deliverable in a different light. In a conversation with the test engineers, I mentioned my admiration for the test plans generated by the design group. After the sardonic laughter subsided, the manager of this department showed me five sheets of paper that had been torn from a spiral-bound document. "This is what's left of that gorgeous test plan that you liked so much. We tore these pages out and threw the rest away."

I later learned that although the test plan looked terrific, it provided almost nothing of value to the test engineers, its intended customers. In fact, I was told that it typically took several months of pestering for the test group to get the information they actually needed from design engineering. How is it possible that the design group could miss the mark so badly? Very simple: The engineers who created these documents were responding to feedback from their own management and peers, and had almost no interaction with their cross-functional customers.

This situation is a classic example of push versus pull, as shown in Figure 5.29. If a deliverable is "pushed" from one function or group to another, it is very likely that its contents will either overshoot or undershoot what is actually needed by the customer. Undershoot can cause delays, while overshoot wastes the time of both the originator and the user. How can the author of a document or other deliverable ensure that the right content, and only the right content, is captured? The cartoon on the right side of the figure illustrates a fundamental tenant of lean thinking; the use of a "pull" approach. Rather than working in a vacuum, an originator could ask his intended customers (i.e., all internal functions or individuals who have a direct interest in the deliverable) what format should be followed and what content should be included. By having this discussion at the onset of his task, the originator will avoid omitting essential content, while saving the time he might have wasted by including unnecessary topics or details. If creating the deliverable in question is a one-time event, then gaining early feedback will ensure an efficient completion and handoff. If a specific type of deliverable is generated on almost every development project, then a template could be agreed upon to standardize the format and remind originators of essential content to include (see Section 3.5). In either case, a pull strategy avoids waste in the short term, while opening up lines of communication among key development functions over the long term.

A related consideration when creating deliverables can be derived from information theory. The same fundamental rules that are embodied in data-compression algorithms can be applied to any form of document or communication, as shown in Figure 5.30. The first theorem states that information which is already known to the receiver has no value to that individual. In other words, old news is worthless news. If a document repeats information that is available from other convenient sources, those words are just wasting space. Providing a reference to related or supporting documents can save many pages of unnecessary text. Similarly, if the readers of a document are already familiar with a topic, there is no need to provide tutorials or other repetitive boilerplate. Creating this redundant material is time-consuming, and it wastes the readers' time as well. If you were to create a revised version of a document, for example, rather than expecting readers to comb through every page for changes, you could simply attach a "change sheet" to the front that summarizes all new information in a concise and convenient way.

The other theorem mentioned in the figure highlights a second-order effect of including low-value content in a document. Not only is it wasteful from a time standpoint, but the unnecessary content may actually obscure the valuable message of a document. In information theory, valuable information is referred to as "signal," while worthless content is referred to as "noise". The more noise that a document contains, the more likely it is that the signal will be obfuscated. Try talking on your cell phone in a nice quiet place, for example, and then compare the quality of that communication to one that takes place in a crowded airport. By focusing on new, high-value information and avoiding low-value noise, your deliverables will be faster to create, and more effectively received. The famous

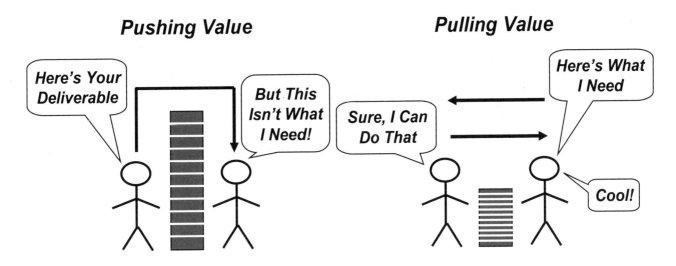

Pushing Value

Pulling Value

Figure 5.29: Internal deliverables should be "pulled" by the customer(s) who will be using them. These internal customers should help define the format and contents of a deliverable. Consider creating a standard template for recurring deliverables that can be easily adapted for each new development project.

Roman orator Cicero once said, "The purpose of communication is not to be understood, it is to make it impossible to be misunderstood." Noise and redundancy make misunderstandings far more likely, and they waste time on both ends of the communication process.

Short-Circuiting the Approval Process

Of all the internal processes that constitute new product development, obtaining approval signatures on documents has the greatest disparity between intent and execution. The intent is admirable; an affixed signature should mean that a person has carefully reviewed the document from their unique perspective, provided constructive comments and suggestions, and ultimately agrees to all of its contents. In practice, however, there is no place in business where there is more gratuitous waste than in document approval. Smaller firms typically have less of a problem – there are fewer cooks in the kitchen. As the scale of a company grows, however, the number of people who *think* that they need to approve every piece of paper increases exponentially. Names are added to the approval list for political reasons (e.g., "My group is just as important as your group"), or are included to reflect hierarchy (e.g., "My employee signs, so I must sign"). Soon the cover sheets of documents require a continuation page to make room for what has become an organizational "who's who" list.

Nor is the situation better with respect to the review and feedback process. You would think that with all of those approval lines, the resulting document would be letter perfect. Alas, as the number of required signatures grows, I believe that the fidelity and quality of a document may actually *decrease*. By diffusing responsibility for the correctness of content among a large group, true ownership becomes unclear. How many of those

From Information Theory –

1) Maximizing Information Value

> **"There is no information value if the content is already known or expected. Information value increases when communication focuses on the <u>unknown</u> or <u>unexpected</u>."**

2) Enhancing Signal and Minimizing Noise

> **"Signal is the valuable information in a communication; noise is anything else that can obscure that valuable information."**

Figure 5.30: The transfer of information that is already known or expected by the receiver has no value. Deliverables should be focused on providing information that is new or unexpected. Extraneous or redundant content represents "noise" that can waste peoples' time and obscure valuable information.

signatures are *pro forma*; affixed because some other trusted person has (supposedly) already reviewed and approved the document? An excessive list of signatures represents a diffusion of individual responsibility, rather than an indication of it.

First, let me be clear that there is a "right" number of approvers for any internal document (note that external documents, such as contracts or supplier agreements, often have additional approval requirements that are driven by fiduciary control rather than technical competency). The first approval line should, of course, be that of the author. Even if many people have contributed to a document, *one person* should take responsibility for its correctness. The remainder of the approval list should consist of a representative from each discipline that is directly impacted by, or is a customer for, its contents. Only one approver should be designated for each discipline; not a hierarchy of managers, manager's managers, etc. If a document requires the approval of a director-level individual, then that should be the only signature line for that discipline. Others in the organization can certainly make comments or suggestions, but from a formal approval standpoint, these few signatures are all that is necessary.

Finally, the way in which approvals are gathered can either be highly efficient, or almost comically wasteful, as shown in Figure 5.31. The "milk-run" approach is, at best, slow and clumsy. At worst, it can be a never-ending cycle of comments and revisions, all taking place in serial slow motion. The "star" model allows review and feedback to take place in parallel, with all approvers providing comments simultaneously. The originator can then concatenate and rationalize these inputs, and release a revised version for final approval. In theory, at least, this cycle could be accomplished in just two steps; in practice, it may take a few more iterations, but would be far more efficient than the endless cycle that is characteristic of the milk run.

"Milk-Run" Model for Document Approval –

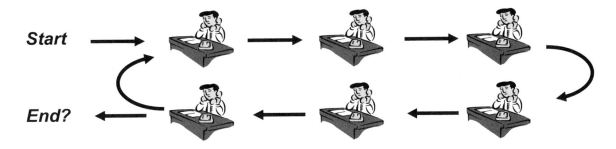

"Star" Model for Document Approval –

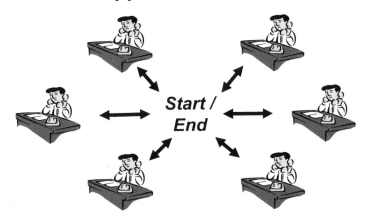

Figure 5.31: Avoid the wasteful and time-consuming "milk-run" approach to gaining approval signatures. Instead use the "star" model, in which a document is simultaneously sent to all approvers for review and feedback. Gather all comments and inputs before generating a revised version, and then distribute the new version with an attached "change sheet" for final approval. Consider giving approvers a set period of time to provide comments, *or their approval is assumed.*

One final note regarding approvals, particularly in reference to the star model described above. Today, many firms utilize a document management system that enables the approval process to be automated. In most situations, these systems are set up to follow the star model. There is a danger, however, in the increased visibility that these systems provide. In one recent case, a firm found that despite automation, their approval cycle was still unacceptably long. It turned out that since every reviewer could see the comments of all the others, as soon as one person rejected the document (often for a minor reason), everyone else stopped reviewing and waited for the revised document to be distributed. What should have been an efficient parallel process had become an automated milk run! If your firm uses such a system, I recommend making both the names and comments of each reviewer blind to all of the others. Each individual should approach a document as though they are the sole reviewer, with all of the personal responsibility that this entails. Automation can be a wonderful thing, unless it is used to avoid providing timely feedback with just a click of the mouse.

Pick the Right Media for the Job

Back when dinosaurs roamed the Earth (i.e., when I first began my product development career), there were few choices of communications media. If you urgently needed to contact someone, you either walked down the hallway or picked up the telephone. Less time-sensitive communications were either faxed, or heaven forbid, sent by snail mail. Today, business people are "fortunate" to have a plethora of media choices, each of which has its own unique advantages, along with the potential for waste if used inappropriately. In a recent meeting, for example, one of the attendees received an urgent text message asking whether she had received an important voice-mail message. When she picked up this voice mail, the caller referred her to an e-mail that had been sent that morning – three types of media were used to complete a single transaction of information.

In communications theory, there are two factors that are used to determine the optimal choice of media: the *type of communication*, and the *bandwidth* required, as shown in Figure 5.32. The type of communication depends on the number of senders, the number of receivers, and whether the exchange will be *two-way* (i.e., synchronous) or *one-way* (i.e., asynchronous). If you wish to discuss something with a teammate, for example, this would be a one-to-one, two-way communication, since there is one sender, one receiver, and the exchange would be synchronous. Conversely, if you wanted to send out a meeting notice, there would be one sender and multiple receivers, meaning that this is a one-to-many communication, and since the memo can be sent asynchronously, it would also be a one-way notification. I'm sure you're wondering what all this means to you, so I'll get to the point. It is the type of communication that should drive your choice of media. E-mail is ideally suited to one-way exchanges, while face-to-face or telephone would be the obvious choice for relatively urgent, two-way discussions. As obvious as this might seem, it is amazing how often people use e-mail to send an urgent message, or call someone to tell them to pick up an e-mail. In each case, the choice of media is inappropriate, resulting in either a poor outcome, wasted time, or both. E-mail should never be used to send urgent messages, since the whole point of this tool is to allow the receiver to disposition their communications when time permits. Similarly, calling someone just to tell them to pick up an e-mail, wastes the receiver's time and interrupts their concentration. If a communication is urgent, it should be handled on the phone (you can always document your conversation in a follow-up e-mail). If there is no real urgency, then send an e-mail and keep your phone on the hook.

Additional waste can occur when the second factor from communications theory is ignored; the bandwidth required to conduct the exchange. You probably have heard this term used in the context of your Internet connection; broadband providers are fond of touting their high bandwidths, meaning that more information can be transferred to the user per unit time. This concept is directly applicable to interpersonal communications. If you have a complex topic to discuss, requiring detailed explanations and responses to questions, then you should use a high-bandwidth media for the exchange. A low-bandwidth

Project Activity	Type of Communication	Bandwidth Required	Least-Waste Option	Second Choice
Coordination Meetings	Few-to-Few, Two-Way	Moderate	Face-to-Face, Stand-up	Brief Telephone Conference
Collaboration Meetings	Few-to-Few, Two-Way	High	Face-to-Face, Event Driven	Video Conference, Event Driven
Distribution of Documents	One-to-Many, One-Way	Low	Post on Project Intranet Page	E-mail Attachment
Review / Approval of Documents	One-to-Many, Two-Way	Moderate	E-mail - Star Distribution	Hardcopy - Star Distribution
Routine Memos	One-to-One, One-Way	Low	E-mail	Fax / Overnight
Transfer of Detailed Information	One-to-One, Two-Way	Moderate	Hardcopy Plus Face-to-Face	E-mail / Fax Plus Telecon
Negotiations	One-to-One, Two-Way	High	Face-to-Face	Video Conference or Telecon
Formal Requests	One-to-One, One-Way	Low	Formal Letter	Faxed Letter
Team Training	One-to-Many, Two-Way	High	Face-to-Face	Real-Time Video

Figure 5.32: It is important to select the appropriate media for project-related communications. In particular, be sure that the media you select has adequate "bandwidth" to handle the situation. Also consider the number of individuals involved in your correspondence; a small amount of waste may be acceptable in one-to-one exchanges, but when a communication is one-to-many, the potential for waste grows geometrically.

choice would be sufficient for unambiguous notifications, distribution of documents, and the like. The highest bandwidth form of interpersonal communication is face-to-face interaction; you get all of the benefits of two-way synchronicity, and the added information content that facial expressions and body language provide. The poorest choice for detailed discussion of a complex topic is e-mail.

I won't belabor this subject; the interested reader can go through the recommendations provided in Figure 5.32. Instead, I will leave you with an admonition. If you are responsible for a one-to-many communication, you have a special obligation from a waste-reduction perspective. It's one thing to use a poor choice of media in a one-to-one situation, since at worst you will squander only one other person's time. For one-to-many situations, however, the waste you create is multiplied by the number of receivers; a geometric explosion of wasted time. So if you are calling a meeting, for example, make sure that only essential people are invited to attend. If you are sending out an e-mail, address the memo only to those who have a need to know (and stop pasting the rest of the org chart onto the "CC" line). A form of "golden rule" applies here; when it comes to interpersonal communications, do unto others as you wish to heck they would do unto you.

Stem the Tide of E-mail Overload

As I've traveled the world of new product development, I've come across some very clever ways to reduce e-mail waste and improve poorly run meetings. I won't bother preaching to the choir on either of these subjects; I'm sure you are already well-motivated to learn some practical solutions. In the final two subsections, I will describe several practical rules for improving the use of e-mail and the facilitation of meetings. Each of these recommendations has been successfully employed by a real-world firm. It is up to you to select a handful of these suggestions that are compatible with your firm's culture and working environment and implement them.

A list of rules for reducing e-mail waste is provided in Figure 5.33. The first rule comes from a small firm whose president was fed up with being copied on virtually every correspondence within his organization. In desperation, he announced a new company-wide policy: Anyone within the firm was allowed to "block CC" if they wished. This simple feature, provided by MS Explorer and other e-mail applications, filters out carbon copies (yes youngsters, that is what "CC" stands for), and only allows through those e-mails that are directly addressed to the recipient. Since most people take the address line much more seriously than the CC line, this firm saw an almost immediate decrease in e-mail traffic. Within weeks, the number of e-mails passing through their internal network had declined by *sixty percent*.

Rule 2 is a reference to my earlier comment regarding the misuse of e-mail as a tool for detailed discussions of complex issues. Once your "chain letter" gets beyond a cycle or two, pick up the telephone and save both the receiver and yourself a ton of time. Rule 3 is just good common sense. In a time when almost every intra-organizational document can be referenced by a hyperlink, attachments to internal correspondence should be obsolete. To show how wasteful unnecessary attachments can be, I recently heard that an employee had become enamored with a humorous Quick-Time video that he had downloaded from www.JibJab.com. He decided to share his taste in humor (which was over five megabytes in size) with three hundred of his closest friends (i.e., his coworkers), resulting in a system crash and hours of dark screens.

Rules 4 and 5 address a common problem; poorly written, stream-of-consciousness e-mails that never seem to get to the point. Every e-mail that you create should be clearly titled and on-topic from the very first line. A few words of pleasantries are appropriate in some cases, but anything beyond "how's the weather" is wasteful in a professional environment. For those e-mails that contain important or complex information, consider borrowing an approach that is employed in scholarly literature. Use the first few sentences of your e-mail as an "abstract" that summarizes the key points of the correspondence, in bullet form if possible. After this brief introduction, you can indicate that "more detail follows" and proceed with a comprehensive discourse on the subject. Interested readers can dig deeper, while peripheral individuals need only scan the abstract to gain a high-level overview of the topic.

Of course brevity is a virtue in e-mail correspondence, but Rule 6 offers an interesting twist. Another frustrated CEO established an equally innovative rule within her organization. She asked the information technology group within her company to

---

Rule 1 – Limit "CC's" to only those that are ABSOLUTELY ESSENTIAL. Make a rule that employees can choose to BLOCK all CC e-mails.

Rule 2 – No more than two "cycles" back and forth between correspondents. If the issue is not resolved by that point, USE THE TELEPHONE!

Rule 3 – No unnecessary forwarding of attachments; use a hyperlink instead.

Rule 4 – Always include the POINT and URGENCY of the e-mail in both the subject line and the first few lines of the text.

Rule 5 – Consider using the first few sentences of an e-mail as an ABSTRACT that summarizes the remainder of the communication. Below the abstract, add additional detail prefaced with the comment, "More detail follows...".

Rule 6 – KEEP IT BRIEF! No e-mail should be more than twenty lines in length (consider using a network filter to block any that are longer).

Rule 7 – Start the subject line with "ACTION" whenever immediate action is required by the addressee. Actions should be identified at the beginning of the e-mail.

Rule 8 – Try using the SUBJECT LINE to communicate the ENTIRE message, followed by "EOM" which stands for "End of Message".

Rule 9 – Limit the number of times during the day that you respond to e-mails. Turn off the e-mail alarm, so YOU control when you deal with e-mail.

Figure 5.33: E-mail can be both a blessing and a curse. The e-mail rules listed above are all in use in real firms on a daily basis. Select and implement the ones that apply to your company's environment and culture, and you can save your organization literally hundreds of hours per week.

implement a network filter that would block any internal e-mails that were longer than twenty lines (personally, I think it should have been ten). Again, the results were immediate and measurable; forty percent of e-mails were blocked during the first week, but after a month almost every internal correspondence was passing through the filter, indicating that a great deal of writing and reading time was being saved.

The final three rules are my personal favorites. Rule 7 suggests that you use the capitalized word "ACTION" in both the subject line and the first sentence of any e-mail that requests help or support from the receiver. Naturally, if there are multiple recipients, you should indicate who is being asked to take action. This convention allows users to quickly scan their e-mails for those that require a prompt response, and delay dispositioning the rest until a more convenient time. Rule 8 may seem kind of cute, but it can also save appreciable time when applied consistently over the long term. Try conveying your entire message within the subject line of the e-mail, followed by EOM (i.e., "end of message"). I've begun using this technique in many of my exchanges with clients, and it seems to be catching on. If you need to reschedule a meeting, for example, you would type into the subject line, "Meeting at 3:00 moved to 4:00 (EOM)". You'd be surprised how often this will work, and each time you use this approach you are saving the recipient(s) the time it takes to open an e-mail. A few seconds saved per e-mail, times dozens of e-mails per person each day, times hundreds of people in an organization...you do the math.

Finally, Rule 9 harkens back to the time-slicing discussion in Section 5.3. I've already beaten this drum, so I'll spare you an encore. Personally, I check e-mail a few times per day, and only on my terms. Just go cold turkey and turn off the e-mail alarm; you will be surprised how good it feels to be the master of your own fate.

Tighten Up Those #@%! Meetings!

Last but certainly not least among our quick-hit opportunities are those poorly run meetings. I'm sure you've sat through countless one-hour meetings that have felt like the longest month of your life. Following the basic rules described in Figure 5.34 can save many hours of wasted time, improve the value of your meetings, and restore your coworkers' will to live.

Challenge yourself to implement Rule 1 for the next meeting you call. Just because MS Outlook has a default duration of one hour doesn't mean you need to schedule one-hour meetings. Everything grows to fill the time allowed, so the more time you allocate, the more time you will spend. I've found that thirty-minute meetings can often accomplish the same objectives as hour-long ones. Select a duration that fits the subject, rather than taking a one-duration-fits-all approach. Rule 2 supports the goal of shorter meetings by eliminating one of the sacred cows of old-school facilitation: the detailed agenda. I suggest skipping the use of a multi-topic agenda in favor of holding single-topic meetings. The motivation for this rule is to avoid having attendees sit around waiting for their subject to be discussed. If the same group of attendees is involved in all agenda items, then by all means use this tried-and-true approach. If only a small percentage of attendees are required for each topic, split the meeting into several smaller, more focused ones.

Rules 3 through 6 require little discussion, but Rule 7 is another personal favorite. At what point in the development of our business culture did rudeness become acceptable behavior? If you've called a meeting, you have given all attendees due notice that you will need a period of their undivided attention. People who get up to take "important" calls or ceaselessly bang away on their Blackberrys during a meeting are (unintentionally, I'm sure) being inconsiderate of others, and potentially reducing the value of the meeting's outcome. At the beginning of your next meeting, ask if anyone present is expecting an urgent call (e.g., the imminent birth of a child, a tornado warning, the landing of aliens, etc.). Unless the group agrees that an incoming call is truly urgent, all cell phones and other electronic devices should be turned off, and if necessary, temporarily confiscated. Sorry to imply that professionals should be treated like children, but frankly I've seen longer attention spans and better focus in kindergarten classes than is typical at important business meetings.

The last two rules are so fundamental that they outweigh the importance of all the others. *Is a meeting really necessary*, and if so, *what is the valuable output that will be generated* to justify taking people away from their value-creating work? I would guess that over half of the meetings held in businesses today are completely unnecessary. Here are some meetings that should never have been held:

Rule 1 – Reduce the duration of most meetings. Try restricting meetings to no more than thirty minutes in most cases.

Rule 2 – Have only a single topic on the agenda, or perhaps several closely related items – it's hard to run a multi-topic meeting efficiently.

Rule 3 – Only invite those people who have a need to be there. Uninvited attendees should be discouraged – they can waste the rest of the group's time.

Rule 4 – Foster a culture that discourages lateness. If an attendee is running late, they should notify the meeting holder as to when they will arrive.

Rule 5 – Define the goals of the meeting when it is announced, and identify any pre-work that should be performed or information that is needed.

Rule 6 – Any tangential issues or comments should be captured in a "parking lot" for future discussion.

Rule 7 – Ask attendees at the beginning of the meeting if they have a legitimate need to stay in touch with the outside world, otherwise ALL ELECTRONICS SHOULD BE TURNED OFF! You may need to forcibly remove Blackberrys from peoples' hands.

Rule 8 – Do not begin the meeting until everyone in the room agrees on the "deliverables" that will be created. EVERY MEETING SHOULD HAVE A DELIVERIBLE, OR THE TIME SPENT WILL PROBABLY BE WASTED.

Rule 9 – Ask yourself if a formal meeting is really necessary before interrupting multiple peoples' value-creating work.

Figure 5.34: A few simple rules can help avoid frustrated attendees and valueless meetings. The final rule is perhaps the most important: ask yourself if a formal meeting is really necessary before interrupting the workdays of development team members.

1) The "we need to discuss how things are going" meeting.
2) The "I can't make a decision, so I'll let the group decide instead" meeting.
3) The "I'm feeling uncomfortable and need reassurance" meeting.
4) The "company policy says we need a meeting" meeting.
5) The "I'm too lazy to do the research, so I'll just bring in all of the experts" meeting.

And my all-time favorite:

6) The "let's see how far we get, and we'll pick it up again next week" meeting.

Assuming that a meeting is truly necessary, a tangible deliverable should be identified as its objective, both in the meeting notice and in the opening moments of the meeting itself. Acceptable deliverables include: a plan of action, an agreement, a decision, a signed drawing or document, an approval to proceed, and so on. Each of these outcomes allows the development process to move forward and justifies the time spent by all parties. Incidentally, meeting minutes are *not* a legitimate deliverable, unless they are used to document one of the valuable outcomes mentioned above. Distributing minutes for a worthless meeting simply compounds the waste. The next time you think a meeting might be needed, challenge yourself to clearly define the tangible outcome that will result. If you cannot define the deliverable, step away from MS Outlook and leave those haggard design team members alone.

Conquering Batches, Queues, and Resource Bottlenecks

5.6

Section

There is much that a manufacturer can do to optimize its production environment. However, no matter how lean a factory has become, it will grind to a halt at the first outage of materials. If all of the pieces and parts of a product are not available when needed, it is impossible to ship that item in a timely manner. This issue, of course, is addressed by one of the mainstays of lean manufacturing, the just-in-time (JIT) inventory management methodology. In the factory, production is enabled by the prompt availability of materials, whereas in the product development arena, the enabling factor is people. Even the most advanced development process cannot function without adequate resources and skills being available to provide the impetus that drives a project forward. In fact, suboptimal resource management is prevalent in almost every firm that I have observed.

As in previous sections, when there is a definitive book on a given subject, I will highlight that reference in this introduction. On the topic of resource and capacity optimization, there are *two* books that I highly recommend. The first deals with the management of product development resources by applying the concepts of batches and queues. This excellent book, entitled *Managing the Design Factory*, by Donald Reinertsen, offers a unique and insightful look at how people and skills can be effectively allocated in a multi-project environment. A somewhat different, but equally valid, viewpoint can be gained from reading *Critical Chain*, by Eliyahu Goldratt (the author of *The Goal*). Although these writers have different perspectives, all roads lead to Rome; both approaches stew down to a similar set of conclusions and recommendations. My contribution to this critical topic will be to highlight those practical conclusions, and describe some straightforward tools and techniques for directly attacking this issue. Resource management is the last frontier of lean product development; if you can conquer this challenge, your design process will be in a league of its own.

Resource Bottlenecks and the Fallacy of Multitasking

When it comes to resource management, there are a wealth of analogies. In the end, however, it is irrelevant whether you think of yourself as a "bottleneck," the "weak link in the chain," or the slowest boy scout on the hike (let's see if you've done your reading). All that matters is that there is a long queue of people waiting for you to service their needs, and all of them are pissed. A resource capacity constraint can be described in several ways, as shown in Figure 5.35, but ultimately it comes down to the presence of a queue. Whether referring to an individual or an entire functional department, if the wait-time is significant, you've identified a resource bottleneck. Just in case you've missed the point of the above analogies, resource bottlenecks limit the capacity and speed of the entire product development process.

Going back to the line of people waiting at your cubicle door (or opening, as the case may be); what is the best way to pacify this unruly mob? If you approach this situation in the same way as most designers, you will try to keep everyone happy. Whenever someone shows up at your desk, you pull out their work and look as though you've been slaving away at it all day long. Once they leave, you switch to another one of your critical tasks, trying to keep all of the balls in the air, as shown in Figure 5.36. After all, you think of yourself as a great multitasker, and this is what multitaskers do, right?

Analogy #1 – The "Weakest Link"

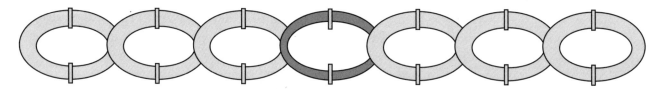

▶ *The chain always breaks at the weakest link.*
▶ *Reinforcing any other link <u>does</u> <u>nothing</u> to improve the strength of the chain!*

Analogy #2 – The "Bottleneck"

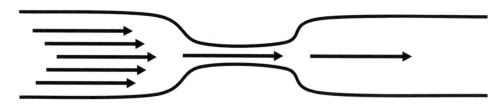

▶ *A bottleneck determines the capacity (or speed) of a system.*
▶ *Expanding the capacity of a bottleneck dramatically increases the overall capacity (and speed).*

Figure 5.35: The capacity of an entire product development organization will be limited by the resource that is in shortest supply (the capacity constraint). The only way to improve development capacity is to increase the workflow through this bottleneck.

Typical Multitasking Environment

▶ *No Clear Prioritization*
▶ *Impossible Workload*
▶ *Chronic Overtime*
▶ *Low Morale*
▶ *"Just Do It All" Syndrome*

With Prioritization and Time-Slicing

▶ *Uniform Prioritization of Work*
▶ *A Clear Work Plan for All Tasks*
▶ *Overtime Used Only as "Reserve Capacity"*
▶ *Making Progress Improves Morale*
▶ *Workers Always Know What to Work On!*

Figure 5.36: Multitasking without clear prioritization of tasks is extremely wasteful. By setting priorities, and applying time management techniques such as time-slicing, the timely output of a constrained resource can be dramatically improved.

Here's the problem with the kind of multitasking described above; it makes no sense at all. In fact, trying to keep everyone happy is the *worst* strategy you (and by extension, an entire support department) can employ from a capacity management standpoint. Let's consider a specific example. Suppose you find yourself on the critical path for three high-priority projects, and the team leaders for these projects are bugging you constantly. Each project requires a week of your effort to satisfy their immediate needs. If you juggle all three projects simultaneously, it will take you three weeks to complete all of the required work, as shown in Figure 5.37. Despite your best intentions, however, all three projects must wait a full three weeks for their respective outputs.

Now suppose that you are a truly enlightened multitasker. Instead of randomly attacking your ponderous workload, you know that the only way to optimize the through-put of a resource bottleneck is to *prioritize the work through that constraint*. Hence, you ask for a meeting with the team leaders from all three projects (and your functional manager, if appropriate) and set some priorities. Now everyone agrees that you will complete work on Project A first, Project B second, and then service the needs of Project C. It will still take you three weeks to complete all of the required tasks, right? However, Project A will

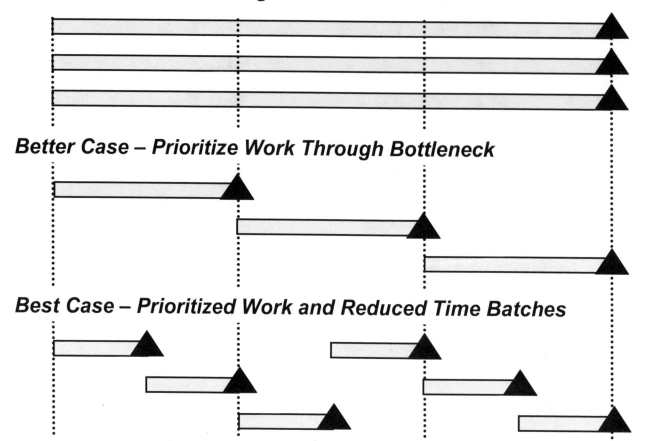

Worst Case – Multitasking With No Prioritization

Better Case – Prioritize Work Through Bottleneck

Best Case – Prioritized Work and Reduced Time Batches

Figure 5.37: The worst way to manage a resource bottleneck is to treat all tasks as though they have equal priority. The timely output of a resource constraint can be improved by setting clear priorities, and by dividing the workload into smaller increments (i.e., reduce the length of time batches).

receive what it needs in *only one week*, Project B will be satisfied in *two weeks*, and Project C will not have suffered at all from the prioritization of your work! Two of the three projects are better off, from a schedule standpoint, as a result of establishing priorities through a capacity constraint. In fact, if you take into account the inefficiency and turbulence associated with juggling multiple projects without prioritization, all three projects will be better off with priorities in place.

This result is often surprising to people, but there is no ambiguity here. *You should always prioritize the work through any resource constraint.* It doesn't even matter what priorities you set; *any prioritization is better than no prioritization.* That being said, there are certainly better and worse ways to structure your work agenda. At the bottom of the prioritization barrel is the classic first in, first out (FIFO) approach. As egalitarian as this method might seem, it is barely an improvement over random juggling, since the most important job in your queue could be waiting behind the least important task. It would be far better to understand the importance and urgency of each activity on your plate, and set your priorities accordingly. What if your management refuses to help you rank-order your tasks? Then set your own priorities and get to work. This is how people who are truly effective at multitasking handle their workloads; they recognize that they must focus on one activity at a time to achieve any real productivity.

As powerful as this basic concept might be, there is still more that we can do to optimize the throughput of a resource bottleneck. Suppose that the three, one-week tasks mentioned above could be subdivided into smaller increments of work. For example, it might be possible to deliver an intermediate output to each of the project team leaders that would allow their projects to move forward along their respective critical paths. By reducing the length of the "time batch" for each activity, you can further reduce the wait-times for all three projects, as shown at the bottom of Figure 5.37. In principle, if each week-long activity could be divided into two halves, even the lowest priority project would receive a useful output in just a week and a half. By applying these two simple concepts, prioritization of a queue and defining smaller increments of work, you can dramatically increase your effective capacity, while significantly reducing your blood pressure.

Some Practical Methods for Relieving Capacity Bottlenecks

The most challenging aspect of resource management is finding and relieving resource bottlenecks. Identifying these constraints on a day-to-day basis is relatively easy; just look for individuals or support functions with the longest wait-times. Unfortunately, nothing stays the same for very long in new product development. Within weeks, the capacity constraint may have moved to other functions or individuals. It is common for "peaks" of workload to occur on a transient basis, only to be followed by "troughs" of relatively low demand. Moreover, it is very difficult to predict where bottlenecks will appear next, even if you have sophisticated resource tracking tools at your disposal. In this rapidly changing environment, whatever measures you take to relieve capacity constraints must be quick and agile.

Your most potent weapon in the battle to alleviate resource bottlenecks is *cooperation*. In the example provided in the previous subsection, the output of a constraining resource could be dramatically improved only after a cooperative agreement was reached on work priorities. Likewise, the subdivision of work into smaller increments may require collaboration among both internal customers and project team leaders. Knowing human nature, you might imagine that this kind of supportive environment is difficult to achieve. In fact, without strong motivation, education, and an admonition from executive management, it can be darned near impossible. Although everyone is better off in a cooperative workplace, it is hard to overcome the self-interest displayed by many aggressive managers and team leaders.

A logical hierarchy can be followed when seeking cooperation on the utilization of a resource bottleneck, as shown in Figure 5.38. You should first try to reach a mutually beneficial solution among all involved parties. Remember that even if a task takes a back seat to other work in a queue, it may still be better off than if clear priorities had not been set. If the above negotiation degenerates into a rancorous row (as is fairly likely), be prepared to elevate the discussion to a higher, multi-project authority. If the projects involved are of sufficient importance to your firm, it may even be necessary to exercise the elephants (an old expression for getting executive management involved in making a decision).

Before we leave the subject of prioritizing resource bottlenecks, I'll share with you a personal story. A number of years ago I took a trip to the Masai Mara, in Kenya. Since my wife and I are both animal lovers, we relished the opportunity to experience the greatest concentration of large mammals in the world. While watching an enormous herd of Thompson's gazelles, I noticed a baby gazelle wandering away from the group. As luck would have it, there was a lioness perched on a rock very near to where the baby was straying. Suddenly, the lioness bolted toward the baby and began chasing the poor thing down, as illustrated in Figure 5.39. Surprisingly, however, the lioness didn't catch the

Executive Team Makes Final Call on Conflicts With Strategic Impact

⬆

Conflicts That Cannot Be Resolved Are Elevated To a Multi-Project Authority

⬆

Project Managers and Team Members Work Cooperatively to Handle Most Resource Conflicts

Figure 5.38: Cooperation is the key to maximizing the timely output from a resource bottleneck. If all involved parties (the worker and all individuals who are requesting work) can agree on priorities, then a wasteful multi-tasking situation can be transformed into a series of focused and efficient tasks.

baby. Instead, at the very last moment, she spotted a larger gazelle, and began chasing this new quarry, evidently swayed by the prospect of a more substantial lunch. As she approached her new prize, an even larger animal caught her eye and again she changed direction. In the end, the lioness was left panting in the middle of the savanna, with nothing to show for her efforts.

Later that evening, I asked our very knowledgeable guide about the drama we had witnessed. It didn't make sense to me that the lioness would waste all of her energy and end up with nothing to show for it. Our guide told us that the big cat was just getting exercise. As he succinctly put it, "If that lioness was hungry, she would have picked a victim, and not stopped until she had her meal." In the jungle that is new product development, it is all too common for managers to continuously shift priorities. Everything becomes the number-one priority some of the time. I've come to call this behavior the "Gazelle Syndrome". The bottom line is that if you are just looking for exercise, then go ahead and keep changing those priorities. On the other hand, if you wish to get the maximum output from a bottleneck resource, *set priorities for that individual and avoid changing them at all cost.*

Assuming that your resource bottlenecks have been effectively prioritized, there is another important step you can take to maximize throughput. In Section 5.3 we discussed the concept of "project time"; a period during each workday that is set aside for high-concentration project work. Project time is a great idea for the average team member, but it becomes a virtual mandate for resource bottlenecks. In fact, why stop at two or three hours of protected time? The electronics superstore Best Buy, for example, has established a policy of allowing employees to work at home when they are under significant schedule pressure. In a recent *60 Minutes* interview, Best Buy's CEO observed that the productivity of individuals who have participated in this program has dramatically increased, and their morale has improved as well.

If off-site work is not an option in your situation, consider creating a "filter" to protect resource bottlenecks, as illustrated in Figure 5.40. A filter screens out interruptions that would otherwise distract a resource bottleneck, and dispositions all but the most critical ones. A mid-level manager can serve as a filter for his direct reports, or a team leader can be a filter for critical-path team members, and so on. The goal is to reduce any turbulence or disruption, so that those resources that are in high demand can apply the greatest percentage of their time to value-creating work.

Finally, it is important to be as proactive as possible when dealing with potential resource constraints. Although every product development organization has, by definition, one or more resource constraints, I've seen many instances in which these bottlenecks could have been easily avoided. The most common situation occurs when an individual or group receives their work assignments from multiple sources. One manager assigns a full-time workload to the resource bottleneck, and then a second and third manager does the same. Since each of these "customers" is unaware of the others, they feel no shame in demanding immediate attention. Of course, one would think that the overloaded resource would scream bloody murder. The problem is that in many firms, *everyone* is screaming about being overworked. It is hard to tell whether an employee or support group is in real pain, or just "crying wolf".

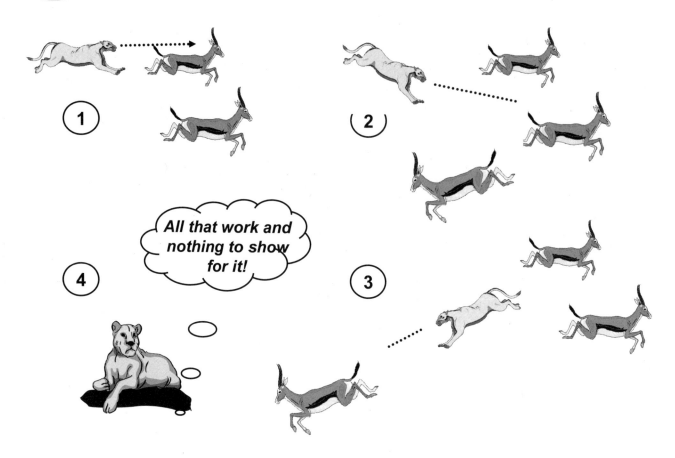

Figure 5.39: It is common for managers to change priorities on a continual basis. Just like the lioness in the illustration, if priorities are not set and maintained, there is a strong possibility that little or no work will get done. The author refers to this situation as the "Gazelle Syndrome".

This problem can be avoided through the use of a resource-loading tool such as the one shown in Figure 5.41. The template that I've provided represents a monthly snapshot of the workload for a functional department, but the same format could be used for tracking the workload of a project team or support organization as well. Along the top of the chart are the names of all individuals who are involved in project work. Below each name is an estimate of how many hours that person will have available over the next four weeks. This should be a realistic estimate, taking into account vacation time, business travel, and any other commitments that would take the resource away from product development activities. Projects are listed in order of priority along the vertical axis. On a monthly basis, the available time for each employee is allocated to various projects through negotiations with their team leaders. The highest priority projects will be fully staffed, but as the available hours are consumed, some lower priority activities may not receive all of the resources that they desire. Near the bottom of the list, there may be projects that are given no attention at all during the next four-week period. This is a necessary evil if the higher priority projects are to meet their schedule commitments.

Examples of Filters –

► **Rule that all senior management contact with team must first pass through team leader.**

► **Rule that no "firefighting" assignments can be given to those individuals working on critical-core tasks.**

► **Rule that workers can graciously redirect all disruptive contacts to team leader (and continue creating value).**

Figure 5.40: If a resource constraint is driving the schedule of one or more important projects, it may make sense to protect that individual from any disturbances through the use of a "filter".

The projects that have been allocated full staffing, I've designated with the letter "A," while development efforts with only partial staffing have been assigned the letter "B". Those poor neglected projects near the bottom (e.g., Dream 1.0, Wish 1.0, etc.) fall into the "C" category; they are ladies-in-waiting until resources from higher priority projects become available. This type of resource-loading tool does not have to be highly accurate to be of tremendous utility. At a glance, a manager or team leader can determine which employees are assigned to which activities, and whether any individual is severely overloaded. This template also provides the means for detecting chronic resource shortfalls; disciplines or skill-sets that are almost always in short supply. In the final subsection, I'll discuss how these persistent resource bottlenecks should be addressed.

Priority	Project List (Current & Planned)	Tom	Dick	Harry	Sue	Jane	Liz	Fred	Cathy	Ron	Tim	Sara	Nada	Dave	Renee	Cassie	Naresh	John	Thor
	Available Hours*→	80	120	120	160	120	160	160	160	140	80	120	120	160	120	160	160	160	140
A	*Widget 1.3*	40				80		160		40					80			160	
A	*Thingamajig A3*		80		120	40						80		120	40				
A	*Dohicky Update*			100			40			100			100				40		100
A	*Whatchamacallit A*	40				120				40						120			
A	*Bluesky 5.3*		40			40			120				40			40		120	
B	*Widget 1.4*			20									20						
B	*Thingamajig B6*				40														
B	*Mini-Dohicky*									40									
B	*Whatchamacallit B*																		40
B	*Bluesky 6.0*													40					
C	*Dream 1.0*																		
C	*Wish 1.0*																		
C	*Prayer 1.0*																		
C	*Hope 1.0*																		

* Hours available for product development work in current month.

Figure 5.41: A simple method for allocating employee's workloads on a monthly basis. This matrix tracks the time that individuals have available for product development work, and allocates that time to projects in priority order.

A Step-by-Step Process for Eliminating Capacity Bottlenecks

I'm willing to bet that you are already acutely aware of the chronic resource bottlenecks that are limiting your time-to-market. There's that support department that is notorious for slipping schedule, or the individual that always has a mountain of work piled on his desk. In the short run, the suggestions I've provided above can help to mitigate this problem, but in the fullness of time, something more permanent must be done. Again, there is a straightforward hierarchy that can be followed to reduce or eliminate any tenacious resource constraint, as shown in Figure 5.42.

Your first step should be to convene a *kaizen* event to focus cross-functional attention on the issue. The brainstorming portion of this event may uncover process inefficiencies that are exacerbating the resource shortfall. If process improvements appear to be a viable solution, then identify a more efficient process, and assign action items to enable immediate implementation. Be sure to decide how you will measure the effectiveness of your modified process, and plan to gather the same group together after an agreed-upon period to review your metrics and determine if any further action is required.

Step 1 - *Identify resource bottlenecks and hold focused "kaizen" events to select and apply lean tools and methods.*

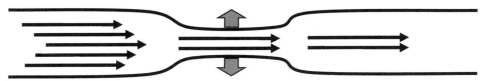

Step 2 - *Utilize "level loading," cross-training, and occasional overtime to relieve persistent resource constraints.*

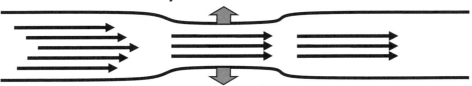

Step 3 - *Only when the above methods fail to eliminate a persistent bottleneck should permanent hiring be considered.*

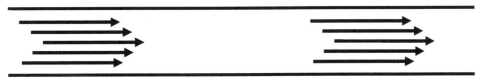

Figure 5.42: The first step toward elimination of capacity bottlenecks is to identify the individuals or groups involved and then use lean improvement techniques to rectify the situation. If the problem persists, the next step should be to utilize level loading and cross-training to alleviate the capacity constraint. Hiring of additional staff should be treated as a last resort to relieve intractable resource limitations.

If a chronic resource bottleneck cannot be solved through process improvements, your next step should be to consider utilizing "level loading" to dynamically adjust workloads among individuals who possess the appropriate skills. I've seen as much as a fifty percent increase in work capacity as a result of an aggressive implementation of level loading. Naturally, this technique only makes sense if there is more than one person in your firm with the requisite skills and knowledge. If a single person has been identified as a "point failure" within your organization, a good solution would be to engage in the aggressive cross-training of employees in related fields. Cross-training is one of the least expensive, most effective, and frequently ignored methods for eliminating long-term resource issues. As a final desperate measure, you might consider requesting occasional overtime to handle peaks in workload. I can't state strongly enough, however, that *this is not a permanent solution.* Not only does institutionalized overtime frequently backfire in the form of poor employee morale and costly attrition, but it is (in my humble opinion) a morally questionable practice. Employees should not be forced to bear the burden of poor planning, ineffective resource management, or wasteful business processes.

And then there's the six-hundred-pound gorilla sitting in the corner. You could, of course, hire additional employees to alleviate your capacity bottleneck. Why have I delayed mention of this option until the bitter end? Because the hiring of new employees should be motivated by the growth of your firm, not as a knee-jerk reaction to slipped project schedules. If you add more workers to a bottleneck situation, what was once a highly visible problem will disappear from view. If the resource constraint was caused by a legitimate shortfall in staffing, then the disappearance of the bottleneck is the desired result. However, if the constraint was caused by waste and inefficiency, then hiring more people will transform that waste into a drain on your cashflow for years to come.

Focus on Improvement

6.1 - Value-Stream Mapping
and Kaizen Events

6.2 - The Lean Self-Assessment Tool

6.3 - A Proven Strategy
for Deployment

*"A culture that is resistant to change
is what happens in the absence
of effective leadership
and good communication"*

Ron Mascitelli

Value-Stream Mapping
and Kaizen Events

The three sections that make up Part 6 are directed toward a very special audience; those rare individuals who are willing to do whatever it takes to improve their firms. If you think that you might be one of these courageous souls, please join me for a survey of how lean product development can be (and has been) successfully implemented. On the other hand, if you are not inclined to pursue an improvement initiative at this time, you might find the remainder of this guidebook to be of marginal interest.

This first section describes how two of the mainstay tools of lean improvement can be adapted for use in the fuzzy world of new product development. If you are already familiar with *value-stream mapping* and *kaizen events*, you will find that there are some subtle challenges that must be addressed before these methods can make the transition from manufacturing to product development. If you are new to the lean improvement game, never fear; the material that follows is all that you will need to get started. Experience is the best teacher, however, when it comes to implementing something new and different. Idealism has no place in the trenches where change actually happens. It doesn't matter how Toyota does it, or how some high-priced consultant does it, or for that matter, how I do it. What matters is that you find a way to make improvements happen in *your* firm, and then make them stick. I will endeavor to provide you with a solid start, but being an improvement champion or change agent requires a serious commitment. If you lack patience and persistence, you may want to consider taking up a less demanding avocation.

The Fundamentals of Value-Stream Mapping

Value-stream mapping is a systematic methodology for visually representing a business process, identifying waste elimination opportunities, and subsequently designing an improved "future state". Its success in the manufacturing environment is legend; firms around the globe are using this approach to dramatically transform how their products are produced. From its origins in operations, value-stream mapping has diffused outward in recent years to encompass the entire enterprise, and is currently being used to accelerate processes that range from accounts payable to customer service. In fact, the only notable void in the proliferation of this technique is in new product development. Although there are a handful of consultants and internal improvement specialists that have demonstrated success in this realm, most firms have yet to step up to the plate. This may be because new product development is the most complex, cross-functional, risky, irregular, and frankly, illusive process in any manufacturing business. Or it could be because engineers and designers are, how can I say this delicately, a pain in the tush to sell on new methods. Being an engineer and designer myself, I can speak of my peers' stubbornness with some confidence. We're all nice people, but when it comes to telling us how we should do the creative things that we do, we can be skeptical to the point of obstinacy. Yet despite the barriers of process complexity and organizational intractability, firms that have followed the simple value-stream mapping methodology described below have achieved significant improvements in time-to-market and project capacity.

We will first discuss some basic terminology and fundamental concepts, and then walk through a real-life, step-by-step example. In my opinion, the most critical factor in achieving success as a process cartographer is whether you clearly define the beginning and end points of the process under scrutiny. Attempting to take on the entire front-to-back development process, particularly as a first effort, is not advisable. Your greatest probability of success occurs when small, well-defined portions of the process are addressed systematically, and in priority order. This is not to say that you should *never* map the entire development process, but I've found that beginning with a few modest efforts will give you and your improvement team the experience (and track record) you will need to take on the Big Kahuna. To this end, the terms *trigger point* and *end point* should be understood by everyone who will be involved in your mapping exercise, as defined in Figure 6.1. The trigger point is a moment in time that identifies the start of the process under review. This point must be unambiguous, and should be the same for all variations of the process that the mapping exercise will encompass. Similarly, the end point must be clearly understood, and all process variations should end at this same point in time.

The next three terms in the figure reflect three different ways in which time can be measured relative to the flow of value within a business process. The first category is *calendar time*, which indicates (not surprisingly) the passage of time on the seven-day-per-week calendar. This is the time metric that impacts your product's market success; time-to-market, for example, is measured in calendar time. The second category, *work time*, represents the number of hours or days of actual effort required to complete a step in the process being mapped. Work time should include all individuals who are active on a process step, so if three people spend time on the creation of a document, for example, all of their applied hours would be summed to arrive at the work time for that task. When this situation occurs, however, I have found it useful to note the number of individuals who are involved, as well as the total combined work time for all parties. This information will be used later when we determine which process steps have the greatest potential for improvement. The third category is referred to as *value-added time*. This represents an ideal; a measure of the theoretical minimum work time required to complete a process step. You could think of value-added time as being what is left over after all Type 2 waste and Type 1 enablers are eliminated from the task under consideration. I must admit that it can be challenging to estimate the value-added time of some types of product development work. For example, if a designer spends a full day working to complete a drawing on a CAD system, how much of that time is value-added? If she was interrupted to attend a meeting, or spent time searching for information, we could deduct those periods as either enablers or waste. But what about the time she spends staring at the computer screen

Trigger Point –	A milestone or other well-defined point in time that represents the beginning of the value-stream map (VSM).
End Point –	A milestone or other well-defined point in time that represents the end of the VSM.
Calendar Time –	The time on a 24/7 calendar that it takes for a step in the process to be completed (abbreviated "C/T").
Work Time –	Total work hours required to complete a step in the process, including all involved individuals (abbreviated "W/T").
Value-Added Time –	A theoretical ideal – an estimate of how many hours would be required to complete a process step if all waste was eliminated (abbreviated "VA/T").
Current-State Map –	A map of a process that has been selected for improvement. The current-state map should capture the process as it actually occurs, with all of the waste, turbulence, delays, etc.
Future-State Map –	A map that captures improvements to the current-state process. The future-state map should be clear and easily understood by those who will be participating in its implementation and use.

Figure 6.1: Several key value-stream-mapping (VSM) terms are defined above. It is important that everyone involved in a mapping exercise understand exactly what process is being addressed (i.e., the trigger point and the end point), and the meaning of the three categories of time.

thinking? My suggestion is to not put too sharp a point on value-added time when mapping new product development processes. A reasonable guess will give you all that you will need to set priorities and identify improvement opportunities. The final two terms defined in the figure represent the "before and after" condition of the value-stream mapping methodology. The *current-state map* represents what exists today, with all of the warts and whiskers, whereas the *future-state map* reflects your new and improved process (*sans* warts, whiskers, and waste).

Now that we have the terminology down, what are the basic steps involved in value-stream mapping? I can summarize them in one sentence: Map the process you have, set priorities for waste elimination, brainstorm on improvements, and generate an improved new process. It just couldn't be more logical, as shown in Figure 6.2. A word of warning, however; I've seen value-stream mapping efforts turn into overwrought, time-wasting nightmares. Remember that the ultimate goal of this improvement activity is to yield a future-state value-stream map that can be immediately understood and easily implemented. Hence, your current-state mapping activity should be treated as a means to an end; keep it simple and informal. Once you have defined an improved process, you might invest some time prettying up your future-state map. Your goal should be to create a clear and concise future-state diagram, rather than a piece of abstract art worthy of Jackson Pollack.

The first step is to create a current-state value-stream map for your selected process segment. You should endeavor to make your map as realistic as possible, so try to include all of the delays and frustrations that may be experienced when this process is active. It is critical that you capture all of the waste that is present in the current state, otherwise it will be invisible to your improvement team and will not be addressed. If you are lacking some needed information, ask your team to agree upon a best estimate and continue with your mapping exercise. You can always refine your data later if it becomes necessary. Begin your mapping effort by identifying the trigger and end points of the process to be analyzed. Make sure that these milestones are clear, well-defined, and measurable. Next, list the major steps within your selected process on sticky notes. Keep your first map at a high level; you will use a "drill-down" technique later to get into the details. I suggest identifying no more than about twelve steps for the highest level of your current-state map. A typical value-stream mapping format is shown in Figure 6.3.

Now you are ready to set some initial priorities. This is where my approach to value-stream mapping departs from the conventional wisdom. Having seen so many of these exercises turn into temporal sinkholes, I have become obsessed with achieving the maximum improvement value per time spent. Hence, I immediately try to focus my team's attention on those steps within the high-level process that have the greatest potential for waste elimination. To accomplish this, we must use the three categories of time defined above. Each sticky note (representing a step in the high-level process) should display three numbers: the calendar time (C/T), the work time (W/T), and the value-added time (VA/T), as shown in Figure 6.4. As always, just use your best estimates. The primary purpose for including these numbers is to help you prioritize waste opportunities, and to determine the degree of improvement that you might achieve once a future state is defined. You should first identify those process steps that have the greatest calendar time relative to the duration of the overall process; these represent the best opportunities for cycle-time improvement. Beginning with these heavy-hitters, compare the calendar time to the work time for each process step. Those steps that have the greatest differences between calendar-time spent and work-hours applied should receive your highest priority for improvement. I use red / yellow / green visual designations for the improvement potential of the process steps within the current-state map, as shown in Figure 6.5. Steps with large differences between calendar time and work time are given a red designation, while those with moderate differences could be assigned a yellow. If the two times are close together, this implies that there is little wait time or other process-driven delays that occur during this step, and a green designation would therefore be appropriate. Recall I mentioned earlier that if a process step involves more than one person, that fact should be noted along with the combined hours for all contributors. Here is where that information is needed; when comparing calendar time to work time, you should only use the work-time hours required by one contributor – the one who spends the most time. Work performed in

Step 1) Map "Current-State" Process

Step 2) Prioritize Waste Opportunities

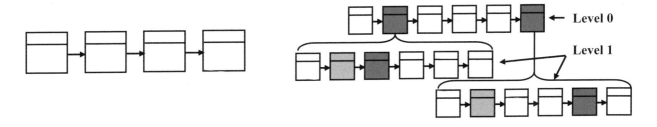

Step 3) Brainstorm on Improvements and Assign Responsibilities

Step 4) Map "Future State," Perform Demonstration, and Deploy

Process Improvement	Responsibility	Due Date

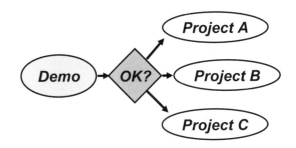

Figure 6.2:   Value-stream mapping can be thought of as a four-step process. The first step is to create an accurate map of the "current state," followed by a prioritization exercise to focus the team's attention on the greatest waste-reduction opportunities. The third step is to brainstorm on possible improvements to the current-state process. These suggestions are then rank-ordered and a select group is implemented in a future-state version of the process. After testing the future state through a demonstration project, the successful new process is implemented across the organization.

parallel is dominated, from a time-to-market standpoint, by the longest pole in the tent. Hence, we use just the long pole to identify improvement opportunities that involve wait time or other process-driven delays.

Once you have identified the highest priority opportunities based on calendar time versus work time, there is one more criterion that should be considered. Although the precision of value-added-time estimates is usually fairly poor, it is worthwhile comparing the work time for each high-level process step with its value-added time. Again, if the difference is substantial, this is a sign of high waste elimination potential, and that step should be given a red designation. At this point, you will have a high-level current-state map that displays your priorities for improvement. You will now use a drill-down technique to determine the root causes of waste for each high-priority opportunity. I call this technique "value-stream expansion," as shown in Figure 6.5. Each process step in the "Level 0" (i.e., high-level) map that is designated as a high priority is expanded to "Level 1". This more detailed level should consist of approximately twelve steps, and again the improvement potential of each step is evaluated and a priority is assigned. For relatively

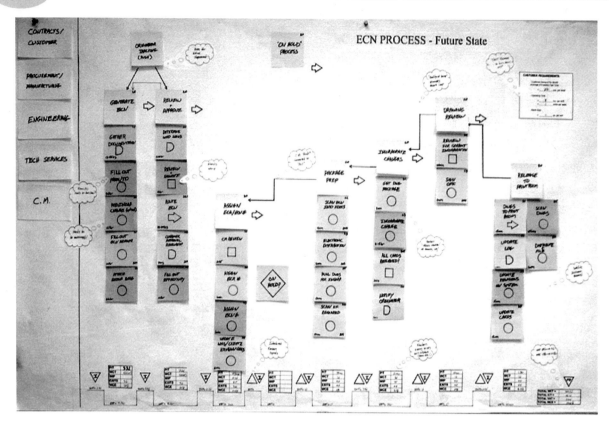

Figure 6.3: A typical small-scale value-stream map; in this case for the future state of an engineering change notice (ECN) process.

simple processes, it may be that a Level 1 expansion is all that is needed to isolate the root causes of waste for that segment of the process. If this is not the case, a Level 2 expansion can be generated that provides even greater detail. The motivation for using this expansion technique should be obvious; if you were to create an entire front-to-back current-state map at Level 2, for example, you would almost certainly waste time and a great deal of wall space. Evaluate your "red" opportunities in order of priority, expanding each until enough detail is provided, and then move on to the next high-priority opportunity.

Now as a group, begin brainstorming on how each wasteful step in the current-state process could be improved. Capture ideas on a flip chart, being careful to identify which ideas apply to which process step. Once a healthy list of possibilities has been generated, ask the group to score each suggestion based on two criteria: the *impact* that the improvement would have if successful (on a 1-to-5 scale), and the *ease of implementation* of the improvement (on a 1-to-5 scale, with a "5" meaning *easy*). Multiply the two scores together for each suggestion and use the results as a way of ranking the ideas for implementation. Take the top-scoring ideas and create an action list for your team, including responsible individuals and due dates.

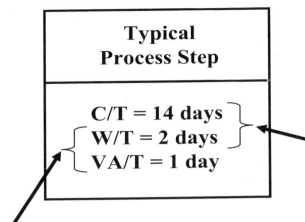

Typical Process Step

C/T = 14 days
W/T = 2 days
VA/T = 1 day

▶ *Start by selecting the process steps that have the longest C/T relative to the overall duration of the process.*

▶ *Next, look for steps that have a large difference between C/T and W/T.*

▶ *Finally, consider the difference between W/T and VA/T as a "tie breaker". A greater difference here implies greater long-term potential to improve.*

▶ *Keep in mind that this does not need to be an exact science. Your goal is to focus your improvement efforts on high-priority, fruitful opportunities.*

Figure 6.4: The three time catagories shown in the block above are used to determine where an improvement team should focus their attention when designing a future-state process. The most important consideration should be the relative value of the calendar time (C/T) when compared to the overall cycle-time of the process.

All that remains is to create a future-state value-stream map that captures the improvements that have been selected for implementation. Again, an expansion approach may be useful here; rather than mapping the entire process in great detail, you should consider keeping the steps that haven't changed at a high level, and only showing detail for those steps that have been significantly modified. The purpose of the future-state map is to communicate the new and improved process both to implementers and to those who will be executing the process. Include as much detail as is needed to accomplish this goal. At this point, I typically select a "showcase project" to demonstrate the future-state process and provide feedback prior to broader deployment. This implementation strategy is discussed in detail in Section 6.3.

The value-stream-mapping methodology that I've suggested is about as simple and straightforward as it gets. You can make this approach more complex and cumbersome if you feel that it is too understandable. Just keep in mind that if you don't find sufficient waste during your improvement event to pay yourselves back for the time your team has invested, your firm will actually be worse off. Here is a good rule to follow: Every once in a while, pull your face out of the trees long enough to see the forest. You may discover that there are far greater opportunities for waste reduction hiding just around the next stand of trees.

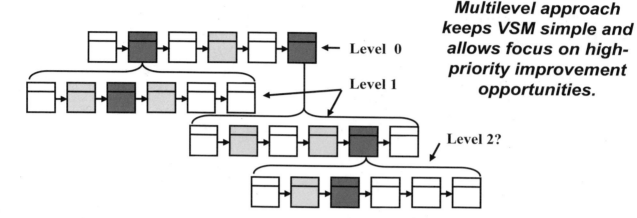

Level 0

Level 1

Level 2?

Multilevel approach keeps VSM simple and allows focus on high-priority improvement opportunities.

► *"Level 0" map provides an overview of key steps in the process.*

► *Improvement priority is determined by the differences between C/T and W/T and between W/T and VA/T.*

► *"Level 1" maps are created for each high-priority step (reds).*

► *If the level of detail is sufficient to identify a solution, the mapping process stops.*

► *If not enough detail is present, continue the expansion process to "Level 2" and beyond.*

Figure 6.5: Value-stream maps can become unwieldy when mapping a large portion of the product development process. By using a "value-stream expansion" approach, the number of process steps and the detail required in your map can be minimized, while still providing substantial insight into those steps with the greatest improvement potential.

Current-State Waste and Future-State Improvement

Let's walk through a simple real-life example of value-stream mapping to solidify your understanding. A few years ago, I came across a small firm that manufactures hydraulic and pneumatic components. Since their products were mainly commodities, they differentiated themselves in the marketplace by offering special order and custom engineering services. Hence, many of their sales calls resulted in the need for a customer proposal. Unfortunately, over the past several years their ability to respond quickly to proposal requests had dramatically diminished. This represented a perfect opportunity to apply value-stream mapping.

A cross-functional team was formed to attack the problem of unacceptably long proposal response times. Following the methodology described above, they began their

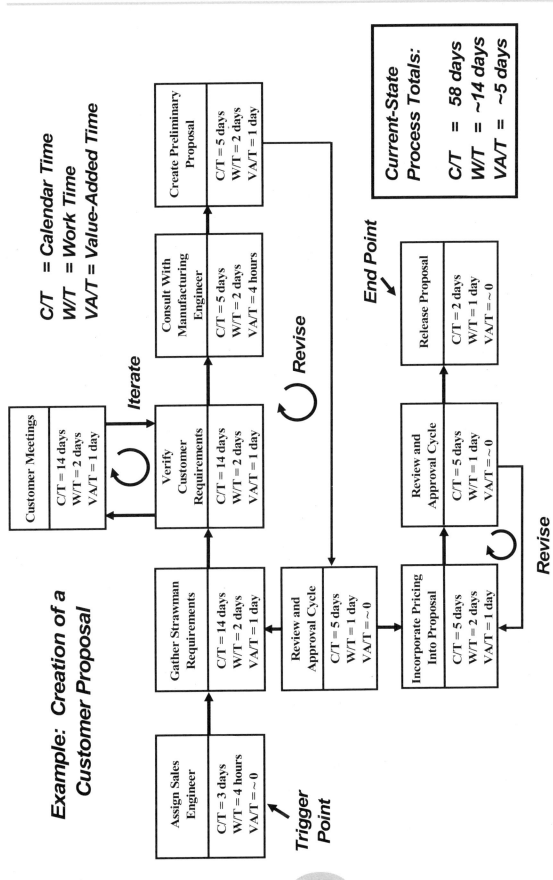

Figure 6.6: An example of a current-state value-stream map for a typical development-related process: in this case the creation of a customer proposal. The current-state process has an average total calendar time (from trigger point to end point) of fifty-eight days.

263

exercise by creating a current-state value-stream map, as shown in Figure 6.6. (Note that in this situation, the process was sufficiently straightforward that only one level of expansion was necessary.) The first step in the process (i.e., the trigger point) was the assignment of a sales engineer to manage the creation of the proposal. The sales engineer would then begin gathering strawman requirements and other technical information at a rather leisurely pace. Once the engineer felt prepared, he would hold a series of meetings and conference calls with the customer to discuss requirements, each of which was followed by technical discussions within the firm's design group. Once a preliminary design approach was identified, the sales engineer would collaborate with a manufacturing engineer to create a draft proposal that would subsequently be reviewed by management. After going through one or more revision loops, the proposal was submitted to finance for pricing, and reviewed yet again by management. Finally, the proposal was released to the customer (i.e., the end point).

For each of the process steps described above, the improvement team estimated the calendar time, work time, and value-added time. When all of the steps were totaled, it was found that the overall calendar time of the process averaged fifty-eight days; a number that matched recent experience. The team was encouraged (and a little dismayed) by the huge gap between total calendar time and total work time. It appeared that there were forty-four days of wait time and other process-driven delays that could potentially be eliminated. Excited by this bounty of waste elimination opportunities, they proceeded to prioritize each step in their current-state process using red / yellow / green designations, as shown in Figure 6.7. Several steps had calendar times of more than a week, but work times of just a few days. These steps were identified as the highest priorities for improvement and were assigned a red status. Other steps showed lesser potential, but were still considered worthy of attention. These were assigned a yellow status. Only the final step in the process showed sufficiently low potential that it was given a low priority.

With priorities in hand, the team began brainstorming on ways to improve the process. Their results are shown in Figure 6.8. Each suggestion was scored based on its potential *impact* and *ease of implementation*, and the product of these two numbers was used as a means of ranking the improvement ideas. Most of the suggestions shown in the figure were considered promising enough to implement in the future state of the process, so action items were assigned and due dates were set. Once this improvement plan was solidified, the team reassembled to create a future-state map that captured their innovative solutions, as shown in Figure 6.9. The time required to assign a sales engineer was shortened from three days to one, and the delay in gathering strawman requirements was slashed from fourteen days to five. Rather than employing a series of inefficient customer meetings and teleconferences, a focused customer negotiation meeting was implemented that would be attended by all functions that were needed to arrive at a viable real-time solution. One entire approval loop was eliminated by sending the draft proposal to pricing prior to management review, resulting in a savings of another dozen days.

The resulting future-state map indicated that the new process should achieve a customer response time of just sixteen days – a net saving of forty-two days! A demonstration run of the new process uncovered a few minor bugs that were easily corrected. Once the future state was finalized, it was deployed across the organization and tracked

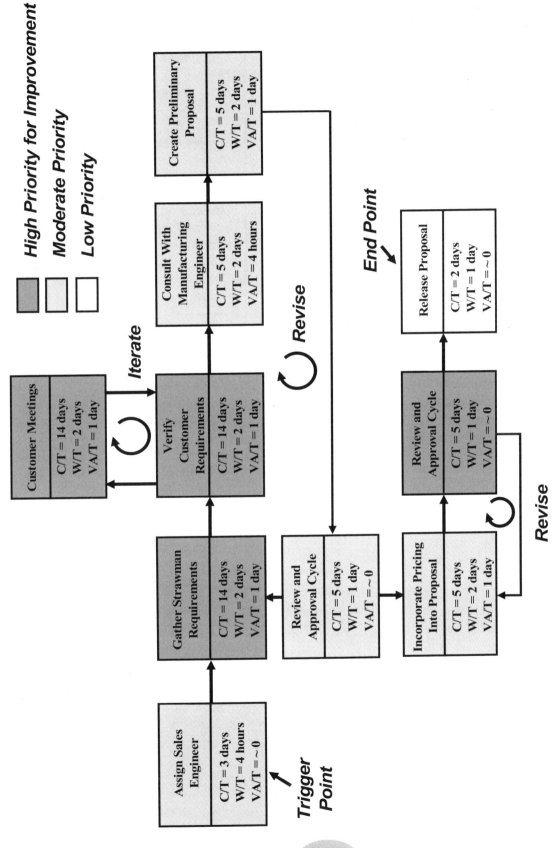

Figure 6.7: Continuing with the value-stream-mapping example, the current-state map has been prioritized, based on which steps within the process have the greatest potential for improvement. The three time categories shown in each process block are used to establish this priority.

High Priority for Improvement

Moderate Priority

Low Priority

Customer Meetings

C/T = 14 days
W/T = 2 days
VA/T = 1 day

Iterate

Verify Customer Requirements

C/T = 14 days
W/T = 2 days
VA/T = 1 day

Consult With Manufacturing Engineer

C/T = 5 days
W/T = 2 days
VA/T = 4 hours

Create Preliminary Proposal

C/T = 5 days
W/T = 2 days
VA/T = 1 day

Revise

Assign Sales Engineer

C/T = 3 days
W/T = 4 hours
VA/T = ∼ 0

Trigger Point

Gather Strawman Requirements

C/T = 14 days
W/T = 2 days
VA/T = 1 day

Review and Approval Cycle

C/T = 5 days
W/T = 1 day
VA/T = ∼ 0

Incorporate Pricing Into Proposal

C/T = 5 days
W/T = 2 days
VA/T = 1 day

Revise

Review and Approval Cycle

C/T = 5 days
W/T = 1 day
VA/T = ∼ 0

Release Proposal

C/T = 2 days
W/T = 1 day
VA/T = ∼ 0

End Point

6.1

265

Improvement Suggestion	Impact	Ease	Priority	Recommended Approach
1. Eliminate first iteration loop to determine customer needs.	5	3	15	Hold focused customer-needs negotiation meeting.
2. Reduce time to gather strawman requirements.	5	2	10	Use a template or checklist to accelerate information gathering.
3. Reduce time required to consult with manufacturing engineer.	3	3	9	Involve manufacturing engineer in customer meetings or use a "feed forward" of information.
4. Eliminate first approval cycle.	4	3	12	Use customer-defined template and feed forward of preliminary information.
5. Reduce final approval cycle.	4	4	16	Use a reservation system to enable immediate review.
6. Reduce time to assign sales engineer.	3	3	9	Implement real-time priority system to eliminate queue.

Figure 6.8: Continuing with the value-stream mapping example, the improvement team has brainstormed on possible improvements to the current-state process. After a list of suggestions was generated, the team scored each suggestion based on the impact that the improvement might have, and the ease with which it could be implemented. A 1-to-5 scale was used for each of these criteria, and the product of the two scores represented a useful priority metric for selecting improvements.

over a period of several months. The actual data supported the future-state estimate made by the improvement team; the average response time had dropped to roughly two weeks. You might have noticed that even after this significant improvement, there is still potential to squeeze out more waste. The future-state process totals indicate that there were still seven days of process delays, and several days of difference between total work time and total value-added time. As it turned out, the same improvement team decided to readdress this process after six months of initial success, and was able to drive another four days out of the response time. The real payoff came when the firm calculated how this dramatically accelerated process impacted their win rate for customer proposals. They found that the improved customer response time had resulted in a thirty percent increase in sales orders – an enormous payback for just a few days of value-stream-mapping effort.

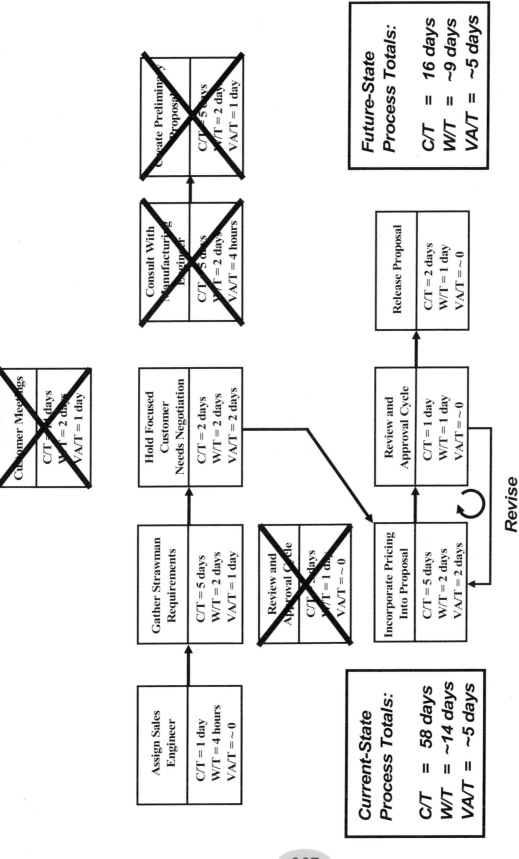

Figure 6.9: Completing the value-stream mapping example, the above diagram represents the future-state process that was implemented by the improvement team. The projected total cycle-time for this future state is sixteen days, representing a potential savings of thirty-two days over the current state.

Short Attention Span? Try a Mini-Kaizen Event!

There is no question that value-stream mapping can enhance the performance of any business process. However this methodology has one major drawback; it requires a significant investment of time and resources to do it justice. In some situations, this investment may become a roadblock to improvement, representing too large a commitment and having too much potential for disruption of ongoing business activities. What is an improvement champion to do in circumstances such as this? Why not slice away waste by using a smaller knife? The mini-*kaizen* event represents a surgical improvement tool that can yield significant benefits in a fraction of the time required to perform a value-steam mapping exercise. Essentially, the mini-*kaizen* is the same as "Step 3" of the value-stream methodology shown previously in Figure 6.2. As its name implies, it is short (hence the "mini"), and it enables incremental continuous improvement (the "*kaizen*" part).

Instructions for holding a mini-*kaizen* event are shown in Figure 6.10. The best application of this lean method is as a highly focused problem-solving session. A specific waste elimination opportunity is selected, often derived from an employee suggestion. For example, someone might point out that there is an internal document or procedure that appears to be unnecessarily time-consuming or of questionable value. However the opportunity is selected, it must be possible to treat it as a stand-alone improvement initiative, rather than as an integral part of a larger process. Basically, the mini-*kaizen* event is just a brainstorming exercise, followed by the rank-ordering of suggestions, and ultimately the creation of an action list for the implementation of selected ideas. A template for performing the brainstorming and ranking tasks is provided in Figure 6.11. Again, this activity is at the heart of the value-stream methodology; we have simply bypassed the mapping and prioritization steps, and jumped directly to improving a specific wasteful situation.

The mini-*kaizen* event is not a substitute for a more strategic, value-stream-mapping approach to improving new product development. Realistically, you can't just add up a bunch of mini-*kaizens* and end up at the same future state that would have resulted from a value-stream-mapping event. Without a global perspective, improvements will be incremental and localized. That being said, the exceedingly low barrier to entry for this method makes it attractive, particularly for organizations that respond best to quick hits and immediate gratification. In fact, a few successful mini-*kaizens* might be sufficient to get management interested in a more substantial commitment to improvement. From my perspective, a mini-*kaizen* event is like arthroscopic surgery; it provides a way of taking aim at chronically annoying situations within a firm, without the patient suffering much discomfort.

Instructions for Holding a "Mini-*Kaizen*" Event

Step 1 – Select an opportunity for waste elimination. To be a candidate for a mini-*kaizen* event, an opportunity should meet all of the following criteria:

  • It must be specific and well-defined – typically a small-scale improvement.
  • The improvement team must have the authority to make necessary changes.
  • The scope of work should be limited to a few days of effort.

Step 2 – Form the improvement team based on the nature of the chosen opportunity.

Step 3 – Hold a team meeting to precisely define the scope of the waste problem, and identify metrics that can be used to measure success.

Step 4 – Hold your mini-*kaizen* event. Start with a review of the results from Step 3, and then begin a brainstorming session, with the goal of identifying a number of viable ways in which the waste problem can be solved. Capture these suggestions using the template provided in Figure 6.11.

Step 5 – Rank improvement suggestions based on two criteria: 1) The IMPACT that the suggestion would have in solving the waste problem, and 2) The EASE OF IMPLEMENTATION of the suggested improvement. Use a 1-to-5 scale for each criterion, with a "5" implying high impact and easy implementation.

Step 6 – Multiply the two scores from Step 5 together to generate a priority ranking. Based on this ranking, select one or more improvement suggestions for immediate implementation and evaluation. Assign action items, responsibilities, and due dates to accomplish this goal.

Figure 6.10: Instructions for holding a "mini-*kaizen*" event. These quick-hit exercises can be used to attack a specific waste problem and provide an immediately implementable solution.

Suggested Application of Lean Method to Improve Development Process	Ratings (1-5)		Priority Ranking
	Impact	Ease	

Figure 6.11: A template used during a mini-*kaizen* event to capture suggestions for process improvement. Note that two criteria are used to determine the applicability of suggestions. The product of these two scores becomes the priority ranking shown in the column on the right.

The Lean Self-Assessment Tool

Now here's a change of pace. You have been diligently reading away now for a few hundred pages, without a single interactivity break. Well, in this section you will have a chance to assess your firm's product development performance, and compare your results with those of other companies. A self-assessment tool is a qualitative questionnaire designed to measure the subjective benefits of an improvement initiative. Certainly it is no substitute for quantitative metrics, but as you will learn in Section 6.3, product development is a difficult process to quantify, and even more difficult to assess over periods of months rather than years. Moreover, perception can be as important as reality for a process that is substantially driven by collaboration, interaction, morale, and personal productivity. These days, subjective surveys affect the outcomes of elections, influence which products make it to market, and even determine who becomes the next American Idol. Don't shy away from this method because you can't put a decimal point after the result; in the nebulous world of new product development, a heuristic assessment may be your best read on the progress you have made toward a waste-free future.

A Qualitative (but Useful) Measurement Approach

I have used a self-assessment diagnostic tool for several years as a way to illuminate fundamental problems within a development organization. My approach involves sixty questions and makes use of an automated spreadsheet, but there is no reason why you couldn't use a more basic questionnaire to focus in on specific areas that are in need of improvement. You can use the fifteen-question version presented in the next subsection as a guide to the types of questions you may wish to ask. I suggest having several individuals from each function involved in new product development take the survey. If you have boundless energy, you could try for a statistically valid sampling, but you would need to involve hundreds of people to achieve a statistical error of below ten percent. Instead, keep track of who takes the initial (i.e., baseline) self-assessment, and then ask those same individuals to be part of your sample group throughout the duration of a typical development project. By polling the same people each time, you can substantially reduce the statistical variability in your results, and can therefore gain useful insights from a more manageable sample group.

The results of your first application of the self-assessment tool will help you formulate an improvement plan by indicating which areas or activities require immediate waste-eliminating attention, as shown in Figure 6.12. After implementing your selected lean improvements, you should plan to reapply the self-assessment questionnaire at regular intervals as the new methods take hold. I've found that obtaining a new sampling every three months or so is about right; there needs to be enough time between samples to allow working conditions to change (hopefully for the better). After each three-month interval, poll the same individuals again, and post the comparative results on the team's visual project board (or in a prominent location along with other improvement data). Each time you iterate the self-assessment, you should update the visual display to show progress. If no improvement is evident after a couple of iterations, gather the sample group together and determine the root cause of this problem. Revise your improvement plan, re-baseline your visual display, and proceed as before. Not only will the self-assessment tool provide you with insight into the experiences of actual team members, but allowing them to actively participate in the improvement process will enfranchise these individuals, and hopefully gain you valuable allies as you continue along your lean implementation journey.

Take the Lean Self-Assessment Challenge

Grab a pencil and prepare to evaluate your own product development organization. I've provided a fifteen-question, generic self-assessment questionnaire in Figure 6.13. Answer each question as honestly as possible, but don't spend a lot of time on each one; your first impressions are probably the most accurate. If the potentially wasteful situation described in a question occurs frequently within your new product development process, give that question ten points. If the situation occurs sometimes (meaning from twenty to eighty percent of the time), assign it a score of five points. Finally, if the condition rarely occurs, give that question a zero. When you've completed all fifteen questions, total your scores and continue reading. I'll be waiting.

Okay class, time's up, pencils down. How did your firm fare? You can compare your results to those of a number of other firms by using the scale provided in Figure 6.14. I use this exact survey as an exercise in virtually every workshop that I present, and the conclusions indicated in the figure seem to be quite consistent. A low score (i.e., below thirty points) is a rarity, but if your total is within this range, you might want to take some objectivity training. Even a total score of less than sixty points is uncommon, and can either mean that you work for Toyota, or that you may be underestimating the amount of waste that surrounds you and your development teams. Far more typical is a score of between sixty and one-hundred-twenty points (with a large clustering in the range between ninety and one-hundred-ten points). A total score that falls on the low side of this range would indicate that your organization has significant near-term improvement potential. The higher end of the range implies that there is a compelling need for waste elimination. Finally, if your total score exceeds one-hundred-twenty points, your teams are in need of CPR stat. Don't panic, however; you have an excellent chance of recovery, provided that you immediately begin taking your lean improvement medicine.

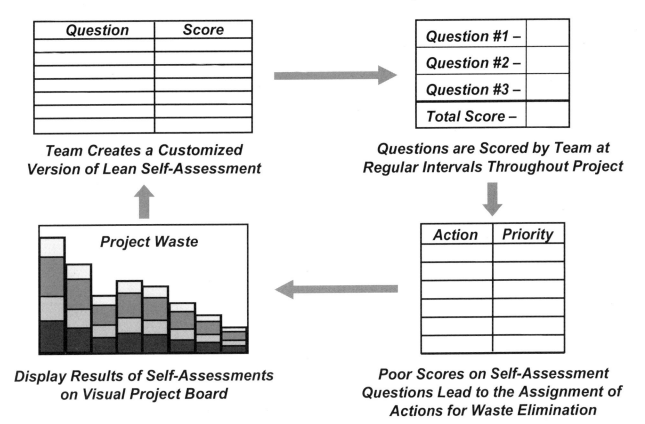

A Lean Self-Assessment Tool
Enables Continuous Measurable Improvement –

Question	Score

**Team Creates a Customized
Version of Lean Self-Assessment**

Question #1 –	
Question #2 –	
Question #3 –	
Total Score –	

**Questions are Scored by Team at
Regular Intervals Throughout Project**

Project Waste

**Display Results of Self-Assessments
on Visual Project Board**

Action	Priority

**Poor Scores on Self-Assessment
Questions Lead to the Assignment of
Actions for Waste Elimination**

Figure 6.12: A well-crafted self-assessment questionnaire can provide a useful, albeit qualitative measure of improvement over time. The same questions are asked of a design team at regular intervals over the duration of a project, and the results are posted on the visual project board.

Now here's a reward for your honesty (and a balm for your newly found humility). Each question in the self-assessment that you have just completed can be linked to several applicable lean methods presented in this guidebook, as shown in Figure 6.15. If you gave a question a "ten" score, you can use the material in the indicated sections to begin forming a plan for improvement. Of course if you gave almost every question a ten, you might as well go back to the beginning of the book and read it again with feeling. My experience with self-assessments of this type has generally been very positive. Although the results are far from definitive, this tool represents a highly visible way of focusing attention on improvement goals, while highlighting any backsliding or discontent within your teams.

Symptoms of Waste (Consider a typical product development team – answer honestly!)	Score		
	Frequently (10)	Sometimes (5)	Rarely (0)
1) Is more than one hour of a typical team member's day spent in meetings?			
2) Do poorly defined requirements cause significant delays in product launch?			
3) Is product development work interrupted by "emergency" customer / factory support?			
4) Are critical decisions delayed for weeks or months due to a slow decision process?			
5) Do handoffs between the design team and the factory require corrections or iterations?			
6) Do your new product development projects overrun target costs and miss margin goals?			
7) Are your development projects characterized by multiple, disruptive design changes?			
8) Are the production dates of new products delayed because of slow starts to projects?			
9) Is your design review process ineffective at identifying errors or risks early in a project?			
10) Do you or your team spend too much time in status meetings or management reviews?			
11) Are your design team members typically working on more than one project?			
12) Are priorities among multiple projects unclear, or do they change often?			
13) Do your projects suffer from persistent slips in task completion dates and milestones?			
14) Are there job functions (or individuals) that are an obstacle to meeting launch targets?			
15) Do delays on one project have a "cascading effect" on the schedules of other projects?			

Figure 6.13: Take this abbreviated version of a lean self-assessment yourself. Answer each question honestly, and then total your score when completed. Your total score is interpreted in Figure 6.14.

Total Score	Potential Benefits of a Lean Product Development Improvement Initiative
0 – 30	Get Real! You're in denial.
30 – 60	Possible minor improvements.
60 – 90	Significant near-term gains possible.
90 – 120	Major opportunity – dramatic and immediate.
120 – 150	Thank you for your honesty – get started ASAP!

Figure 6.14: How to interpret your total score from the self-assessment questionnaire provided in Figure 6.13. Most companies seem to score themselves in the range from ninety to one-hundred and ten, indicating that there is substantial room for improvement.

If you scored a "10" on:	Consider lean methods discussed in:
Question 1	Sections 5.2, 5.3, 5.5
Question 2	Sections 3.3, 3.4, 4.1, 4.2, 4.3
Question 3	Sections 4.2, 5.3, 5.6
Question 4	Sections 2.3, 3.2, 4.2, 4.3, 5.2, 5.5
Question 5	Sections 3.3, 3.4, 4.2, 4.3
Question 6	Sections 2.3, 3.3, 3.4, 4.2
Question 7	Sections 2.3, 3.3, 3.5, 4.3
Question 8	Sections 2.2, 2.3, 2.4, 5.2, 5.6
Question 9	Sections 2.3, 3.3, 3.5
Question 10	Sections 3.2, 5.1, 5.2
Question 11	Sections 2.2, 2.4, 5.2, 5.4, 5.6
Question 12	Sections 2.2, 2.4, 4.2, 5.2, 5.4, 5.6
Question 13	Sections 3.2, 5.2, 5.3, 5.4
Question 14	Sections 3.1, 3.2, 5.3, 5.6
Question 15	Sections 2.2, 2.4, 4.2, 5.4, 5.6

Figure 6.15: The questions provided in the lean self-assessment shown in Figure 6.13 have been linked to sections within this guidebook that discuss ways to improve each wasteful situation. If you scored a "ten" on any of the questions, the sections corresponding to that question would be a good place to start your improvement journey.

<u>Notes</u>

6.3

Section

A Proven Strategy
for Deployment

Are you excited about lean product development tools and methods? Perhaps you are visualizing how much better things could (and should, and must) be if waste was banished from your organization. Well, it's time to take action. The final section of this guidebook is dedicated to helping you transition from unfulfilled excitement to blissful contentment. Setting hyperbole aside for a moment, you really do have a challenge ahead of you if you wish to enjoy an efficient, waste-free future. The problem is that although no one benefits from waste within an organization, we all like things to remain just the way they are. When it comes to lean deployment, our enemy is the status quo. How can we motivate people to leave their comfort zone and venture into territory that is uncertain, intimidating, and just plain different? As you will soon see, there is a reasonably straightforward formula for success when it comes to implementing lean product development. The most critical ingredients, however, will have to come from you and your team: discipline, energy, and persistence. Frankly, deployment of new tools and methods within a firm can be a Sisyphean task, so if you enjoy pushing a huge boulder up an endless mountain, you are going to love leading an improvement initiative.

Springs, Entropy, and Other Legitimate Excuses

How is a design organization like a spring? Try implementing a new work method and see how much tension is generated, and how quickly things will return to their original state if constant pressure is not applied, as shown in Figure 6.16. Unfortunately, a typical improvement initiative follows an all too familiar pattern: a couple of months of fanfare and hoopla, followed by a gradual loss of management interest, and ultimately a return to the way things were before. In other words, as soon as the pressure is removed, the spring snaps back to nearly its original position, leaving behind little or no lasting benefit. It is not uncommon for me to revisit firms that I've worked with in the past, only to find that a lack of management discipline and persistence has eroded what took months or years for us to build. The problem is the timeframe; management would like to believe that a highly visible short-term program, with lots of training, tee-shirts, and banners, can make a lasting difference. The reality is that organizational change takes years of constant pressure, continuous feedback, and unflinching commitment.

Returning to my spring analogy, what happens to a spring if it is kept in a distended state for an extended period? It will eventually deform to the new, stretched position, and

277

Like a stretched spring, change puts your organization under tension...

Current State

Future State (Short term)

To make it stick, you must actively enforce the future state for at least six months...

*Back to Current State (If management is not **persistent**)*

or

Future State Sticks (If management holds their ground!)

Figure 6.16: It takes at least six months of continuous use for a new tool or method to become ingrained in the minds of employees. Failure to persistently support and encourage the use of an improved method during this transitional period will result in backsliding to the old status quo.

even resist going back to its original condition. (Actually, I've been informed by several mechanical engineers that this should never happen to a "good spring". You've just got to love how engineers can make a point and miss one at the same time.) It seems that there is a "trick" to achieving lasting change that isn't really a trick at all, it's just common sense: take manageable bites, be open to constructive feedback, and apply persistent pressure for a period of at least six months. Following these three straightforward requirements will give you a high probability of success. Violate any one of them, however, and your chances for lasting improvement will drop precipitously.

Since we're on the subject of enduring change, there is another challenge that is worth mentioning. This one, however, goes beyond human nature to encompass our entire universe; in fact it can be called a "natural law". I'm referring to entropy, that ubiquitous tendency of all things to become more random and chaotic over time. Try cleaning your desk on Monday and see what it looks like by Friday, as shown in Figure 6.17. A one-time cleaning will have little long-term effect on the neatness of your desk. Likewise, a one-time waste reduction initiative will provide little lasting benefit to an organization. As time passes, waste will creep back in, not like the snapping back of a spring due to human nature, but as a long, slow decline in order and efficiency. There is no "solution" to entropy; it is always present and always will be. Its deleterious effects can be controlled, however, through a constant input of organizing energy. How do you keep your home or office from degenerating into a pigsty? Through constant maintenance. How do you keep your car from grinding to a halt? Same answer. Maintenance is the essential response to the randomizing effects of entropy. In the context of an improvement initiative, maintenance should include: 1) A period of high energy input to move an organization to the desired new position, 2) A six-month or longer period of moderate energy input to ensure that no backsliding occurs, and 3) A long-term, low-energy maintenance program that constantly updates tools, measures performance, and applies selected fixes where needed. So gather up your resources and muster your energy; you're in for a long, but hopefully rewarding, battle against both human nature and nature itself.

Metrics of Lean Product Development

Logic tells us that if we cannot measure something, we have no way of knowing if it has changed. The implementation of lean manufacturing techniques, for example, is aided by the measurement of such factors as work-in-process inventory levels, *kanban* size, process cycle-times, number of defects, and so on. Using these metrics, it is possible to quickly and unambiguously determine whether an improvement has been successful and how much benefit has been gained. These same measures can also warn of backsliding, and can represent the foundation of a long-term maintenance program. Clearly, therefore, we must identify a set of metrics for the implementation of lean product development.

It takes about a week for THIS to look like THIS!

Figure 6.17: Yet another reason why organizations fail to successfully implement new tools and methods. The law of entropy, which states that all things will naturally tend to become more random and chaotic, affects our universe in the same way as it affects your messy desk.

This will prove to be more of a challenge than you might expect. New product development is one of the most difficult business processes to quantify, as I'll illustrate with the following example. Suppose your firm plans to develop three new products over the next twelve months. Since these are the only projects on your docket, they represent your only opportunities to measure the success of improvement initiatives. The first project involves the design of an entirely new product platform, one that will be used as the basis for countless variations and extensions over the next decade. The core team will consist of several dozen members drawn from diverse functional departments, with additional support personnel being included on an as-needed basis. The goal of the second project is to update an existing product line to incorporate new technology and added features. A smaller team is required for this project, with most of the core team members being engineers and technicians. Your final opportunity is a cost reduction project that is focused on reducing defects and driving down material and labor costs on a mature product line. Most of the core team members for this effort are manufacturing and industrial engineers. Three projects with essentially nothing in common, either with each other or with projects completed in the recent past. The planned durations are significantly different, the constituency of the teams is different, the technical and market risks are different, and the core team leaders themselves are different. Go ahead, start measuring.

Recurring processes with relatively short cycle-times are straightforward to quantify. New product development is, at least in some respects, a *non-recurring* process, with typical cycle-times of six months to two years. This variability from project to project makes it almost impossible to establish "controls" on your measurements. How can we get a grip on this illusive creature? The answer is that we can't, at least not to the degree possible with other, more tractable business processes. Rather than give up, however, we will persevere. I've identified a number of metrics that can be useful in tracking the effectiveness of improvement initiatives in the product development environment, as shown in Figure 6.18. None of these measures is sufficient on its own, and all suffer from the vaguaries highlighted in the example above, but when used properly they can paint a relatively detailed picture of value and waste in new product development.

Since most of the metrics mentioned in the figure are straightforward, I will only highlight the two that I prefer: productivity per engineer and the lean self-assessment. Productivity is defined as the value created per unit time. For example, if a design team spends only one hour of each workday on value-added activities prior to the implementation of lean methods, and achieves two hours of value creation after employing lean improvements, their productivity has doubled. There are many ways to measure productivity, ranging from sophisticated financial calculations to time studies and log sheets. As you might expect, I prefer the more hands-on approach. In particular, I've had success using a weekly time tracking sheet such as the one described in Section 1.2. Each member of a product development team is asked to fill out a "baseline" tracking sheet prior to the implementation of lean tools and methods, and then create a new sheet after several months of using the improved process. Although the results are coarse and subjective, they do represent a direct measure of waste and value, as opposed to other possible metrics that only provide indirect information.

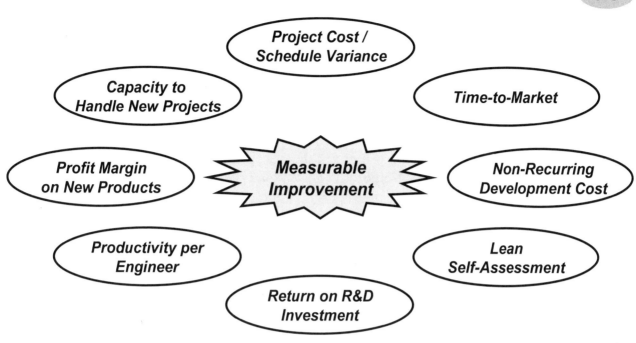

Figure 6.18: Although improvements to the product development process can be difficult to measure, the metrics shown above can be used effectively once they have been tailored to your firm's situation.

Along a similar vein, the lean self-assessment described in the previous section can provide useful, albeit qualitative insights into the success of an improvement initiative. One of the reasons why I prefer these two techniques over other, more analytical choices, is that they are relatively noninvasive. Remember that time spent measuring a process is non-value-added. It may be necessary to determine the amount of progress, but it is nonetheless a tax on the very process you are seeking to improve. I'll settle for a more heuristic measurement approach that requires just a few minutes of team members' time, rather than run the risk of creating more waste than I've eliminated by imposing a draconian tracking system.

Finally, when establishing your measurement system, I strongly recommend using a "balanced-scorecard" approach that involves the use of several countervailing metrics, such as the example shown in Figure 6.19. Generally, there are three categories of metric you should consider: time, cost, and performance / quality. If you focus your measurements on just one of these dimensions, it is possible that the others will suffer as improvements are implemented. For example, if time-to-market is emphasized above all else, there is nothing to stop teams from rushing suboptimal designs to the factory, thereby negatively impacting production cost and product quality. As is indicated in the figure, I typically select more than one metric from each of the three categories. You will also notice that the metrics I've chosen involve varying timeframes. In this way, your improvement team will not be fooled by short-term "blips," nor will you miss long-term trends. Lastly, I suggest creating a normalized score for each metric that captures its relative behavior from measurement to measurement. This reduces the accuracy of the measurement, so it should only be used for creating visual reports or displays of progress. The benefit is in its simplicity; it is far easier to communicate success (or, heaven forbid, failure) using a few unitless numbers on a histogram than it is to explain each metric and its relationship to the others. In my experience, most progress-tracking systems die of their own weight. The more arcane the measurement approach, the more likely it is that waste will be created and knowledge will be obscured. Keep it simple, be mindful of the impact your tracking system has on design teams, and above all else, stay focused on the goal. I'd rather that the members of my improvement team invest their time and energy eliminating waste, rather than measuring it.

	Quantitative or Subjective Metrics (Units Shown in Brackets)	Target	Actual	Normalized Score (1-10 Scale)
Time	**Total Time-to-Market** (Weeks from Kickoff)			
	Schedule Variance of Key Milestones (Days from Planned Completion)			
Cost	**Non-Recurring Design Cost** (Dollars or Hours per Deliverable)			
	Realized Profit Margin (Dollar Difference between Target and Actual Cost)			
Performance	**Performance Against Requirements** (Subjective Rating Based on Number of Initial Targets Achieved)			
	Features Realized (Subjective Rating Based on Number of Planned Features Achieved)			
	Total Project Score –			

Figure 6.19: A "balanced-scorecard" approach can provide a reasonably accurate measure of progress toward your lean goals. Note that three dimensions of the product development process are tracked, and more than one metric is used to evaluate each of these dimensions.

A Logical Approach to Deployment

Now that we have excuses and metrics out of the way, I will describe how a typical lean product development initiative might be structured, and provide you with some practical suggestions to improve your chances of success. Before you can launch a lean development initiative you must determine which improvements will yield the greatest benefits. In previous sections we have discussed several techniques for selecting the appropriate lean tools and methods for your organization. You could embark on a value-stream mapping exercise, for example, that would yield a future-state process map that can be used as a template for improvement. Alternatively, you might either hold a mini-*kaizen* event or perform a lean self-assessment to prioritize your improvement opportunities.

Once an improvement plan has been established, I recommend using a phased deployment strategy, with each phase representing a substantial move in the right direction, but none so ambitious as to risk overtaxing your organization's ability to absorb change. You can reduce the resistance to Phase 1 changes by selecting improvements that require only a minimal time commitment on the part of the organization. Once the benefits of lean product development have been demonstrated, it will be easier to gather the support needed to deploy more aggressive process changes in later phases. As a guide, and with some trepidation, I've provided in Figure 6.20 some recommendations that you might consider for your initial improvement drive. These tools have proven to be the easiest to implement, and have been at the top of the improvement list for almost every company that I've worked with. My trepidation stems from a concern that my readers will use this list as a recipe for improvement, without going through the due diligence required to ensure that these methods are the ones best suited to your unique situation. That being said, you will not go too far wrong if you implement some or all of these lean methods during Phase 1.

After you have determined your long-term improvement goals, you might lay out a phased improvement program such as the one shown in Figure 6.21. Note that Phase 1 is actually not the first activity that should be executed. Your chances of success are greatly increased if you begin your journey toward lean product development with broad initial training in the basic concepts. This "Phase 0" training should motivate your organization to embrace a lower-waste approach, and help design team members to understand the Phase 1 tools that have been selected for implementation. Once the training program is well underway, I suggest selecting a "showcase project" to pilot the lean methods you have identified. This showcase project should have a team leader who is sold on the benefits of lean product development and capable of motivating her team to move in new directions, and the project itself should be selected based on having a high probability of successful implementation. You are looking for a big initial win here to pave the way for subsequent company-wide deployment. A showcase project is also an effective way to harvest early feedback to help tweak the selected improvements so they best suit your company's products and culture. A short-duration pilot project is preferable, since rapid feedback will accelerate your entire improvement agenda.

A Recommended Lean Product Development Toolset for Phase I Deployment	Guidebook Reference
Stand-Up Team Coordination Meetings	Section 5.2
Visual Project Board	Section 5.2
Lean Meetings	Section 5.5
Must / Should / Could Prioritization	Section 4.2
E-mail Rules / Selected "Time-Savers"	Section 5.5

Figure 6.20: Based on the author's experience with a number of firms, the lean methods listed above represent a good starting point for Phase 1 of a lean product development implementation.

As the selected improvements for Phase 1 take hold, it is wise to begin planning your Phase 2 rollout. By overlapping deployment phases, you will maintain a constant level of pressure toward improvement, and accelerate the pace at which change can occur. Each subsequent phase should include additional training, both to reinforce the improvements from the previous phase, and to provide an introduction to the next wave of changes. It is common for firms to think of lean product development implementation as having a beginning, a middle, and an end. In reality, your improvement drive should be ongoing, with new phases being launched at regular intervals. There is never an end to waste, and hence there should never be an end to your drive to eliminate it. This does not need to be an invasive program. Instead, it should become an integral part of the normal course of business; something that is accepted by design team members and management alike. A culture of continuous change for the better is one of the most common and recognizable attributes of the world's most successful companies.

Some Possible Glitches and Gotchas

There are two particularly nasty roadblocks that you may encounter as you embark on your lean product development initiative. I will illustrate these situations through a final pair of stories. The first example involves a major aerospace firm that desperately needed to improve their project scheduling system. Design team resources were being allocated to projects with little understanding of the big picture, resulting in overworked employees and unpredictable slips in schedule. I worked with this organization for several months to develop a detailed strategy for resource allocation, project prioritization, and master scheduling. To ensure rapid acceptance of the new system, all of the key stakeholders in this new and improved process were included in every discussion and decision...or so I thought.

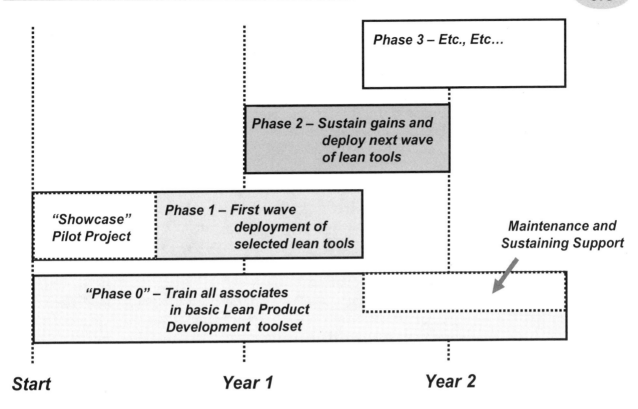

Figure 6.21: A typical phased deployment plan, involving several waves of improvement. Note that a "showcase project" is selected at the beginning of the initiative to allow testing of new tools and methods, and to prove that lean product development can work in a firm's culture.

As our team neared the "go-live" date for the improved scheduling approach, a new face showed up at one of our final meetings. It was immediately clear that this individual was a key figure in the organization, and certainly should have been included on our improvement team. However, the general manager of the firm had omitted his name from my list of suggested team members because this person had a reputation for being resistant to change. This proved to be a major mistake. By not enfranchising him in the process from the very beginning, we had alienated this individual beyond repair. He immediately became hostile to the new approach that we had crafted, and made it clear that his department would not support the improved scheduling system. It came down to either firing this manager or abandoning the improvement initiative. Ultimately, the firm decided to throw out what we had worked so hard to develop, and allowed this individual to lead a new team that would take on the challenge. The lesson to be learned from this painful experience is that no matter how difficult or obnoxious a person might be, if they play a key role in the success of your improvement initiative, *they must be included in all discussions and decisions.* It may have taken us considerable extra time to "pre-sell" this person on our new approach, but ultimately we would have had a successful outcome instead of a disaster.

The second potential obstacle to lean product development implementation is somewhat ironic, because the resistance comes from individuals who should be the most supportive. A few years ago, I came across a large industrial firm that had invested heavily in deploying Design for Six Sigma (DFSS) tools and methods. They had trained all of their engineers and designers in this approach, and had developed an extensive team of internal experts (i.e., six-sigma blackbelts). In fact, a separate entity, referred to as the "six-sigma program office," had been established to promote the utilization of this powerful methodology. As these new tools were taking hold, several of the firm's executives became excited about the lean improvement philosophy, having recognized the unique benefits that this approach could bring to both their manufacturing and development organizations. Not surprisingly, they launched a second improvement program to train employees in the lean methodology, and set up a "lean program office" to support this new thrust. Unfortunately, rather than working together toward improving the business, the two program offices began to war with each other over funding, priorities, and even the usefulness of their respective tools. This battle spilled over into the employee population, resulting in the formation of separate "camps" which supported one methodology over the other. Misinformation was rampant, and emotions began to dominate over logic. In the end, the firm decided to dissolve both program offices and backed away from lean implementation.

With any activity involving Homo sapiens, there is a strong tendency to form cliques. Once a clique has formed, its members become insular to outside ideas and protective of their unique identity. By maintaining separate program offices for their two major improvement drives, the firm played right into this natural human tendency. How could this situation have been avoided? By recognizing that there is *no such thing as an all-encompassing improvement philosophy*. Again I am reminded of the famous quote by Abraham Maslow: "When one becomes adept at using a hammer, everything begins to look like a nail." Tools are tools are tools; the more that we have of them, the better equipped we are to fix what is broken. DFSS is undeniably a successful and sophisticated approach to solving a certain category of business problems. Lean tools and methods are well-suited to attacking a somewhat different set of problems. There may be some overlap, but there is certainly no conflict, as shown in Figure 6.22. In fact, an enlightened company would promote the use of *both* toolsets as a seamless program for continuous improvement. And these two philosophies are not the end of the story. There are many techniques from the Total Quality Management (TQM) era that should still be part of any firm's business activities, and no doubt other methodologies will come along in the future that should be included in the mix as well. There is only one way to achieve a truly sustainable competitive advantage; you must learn faster and better than your competitors. So keep your mind open to new ideas, and encourage your firm to constantly seek a better way.

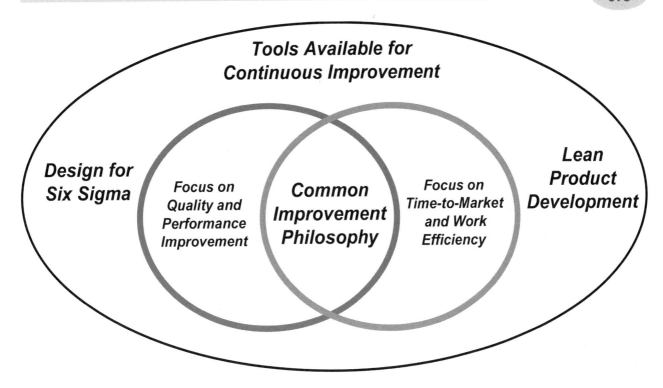

Figure 6.22: Improvement initiatives can often become muddled in such a way that they appear to compete with one another. This is most common among firms that have embraced both Design for Six Sigma (DFSS) and lean product development, where the two sets of tools can appear to be in conflict. In reality, both powerful methodologies should contribute to a seamless toolset for continuous improvement.

A Twenty-Word Recipe for Successful Change

How does one conclude a book of this scope (not to mention length)? Given the waste sensitivity that I'm sure you've developed, my closure will be brief; in fact just the twenty words shown in Figure 6.23. The only way you can improve your organization is to *change the way employees do their work.* Whether you are a development team member or the president of a company, this is your challenge. The few words of advice that I've provided represent a pathway to achieving successful organizational change. First, you must find allies. A lone voice in the wilderness will never succeed (even if the voice is as loud as mine). Look for others within your peer group who share your frustrations and recognize the waste that surrounds them. Then collaboratively select just a handful of the tools you've learned from this guidebook as a starting point. Even one or two notable successes will pave the way for a more significant undertaking. As you choose your initial tools and methods, be mindful that nothing succeeds like success; pick techniques that have an almost certain chance of working in your culture and with your products.

Figure 6.23: The author's concise recipe for successful implementation of lean product development (and yes, there are actually twenty words).

Next, take your selected tools and apply them to a showcase project or team. Once the team has begun to utilize the improved methods you've crafted, be persistent in reinforcing their use; even the most supportive project team will discard new ideas when their schedule gets tight and their nerves become frayed. As you begin to observe tangible improvement in the performance of your showcase project, advertise this success throughout your organization. In this way, you will begin to create a "pull" for the new ideas that have proven to be beneficial. Gradually broaden your improvement program, using the phased approach that was described earlier in this section, and be sure that at every step you take pains to avoid backsliding. I recommend persistence rather than insistence. Gentle positive pressure works far better for sustaining improvements than preaching and badgering.

Well, all that is left for me to do is to wish you great success in your improvement endeavors. May the time you save by eliminating waste be applied to that which is most important to you, both in business and in life.

Recommended Reading in Lean Product Development

Bicheno, J., 2004, *The New Lean Toolbox*, PICSIE Books.

Cusumano, M.A., and K. Nobeoka, 1998, *Thinking Beyond Lean*, The Free Press.

Dimancescu, D., Hines, P., and N. Rich, 1997, *The Lean Enterprise*, American Management Association.

Fiore, C., 2005, *Accelerated Product Development,* Productivity Press.

Liker, J.K., 2004, *The Toyota Way*, McGraw Hill.

Kennedy, M. N., 2003, *Product Development for the Lean Enterprise*, Oaklea Press.

Mascitelli, R., 2002, *Building a Project-Driven Enterprise: How to Slash Waste and Boost Profits Through Lean Project Management*, Technology Perspectives.

Mascitelli, R., 2004, *The Lean Design Guidebook: Everything Your Product Development Team Needs to Slash Manufacturing Cost*, Technology Perspectives.

McConnell, S., 1996, *Rapid Development*, Microsoft Press.

McConnell, S., 1998, *Software Project Survival Guide*, Microsoft Press.

McGrath, M. E., 2004, *Next Generation Product Development*, McGraw-Hill.

Perlow, L. A., 1999, "The time famine: Toward a sociology of work time," *Administrative Science Quarterly*, Vol. 44, No. 1.

Poppendieck, M. and T. Poppendieck, 2003, *Lean Software Development*, Addison-Wesley.

Pugh, S., 1991, *Total Design: Integrated Methods for Successful Product Engineering*, Addison Wesley.

Reinertsen, D. G., 1997, *Managing the Design Factory*, The Free Press.

Smith, P. G. and D. G. Reinertsen, 1998, *Developing Products in Half the Time – 2ⁿᵈ Edition*, John Wiley & Sons.

Sobek, D. K. II, et al, 1998, "Another look at how Toyota integrates product development," *Harvard Business Review*, July-August Issue.

Sobek, D. K. II, et al, 1999, "Toyota's principles of set-based concurrent engineering," *Sloan Management Review*, Vol. 40, No. 2.

Suri, R., 1998, *Quick Response Manufacturing*, Productivity Press.

Ward, A., et al, 1995, "The second Toyota paradox: How delaying decisions can make better cars faster," *Sloan Management Review*, Vol. 36, No. 3.

Womack, J.P., and D.T. Jones, 1996, *Lean Thinking,* Simon & Schuster.

Womack, J.P., and D.T. Jones, 2005, *Lean Solutions*, The Free Press.

Glossary

Balanced Scorecard – An approach to performance measurement that recommends combining several distinct metrics when evaluating a situation. This technique avoids the potential skewing of results due to unrealistic emphasis on only a single metric.

Continuous-Flow Process – An evolutionary next step in product development processes. It is a straightforward enhancement of a standard phase / gate process that reduces unnecessary administrative waste and focuses on the critical path of each project.

Critical Core – A more realistic approach to project schedule management, in which priority is given to any activity that is "schedule-critical". A more qualitative way to identify the critical path.

Critical Path – The shortest duration achievable for a project, based on available resources. A slip in schedule of any critical-path task will directly impact the completion date of the project.

Critical-to-Cost – A specification or other attribute of a product that has a significant impact on the manufacturing cost.

Critical-to-Quality – A specification or other attribute of a product that has a significant impact on the manufacturing quality or yield.

Current State – The way things are today. The current state is used as a baseline for lean improvement initiatives.

Deliverable – Any tangible and transferable item, including data, documents, hardware, fixtures, and even decisions that are communicated to the team.

Deliverables Roadmap – A tool for visually representing all of the key deliverables of a project, along with their dependencies, completion dates, and responsible team members.

Design for Manufacture and Assembly (DFMA) – An improvement methodology that focuses on reduction of manufacturing cost through decreasing touch labor and material waste. Tends to have an auto-industry flavor, since the originators used this sector for their initial focus.

Design Overshoot – A "gold-plated" design that provides more performance or features than a given market segment would be willing to pay for.

Design Undershoot – A substandard design that fails to completely solve the "customer problem" for a specific market segment.

Discount Rate – A term used in the calculation of net present value that takes into account the future value of money (i.e., it reflects the financial risk of an investment in a new product by comparing it to what could have been earned if the money had been earning interest).

Enabler – An activity within new product development that is not directly value-creating, but is currently necessary to commercialize a product.

Exception Management – An approach to managing both resources and projects that defines a "region of empowerment" for each team and team member. Status reporting focuses on exceptions that are outside the boundaries that have been defined.

Feasibility Review – A method for identifying projects with high technical risk and addressing those risks through a brief feasibility study. Occurs at the onset of a new product development project.

Finite Capacity – An occurrence characterized by a firm having more moneymaking opportunities than they have resources to pursue them. A factory is said to have finite capacity if demand for its products exceed its maximum output per period. A design organization has finite capacity if there are more profitable projects for designers to work on than they can realistically handle.

Freeze Gate – A modification of the standard "gate review" in which a list of requirements are "frozen" to ensure timely completion of a project. This is an element of the "staged-freezing" methodology for controlling changes to specifications during project execution.

Functional Silos – The tendency of organizations to form high-walled functional departments that can be obstacles to communication and can inhibit the ability of design teams to perform true cross-functional development.

Future State – An improvement to a wasteful current-state process. The future state is a way of visualizing an improved process, often through the use of a future-state value-stream map.

Gold Plating – The act of overshooting customer requirements in a way that will not generate additional price or market share, either by incorporating excessive performance or low-value features.

"How's it Built?" Review – Addresses the critical need for new product development teams to consider manufacturability at the earliest stages of their projects. It is essentially a one-day conceptual manufacturing review.

Integrated Product Team – The optimal structure for a product development team, in which membership is divided into "core" and "extended" team members.

Kaizen – The Japanese word for "continuous improvement". Has a connotative meaning of "take immediate action". Is often used in the context of "*kaizen* events," that can result in dramatic reductions in non-value-added waste.

Lean Scheduling – An approach to project scheduling that uses a "rolling-window" technique to avoid the waste associated with constant replans and excessive detail.

Lean Self-Assessment – Utilizes a subjective questionnaire to gather feedback from development team members regarding the current state of a process, and subsequently on the success of an improvement initiative.

Lean Six-Sigma – A "Frankenstein" improvement philosophy that attempts to merge the "best of Lean" with the "best of Six-Sigma". The result is (as of this writing) not much more than a convergence of buzzwords.

Least Discernible Difference – The point at which the customers for a new product will no longer notice an improvement to performance or the addition of features. It represents a "value threshold" beyond which an improvement no longer imparts benefits to customers.

Market Clock – A theoretical concept that is used to understand how time will impact the sales and profits of a new product. The market clock starts upon the release of a new product, and ends with its removal from the market due to obsolescence or replacement.

Market Risk – A risk to the success of a new product development project that reflects the uncertainties associated with market acceptance, price, competition, etc.

Matrix Organization – A compromise organizational structure that attempts to achieve a balance between strong functional "silos" and a fully projectized approach.

Mini-Kaizen Event – A brief collaborative exercise that yields a prioritized list of opportunities to improve a selected process or business activity. The focus is on identifying improvements that have a high potential impact and are easy to implement.

Muda – The Japanese word for waste. Something that is unacceptable in a business environment.

Must / Should / Could Prioritization – A straightforward approach to prioritizing any aspect of project work, from the specifications or features of a new product to the day-to-day activities of development team members.

Net Present Value (NPV) – A financial metric that represents the "total discounted future cash flows of a proposed product, minus the initial investment required." A positive NPV means that investment in a new product opportunity will be profitable to the firm. A negative NPV means the product opportunity should not be pursued.

Phased Deployment – A proven strategy for implementation of any organizational improvement. Successive phases are employed to roll out improvements in a logical order.

Phase / Gate Process – A common structure for new product development that uses well-defined phases and relatively rigid gate reviews to ensure progress and manage both financial and technical risk.

Project Sensitivity – Conceptually, this term represents the "money value of time" on a specific project. How much would one day (or one week, etc.) of schedule slip cost your company in lost revenue and profit?

Project Time – An application of "time-slicing" that allocates a specific period in the workday for high concentration project work.

Production Process Preparation (3P) – An integrated and highly detailed approach to product and process co-development. This strategy is a mainstay of Toyota Motor Company's product development process.

Productivity – The profit or revenue output of an employee per period worked (often referred to as "output per labor hour").

Profit Margin – The difference between the total cost buildup of a product and its market price. (Note that this definition refers to "pre-tax profits".)

Pugh Method – An approach to filtering and prioritizing the outputs of a creative brainstorming meeting. Several alternatives are compared to a "baseline" design approach, and ranked based on their relative performance benefits.

Resource Bottleneck – A resource shortfall that can have a negative impact on project schedule. Resource bottlenecks can be easily identified by the existence of a queue; a significant wait-time before a new task can be addressed.

Risk – The uncertainties that can affect your profits. Risk can be related to technical challenges, resource limitations, market uncertainty, economic turmoil, or any other unpredictable factors that can ruin your day.

Risk-Corrected Net Present Value – A modification of the traditional net present value calculation that incorporates "discount percentages" to account for market and technical risks.

Seven-Alternatives Process – Derived from Toyota's "3P" process, this technique encourages development teams to consider multiple options for manufacturing process selection, and provides a methodology for selecting the optimal process from a cost and quality standpoint.

Set-Based Design – The "Toyota Way" of new product development. Utilizes multiple design alternatives at every step of the development process, and competes these options to yield an optimal design. Other attributes of the process include integrated product and process co-development (i.e., the "3P" process) and the delaying of design decisions until the latest reasonable point in development.

Six-Sigma Design – A powerful and well-developed improvement methodology based on the breakthrough work performed by designers at Motorola Company in the late 1980's. The primary focus is on reduction of process variability to improve yield, reduce waste, and accelerate time-to-market.

Staged Freezing – An approach to requirements management that allows for partial freezing of specifications or product attributes. A way of controlling changes to those requirements that can directly influence the end-date of a project.

Stand-Up Meetings – Brief meetings held at a specific time and for a specific purpose. Typically no longer than fifteen minutes in duration, and often used as a more efficient substitute for a weekly team coordination meeting.

Stoplight Chart – A technique for providing project status information to management, in which red / yellow / green symbology is used to indicate the relative "health" of specific project tasks. Used in conjunction with an "exception management" philosophy.

Strategic Product - Either: a) a product that is not likely to be profitable, but could have a significant positive effect on the future of a firm, or b) a money-loser that your boss just won't admit was a terrible idea.

Target Cost – The (realistic) market price projection for a product, minus the desired profit (or target) margin. The target cost should be calculated at the very beginning of a new product development project, and then compared to actual cost estimates throughout development to ensure that the desired margin can be achieved once the product is in production.

Target Margin – The minimum profit margin that is desired for a new product. This should be at least equal to the average gross margin for all products within a business unit.

Technical Risk – A risk to the success of a new product development project that results from the application of new or challenging technologies.

Time Batch – Any situation in which development team members must wait for a decision, permission, approval, or information. These generally occur as a result of "regularly scheduled" meetings or approval cycles that fail to provide a timely response to teams.

Time-Slicing – Conceptually, time-slicing is an approach to allocating time and resources, that carves up available time into dedicated "slices" that address specific activities. The "project-time" approach to managing daily work is an example of time-slicing.

Total Quality Management – One of the first truly global improvement initiatives. Its source was the statistical quality methods first proposed by Deming and Juran, and successfully deployed by Japanese firms in the 1970's and 1980's.

Value – Something that a customer would willingly pay for. In other words, value is performance (the solution to a customer's problem) delivered at a specified price. The value of a product is related to both the importance of the problem that is being addressed (from the customer's perspective) and the effectiveness of the product at solving that problem.

Value Engineering – One of the most effective methods for reducing the cost of a product, typically applied during initial conceptual design. Utilizes structured brainstorming on possible design alternatives to enable delivery of customer-mandated performance at the lowest possible cost.

Value Milestones – Objective and directly measurable milestones that allow accurate tracking of value creation (i.e., progress) on a development project.

Value Stream – A theoretical ideal for how value can be created most efficiently. The value stream is the flow of events necessary to accomplish a value-creating activity. For the case of products, there are two primary value streams involved: the non-recurring design value stream and the manufacturing value stream.

Value-Stream Mapping – A technique for identifying a "better way" to execute a process. The methodology involves creating a "current-state" map of a selected process, brainstorming on ways to improve the process, and then generating a "future-state" map that will serve as a roadmap for implementation of the desired improvements.

Value-Stream Organization – An innovative organizational structure that is formed around "value streams" rather than functional departments or project teams. It offers considerable benefits from a standpoint of product focus and time-to-market, at the expense of optimal utilization of development resources.

Visual Project Board – A visual method for presenting project status and planned actions. The visual project board can be posted in a common location to allow both team members and management to have immediate access to project data. It is often used in conjunction with a stand-up coordination meeting.

Waste – A non-value-added activity or task. Waste is the antithesis of value; it is something that benefits no one and should be eliminated wherever possible.

"Waste-Free" Design Review – A simple facilitation approach to technical design reviews that yields a prioritized list of valuable design improvement suggestions in a short period of time.

<u>*Notes*</u>

Allen, D., 2001, *Getting Things Done*, Penguin Books.

Anderson, D. M., 1997, *Agile Product Development for Mass Customization*, Irwin Professional Publishing.

Argyris, C., 1998, "Empowerment: The emperor's new clothes," *Harvard Business Review*, May-June Issue, Pgs. 98–105.

Ballis, J., 2001, *Managing Flow: Achieving Lean in the New Millennium to Win the Gold*, Brown Books.

Barham, K. and C. Heimer, 1998, *ABB –The Dancing Giant*, Financial Times Publishing.

Barnes, T., 1996, *Kaizen Strategies for Successful Leadership*, Financial Times Pitman Publishing.

Belliveau, P., Griffen, A., and S. M. Somermeyer, 2002, *The PDMA Toolbox for New Product Development*, John Wiley & Sons.

Belliveau, P., Griffen, A., and S. M. Somermeyer, 2004, *The PDMA Toolbox for New Product Development – No. 2*, John Wiley and Sons.

Bicheno, J., 2000, *The Lean Toolbox – 2nd Edition*, PICSIE Books.

Bicheno, J., 2001, *The Quality 75*, PICSIE Books.

Bicheno, J., 2004, *The New Lean Toolbox*, PICSIE Books.

Bossidy, L. and R. Charan, 2002, *Execution: The Discipline of Getting Things Done*, Crown Business Press.

Carbno, C., 1999, "Optimal resource allocation for projects," *Project Management Journal*, June Issue, Pgs. 22–31.

Christensen, C. M., 1997, *The Innovator's Dilemma*, Harvard Business School Press.

Clark, K. B. and S. C. Wheelwright, 1993, *Managing New Product and Process Development: Text and Cases*, Harvard Business School Press.

Clavell, J., 1983, *The Art of War by Sun Tzu*, Delacorte Press.

Cohen, L., 1995, *Quality Function Deployment: How to Make QFD Work for You*, Addison Wesley.

Connolly, M. and R. Rianoshek, 2002, *The Communication Catalyst*, Dearborn Trade Publishing.

Cooper, R. G., 1993, *Winning at New Products*, Addison Wesley.

Cooper, R. G., 1995, *When Lean Enterprises Collide*, Harvard Business School Press.

Cooper, R. G., Edgett, S. J. and E. J. Kleinschmidt, 1998, *Portfolio Management for New Products*, Perseus Books.

Cowley, M. and E. Domb, 1997, *Beyond Strategic Vision: Effective Corporate Action with Hoshin Planning*, Butterworth Heinemann.

Cusumano, M. A. and K. Nobeoka, 1998, *Thinking Beyond Lean*, The Free Press.

Cusumano, M. A. and R. W. Selby, 1995, *Microsoft Secrets*, Simon & Schuster.

Cusumano, M. A. and D. B. Yoffie, 1998, *Competing on Internet Time*, The Free Press.

Davidson, J. M., Clamen, A., and R. A. Karol, 2000, "Learning from the best new product developers," *IEEE Engineering Management Review*, First Quarter Issue, Pgs. 30–36.

Dawes, R. M., 1988, *Rational Choice in an Uncertain World*, Harcourt Brace College Publishers.

Deschamps, J. P. and P. R. Nayak, 1995, *Product Juggernauts*, Harvard Business School Press.

Dimancescu, D. and K. Dwenger, 1996, *World-Class New Product Development*, AMACOM.

Dimancescu, D., Hines, P., and N. Rich, 1997, *The Lean Enterprise*, AMACOM.

Dinsmore, P. C., 1997, *Winning in Business with Enterprise Project Management*, American Management Association.

Erhorn, C. and J. Stark, 1994, *Competing by Design*, Oliver Wright Publications.

Fine, C. H., 1998, *Clockspeed*, Perseus Books.

Fiore, C., 2005, *Accelerated Product Development*, Productivity Press.

Fleming, Q. W. and J. M. Koppelman, 2000, *Earned Value Project Management*, The Project Management Institute.

Galbraith, J. R., 1995, *Designing Organizations*, Jossey-Bass.

Galbraith, J. R., 2000, *Designing the Global Corporation*, Jossey-Bass.

Galbraith, J. R. and E.E. Lawler, 1993, *Organizing for the Future*, Jossey-Bass.

George, M. L., 2002, *Lean Six Sigma*, McGraw Hill.

Gilpatrick, K. and B. Furlong, 2004, *The Elusive Lean Enterprise*, Trafford.

Globerson, S., 2000, "PMBOK and the critical chain," *PM Network*, May Issue, Pgs. 63–66.

Goldratt, E. M., 1990, *Theory of Constraints*, North River Press.

Goldratt, E. M., 1997, *Critical Chain*, North River Press.

Goldratt, E. M. and J. Cox, 1984, *The Goal*, North River Press.

Goldratt, E. M. and R. E. Fox, 1986, *The Race*, North River Press.

Gorchels, L., 2000, *The Product Manager's Handbook*, NTC Business Press.

Graham, R. J. and R. L. Englund, 1997, *Creating an Environment for Successful Projects*, Jossey-Bass.

Grief, M., 1991, *The Visual Factory*, Productivity Press.

Groppelli, A. A., and E. Nikbakht, 1995, *Finance – 3rd Edition*, Barron's Educational Series.

Gruenwald, G., 1995, *New Product Development, 2nd Edition*, NTC Business Books.

Hamel, G., 2000, *Leading the Revolution*, Harvard Business School Press.

Harry, M. J., 1994, *The Vision of Six Sigma: Tools and Methods for Breakthrough – 4th Edition*, Sigma Publishing Company.

Harry, M. and R. Schroeder, 2000, *Six Sigma*, Currency Doubleday.

Henderson, B. A. and J. L. Larco, 1999, *Lean Transformation*, The Oaklea Press.

Hooks, I. F. and K. A. Farry, 2001, *Customer-Centered Products*, AMACOM.

Ichida, T., 1996, *Product Design Review*, Productivity Press.

Imai, M., 1997, *Gemba Kaizen*, McGraw-Hill.

Jackson, T. L., 1996, *Implementing a Lean Management System*, Productivity Press.

Kaplan R. S. and D. P. Norton, 1996, *The Balanced Scorecard*, Harvard Business School Press.

Karlsson, C. and P. Ahlstrom, 1996, "The difficult path to lean product development," *Journal of Product Innovation Management*, Vol. 13, Pgs. 283–295.

Kennedy, M. N., 2003, *Product Development for the Lean Enterprise*, Oaklea Press.

Kerzner, H., 1998, *Project Management – 6th Edition*, Van Nostrand Reinhold.

Kerzner, H., 2000, *Applied Project Management*, John Wiley & Sons.

Kidder, T., 1981, *The Soul of a New Machine*, Avon Books.

Laraia, A. C., et al, 1999, *The Kaizen Blitz*, John Wiley & Sons.

Lareau, W., 2000, *Lean Leadership*, Tower II Press.

Lareau, W., 2003, *Office Kaizen*, ASQC Quality Press.

Leach, L. P., 2000, *Critical Chain Project Management*, Artech House.

Lencioni, P., 2002, *The Five Dysfunctions of a Team*, Jossey Bass.

Leonard, D. and W. Swap, 1999, *When Sparks Fly*, Harvard Business School Press.

Leonard-Barton, D., 1995, *Wellsprings of Knowledge*, Harvard Business School Press.

Lewis, J. P., 1998, *Mastering Project Management*, McGraw Hill, Inc.

Lientz, B. P. and K. P. Rea, 1999, *Breakthrough Technology Project Management*, Academic Press.

Liker, J. K., 1998, *Becoming Lean*, Productivity Press.

Liker, J. K., 2004, *The Toyota Way*, McGraw-Hill.

Lipnack, J. and J. Stamps, 1997, *Virtual Teams*, John Wiley & Sons.

Martin, S. H., 2005, *Lean Enterprise Leader*, Oaklea Press.

Mascitelli, R., 1998, *The Growth Warriors: Creating Sustainable Global Advantage for America's Technology Companies*, Technology Perspectives.

Mascitelli, R., 2000, "From experience: Harnessing tacit knowledge to achieve breakthrough innovation," *J. Prod. Innov. Manag.*, Vol. 17, 179-193.

Mascitelli, R., 2002, *Building a Project Driven Enterprise: How to Slash Waste and Boost Profits Through Lean Project Management*, Technology Perspectives.

Mascitelli, R., 2004, *The Lean Design Guidebook: Everything Your Product Development Team Needs to Slash Manufacturing Cost*, Technology Perspectives.

Maskell, B. and B. Baggaley, 2004, *Practical Lean Accounting*, Productivity Press.

McConnell, S., 1996, *Rapid Development*, Microsoft Press.

McConnell, S., 1998, *Software Project Survival Guide*, Microsoft Press.

McGrath, M. E., 1995, *Product Strategy for High-Technology Companies*, Irwin Professional Publishing.

McGrath, M. E., 1996, *Setting the PACE in Product Development*, Butterworth Heinemann.

McGrath, M. E., 2004, *Next Generation Product Development*, McGraw-Hill.

McLeod, T., 1988, *The Management of Research, Development and Design in Industry, 2nd Edition*, Gower Technical Press.

Newbold, R. G., 1998, *Project Management in the Fast Lane*, St. Lucie Press.

Nonaka, I. and H. Takeuchi, 1995, *The Knowledge-Creating Company*, Oxford University Press.

Perlow, L. A., 1999, "The time famine: Toward a sociology of work time," *Administrative Science Quarterly*, Vol. 44, No. 1.

Phillips, J. B., 1999, "Management of modular projects: A templating approach," *Project Management Journal*, December Issue, Pgs. 33–41.

Poppendieck, M. and T. Poppendieck, 2003, *Lean Software Development*, Addison-Wesley.

Project Management Institute, 2006, *The Project Management Body of Knowledge (PMBOK) Guide- 3rd Edition*, The Project Management Institute.

Pugh, S., 1991, *Total Design: Integrated Methods for Successful Product Engineering*, Addison Wesley.

Rand, G. K., 2000, "Critical chain: the theory of constraints applied to project management," *International Journal of Project Management*, Vol. 18, Pgs. 173–177.

Reinertsen, D. G., 1997, *Managing the Design Factory*, The Free Press.

Rosenau, M. D., 1998, *Successful Project Management, 3rd Edition*, John Wiley & Sons.

Rosenthal, S. R., 1992, *Effective Product Design and Development*, Irwin Professional Publishing.

Rother, M. and J. Shook, 1999, *Learning to See*, Lean Enterprise Institute.

Schrage, M., 2000, *Serious Play*, Harvard Business School Press.

Schuyler, J. R., 1996, *Decision Analysis in Projects*, The Project Management Institute.

Sekine, K., and K. Arai, 1994, *Design Team Revolution*, Productivity Press.

Senge, P. M., 1990, *The Fifth Discipline*, Currency Doubleday.

Shimbun, N. K., 1995, *Visual Control Systems*, Productivity Press.

Smith, P. G. and D. G. Reinertsen, 1998, *Developing Products in Half the Time – 2nd Edition*, John Wiley & Sons.

Sobek, D. K. II, et al, 1998, "Another look at how Toyota integrates product development," *Harvard Business Review*, July-August Issue.

Sobek, D. K. II, et al, 1999, "Toyota's principles of set-based concurrent engineering," *Sloan Management Review*, Vol. 40, No. 2.

Suri, R., 1998, *Quick Response Manufacturing*, Productivity Press.

Terninko, J., 1997, *Step-by-Step QFD – 2nd Edition*, St. Lucie Press.

Thut, M., 2000, "Accelerating time to market with technology building blocks," *PRTM Insight*, Volume 7, Number 1.

Tufte, E. R., 1983, *The Visual Display of Quantitative Information*, Graphics Press.

Tufte, E. R., 1990, *Envisioning Information*, Graphics Press.

Utterback, J. M., 1994, *Mastering the Dynamics of Innovation*, Harvard Business School Press.

Uyttewaal, E., 1999, "Take the path that is really critical, *PM Network*, December Issue, Pgs. 37–39.

Verma, V. K., 1995, *Organizing Projects for Success*, The Project Management Institute.

Verma, V. K., 1996, *Human Resource Skills for the Project Manager*, The Project Management Institute.

Ward, A., et al, 1995, "The second Toyota paradox: How delaying decisions can make better cars faster," *Sloan Management Review*, Vol. 36, No. 3.

Wheelwright, S. C. and K. B. Clark, 1993, *Managing New Product and Process Development*, The Free Press.

Wheelwright, S. C. and K. B. Clark, 1995, *Leading Product Development*, The Free Press.

Womack, J.P., Jones, D. T., and D. Roos, 1990, *The Machine That Changed The World*, Harper Perennial.

Womack, J. P. and D. T. Jones, 1996, *Lean Thinking*, Simon & Schuster.

Womack, J. P. and D. T. Jones, 2005, *Lean Solutions*, The Free Press.

Notes

About the Author

Ron Mascitelli, PMP (Project Management Professional, Masters Degree Solid State Physics, University of California, Los Angeles) is the Founder and President of Technology Perspectives. Ron is a recognized leader in the development of advanced product design and development methods. He presents his workshops and seminars internationally, and has created company-specific lean product development training for a number of leading firms, including Lockheed-Martin, Intel Corp., Boston Scientific, Adidas Group, Boeing, Parker-Hannifin, New Balance Shoes, Goodrich Aerospace, Hughes Electronics, Rockwell Automation / Allen-Bradley, and Applied Materials.

Ron served as both Senior Scientist and Director of Research and Development for Hughes Electronics and the Santa Barbara Research Center. His industry experience includes management of advanced product development projects for the Department of Defense, the Defense Advanced Research Projects Agency, Lawrence Livermore Laboratory, NASA, and the Department of Energy.

Since founding Technology Perspectives in 1994, Ron Mascitelli has published over twenty papers and technical articles in major journals, including the *International Journal of Technology Management* and *The Journal of Product Innovation Management*, and is a contributing author for IEEE's *Technology Management Handbook*. He has written four books, including the critically acclaimed *Building a Project-Driven Enterprise* and *The Lean Design Guidebook,* and is the author of *The Lean Guidebook Series*, of which this book is the second installment. Ron currently lives with his wife, Renee, and their many pets in Northridge, CA.